Where In The World?

Volume 3

Where In The World?

Volume 3

Historic People and Places in Clark County, Kentucky

McCormick Bluegrass seed stripper in the field. (Clark County Public Library)

Harry G. Enoch

Bluegrass Heritage Museum
2018

Bluegrass Heritage Museum
217 S. Main Street
Winchester, Kentucky 40391

First printing 2018

ISBN 978-1-387-71624-1

Preface

Did you ever hear the name of a place and wonder "where in the world was that?" Answering that question about quaint and historic places in Clark County, Kentucky, became the basis of a regular column in the *Winchester Sun* called "Where In The World?" The series began on January 6, 2005, with "Bramblett's Lick." This is the third published volume of those collected columns. Previous volumes contained 162 articles published between 2005 and 2016. This volume continues the series with 56 articles that appeared in the *Sun* from June 2016 to March 2018. There are fewer articles in this volume because more recent articles are much longer than the early ones.

Each article describes a historic location or notable person in Clark County, some well known, some not so well known. Some articles were updated from the newspaper version as additional information became available.

In transcribing newspapers and other published material, original spelling was maintained. Some abbreviations were spelled out and punctuation added for clarity. The spelling of creek, road and place names generally follows that used by Clark County GIS on their maps; if not found on their maps, U.S. Geological Survey maps were used.

A considerable amount of research goes into each article. Citations for all the sources used in this research are included here. Maps were one of the essential resources. Readers who wish to find places described in the articles should know where these maps of Winchester and Clark County can be found. Those referred to most often include the following:

1861—E. A. and G. W. Hewitt, "Topographical Map of the Counties of Bourbon, Fayette, Clark, Jessamine and Woodford, Kentucky," accessible at the Bluegrass Heritage Museum and the Clark County Public Library.

1877—D. G. Beers and J. Lanagan, *Atlas of Bourbon,*

Clark, Fayette Jessamine and Woodford Counties, Ky., accessible at the Museum and Library. The Museum has copies for sale.

1926—C. D. Hunter, Kentucky Geological Survey, "Map of Clark County, Kentucky," copies at the Museum and Library.

1937—Gatton blueprint map of Clark County, copy at the Museum.

Modern topographic maps of Clark County, may be purchased from Map Sales, Kentucky Geological Survey, University of Kentucky. Topo maps can be viewed on the web at www.uky.edu/KGS/gis/krgweb/index.html.

Modern county highway maps may be viewed and printed from the Kentucky Transportation Cabinet's website at http://transportation.ky.gov/Maps/Pages/default.aspx.

Photographs were taken by the author unless noted otherwise.

Contents

1
The Midland Trail

June 10, 2016

The Midland Trail posed a mystery to me when I was growing up in Mt. Sterling. We had a Midland Trail Hotel on Main Street, where my grandparents sometimes took us for Sunday dinner. The hotel was so named because it was on the Midland Trail, which was said to follow the highway (US 60) running across Kentucky and into West Virginia. Nobody I asked could tell me anything else about the tr ail. This was long before Google or Wikipedia or even computers.

I learned early that Montgomery County had once been the site of Indian battles, and a place called "Morgan's Station" had been burned by Shawnee raiders who carried off 19 prisoners. I was maybe nine or ten years old then, already fascinated by Indians and eager to learn about those pioneer times. I didn't know what to make of the Midland Trail though. I tried to imagine before it was a highway, when it was just a trail, maybe something like the Oregon Trail. I envisioned people on the Midland Trail travelling by horseback or wagon on their way to or from Virginia. It was only a year or so ago, while doing research on Winchester's Sphar Building, that I learned the actual facts: the Midland Trail had been a highway from the very beginning.

In the early days of the automobile, people were looking for places to explore—they called it "touring"—in their new cars. In 1912, an auto club in Grand Junction, Colorado, formed the Midland Trail Association. Its original purpose was to find a route across Colorado and Utah to the west coast. Within a year, however, the association greatly enlarged its plans and laid out the first transcontinental auto trail in America. Using existing highways, they marked out a route one could follow from Washington, D.C., to Los Angeles. In Kentucky, the Midland Trail went from Ashland to Louisville, passing through Mt. Sterling and Winchester along the way.

By 1925, automobiles were everywhere—more than 20 million of them—but good roads were not. Most roads were unpaved and those that were paved were poorly maintained. There was little effort to coordinate roads between states. One state might build a road to the state line where it dead ended because the adjoining state had no plans for its extension. Bad roads inhibited economic growth and interstate commerce. Enter the federal government with the appointment of the Joint Board on Interstate Highways. The Joint Board, made up of two dozen state and federal highway officials, was charged with developing a nationwide coordinated road system. Roads were to be improved and renumbered so that one could travel coast to coast on a single highway.

The Joint Board decided that the most important north-south highways would receive numbers ending in "1," while secondary north-south highways would end in "5." (Think of US Routes 31 and 25 through Kentucky.) Important east-west highways would be given two-digit numbers ending in "0." The latter began with Route 20 across the South and continued up through Route 90 across the North. All would be coast to coast highways, except one: Route 60. It began in Los Angeles, but instead of going through Kentucky and on to the east coast, it was proposed to turn north at St. Louis and end in Chicago. The likely explanation turned out to be that the five member board appointed to select the route numbers was dominated by men from Oklahoma, Missouri and Illinois.

When Kentucky's governor, William J. Fields, heard the Joint Board's plans, he was furious. "Kentucky was ignored completely." Fields immediately went to work on the Joint Board. He also enlisted the support of the state's business community, which had much to gain by a national road through the state. Kentuckians were joined in their ire by West Virginia, these being the only two states without a coast to coast highway. The plan was particularly disturbing because Kentucky had been on the route of the very first transcontinental highway, the Midland Trail. Fields demanded that US 60 follow the Midland Trail from St. Louis through Kentucky and on to Newport News, Virginia.

A meeting of the American Association of Highway Officials in January 1926 ignored Fields complaints. They designated a secondary highway, US Route 62, to follow the Midland Trail from St. Louis to the east coast.

1926 Rand McNally Roadmap of the Midland Trail in Kentucky.

An angry Fields, along with his congressional delegation, descended on the Bureau of Public Roads in Washington, D.C. Its chief, Thomas McDonald, briefly relented but was then beset by the Midwest trio. They argued that hundreds of thousands of road maps had already been distributed (I have a Rand McNally highway map from that year showing the Midland Trail crossing Kentucky via Route 62) and that they were only weeks away from ordering US 60 highway signs. The battle raged on into summer until it was finally settled at the end of July. Oklahoma backed off and was given their choice of two-digit numbers for a Chicago to Los Angeles highway—they chose Route 66. That November, Fields' persistence finally paid off when the route from Los Angeles to Newport News was designated Route 60. The road crossed Kentucky from Louisville, through Frankfort, Versailles, Lexington, Winchester and Mt. Sterling, to Ashland—the same route as the old Midland Trail.

Route 66 would eventually became one of America's most celebrated highways, while the Midland Trail faded into near obscurity. Yet securing US 60 for Kentucky was a significant achievement for Governor Fields and the state. The national highway brought decades of commercial benefits and tourist dollars to Kentucky, until it was essentially replaced by Interstate 64 in the 1960s.

Sources

Midland Trail, www.wikipedia.com; "Midland Trail Association Formed In Grand Junction," *Leadville* (CO) *Herald Democrat*, November 19, 1912, www.coloradohistoricnewspapers.org/; Susan C. Kelly, "'Kentucky Was Ignored Completely': Governor William J. Fields, The Midland Trail, And The Numbering Of Highway 60," *Register of the Kentucky Historical Society* (2015) 113:3-26.

2
Lost Paintings of the Bush Mill

June 17, 2016

I like stories with a surprise element that turn out well in the end. Such a tale of the search for the lost paintings of the Bush Mill on Lower Howard's Creek. The Bush Mill was a stone structure on four-working levels erected in about 1806 by Jonathan Bush to produce flour for export to the Port of New Orleans. The mill operated under a succession of owners until the early 20th century. The ruins are now protected within the bounds of the Lower Howard's Creek Nature & Heritage Preserve.

About fifteen years ago, while researching the origins of the Bush Mill, I ran across a reference to it in a series of historical articles in the *Winchester Sun* written in the 1920s called the "Clark County Chronicles." The author described the many mills that lined the banks of Lower Howard's Creek, and then added, "Practically all the old mills have passed away, with the exception of the old Bush mill which is still standing and of which two fine oil paintings have been presented to the Clark County Historical Society by Captain C. E. Bush, a grandson of the original builder of the present structure." Charles E. Bush (1851-1931) was a son of James S. Bush and grandson of Jonathan Bush who built the mill.

I asked members of the historical society about these paintings, and no one had seen them or knew what happened to them. Several years later, Clare Sipple, now my bride, found and recognized an unsigned painting of the Bush Mill hanging at Holly Rood Manor in Winchester. We suspected this was one of the missing paintings. Trying to come up with a likely scenario, we wondered if this oil on board, 36 by 38 inches, could have been a copy of an original made for a member of the Bush family. C. E. Bush may have made the copy himself; he was listed in census records as a "painter."

Fast forward to 2013. That summer I received a telephone call from Tom Clark of Clark Art and Antiques in

Lexington. Tom said he had recently acquired a painting from a dealer in Owensboro that I might be interested in. Then he read me the artist's inscription on the back: "Bush's Mill On Howard's Lower Creek, Clark Co. Ky. Sketched from Nature and Painted by Robt Moore. Oct'r 1892." I nearly had a heart attack but managed to say, "Yes, we might be interested."

Not wanting to appear overly eager, Clare and I managed to wait an hour or two before heading to Lexington for a look at the painting. We immediately recognized that the large oil on canvas pictured the Bush Mill in the deeply entrenched Lower Howard's Creek valley. In fact, it was the same view pictured in the copy at Holly Rood.

The work, 30 by 36 inches, did not present well. The paint was very dark, the oil was a network of cracks, and worst of all, there was a large tear in the middle of the canvas. Mr. Clark said the dealer who brought the painting to Lexington had poked a hole in it while getting it out of the car. Nothing could be learned of its provenance except that it had been purchased at an estate sale in Western Kentucky.

We had the painting inspected by art historian, Dr. Estill Curtis Pennington, who pronounced it an authentic Robert Moore and advised that the canvas could be restored to "a highly viable condition, suitable for viewing."

Robert Moore, we learned, was born in Cork, Ireland, and made his way to Winchester by the mid-1850s. He placed a notice in the local newspaper, *The National Union*, announcing his profession: "Robert Moore offers his services to the citizens of Clark County and adjoining counties as a portrait and animal painter. Persons wishing anything done in his line will enquire at the National Union Office."

One of his earliest commissions—a hunting dog, 1861— and one of his latest—a landscape with a sawmill, 1892—are still in the hands of the original owners' descendants in Clark County. Fortunately, the artist signed and dated his paintings. His usual signature was "Robt Moore pinx." ("Pinx," from the Latin *pinxit* meaning "he painted it.")

Many of Moore's known works are of purebred livestock, especially shorthorn cattle, the passion of the times. He painted these subjects for the Taylor, Moore and Sudduth families of Clark County, Brutus Clay of Bourbon, and Dr. John T. Strode of Winchester and later Maysville. His contemporaries thought well enough of him to declare, "During the balmy days of the Shorthorn his services were in much demand." According to Dr. Pennington, Moore's works "though naive, are highly appealing" and are still much sought after by collectors. His damaged painting of the Thomas G. Sudduth bull "Washington" brought over $7,000 at a 2013 auction in Winchester.

Robert Moore's Painting of the Bush Mill, 1892

Moore's skill as a painter did not translate into a comfortable existence. Census records indicate he was unmarried and owned no property. In 1860 and 1870, he resided in Winchester, boarding with others; in 1880, he was an "Inmate" at the "Alms house" in Maysville. Friends described his weakness for ardent spirits.

Following Dr. Pennington's recommendation, a plan was made to acquire, restore and preserve Moore's Bush Mill for the Bluegrass Heritage Museum. A group of donors purchased the painting, and Museum Director, Sandy Stults, secured a grant from The Greater Clark Foundation to pay for restoration. Terry

Boyle, a certified painting conservator in Cincinnati, did the work. The restored Bush Mill, available for viewing at the Museum, brings a quality 19th-century work executed by local artist Robert Moore back to Clark County after an absence of many years. According to Dr. Pennington, "The discovery of this painting is one of the most important events in recent Kentucky art history."

The sad end came for Robert Moore in 1894, two years after finishing the Bush Mill. "Thursday Robert Moore was taken to the Poorhouse. He was quite sick at the time and very feeble. At midnight Mr. Thomas gave him medicine but the next morning he was found dead in his bed." His obituary in the *Winchester Democrat* tells the rest of the story. "He was of gentle, unassuming manners, and always, even in his cups, a gentleman. He was not given to indiscriminate friendships, but his friends were very dear to him.

"For many years he was an enthusiastic Mason, but was dropped many years ago for financial reasons. On account of this feeling of fellowship the members of Winchester Lodge took charge of the remains and they were interred in the Masonic lot in the cemetery. S. D. Goff, who had often befriended the deceased, furnished the coffin, and if the spirits of the departed take cognizance of terrestrial things, his artist soul must be glad that the body does not rest in a pauper's grave."

Robert Moore's grave in Winchester Cemetery has not been located.

Sources

"Clark County Chronicles," *Winchester Sun,* September 13, 1923; *National Union*, November 9, 1860; Edna T. Whitley, *Kentucky Ante-Bellum Portraiture* (Paris, KY, 1955), p. 723; Estill Curtis Pennington, *Kentucky, The Master Painters from the Frontier Era to the Great Depression* (Paris, KY, 2008), p. 73; Estill Curtis Pennington, "Notes on a Painting by Robert Moore," October 1, 2013; *Winchester Democrat*, Tuesday, November 27, 1894.

3
History of a Clark County Plantation

July 1, 2016

In order to get away from Lexington traffic and have a go at country living, my wife Brenda and I moved to Clark County in the fall of 1999. Our new place was an 11-acre wooded site with a 1970s home in the Forest Grove area. Over the years I collected folders full of information on the history of the place. The material goes back to the planting of the Bush Settlement and the influx of immigrants who came here in the 1780s. I thought it might make an interesting story.

The history begins with Capt. Billy Bush, who came to Kentucky with Daniel Boone in 1775. Captain Billy came from Orange County, Virginia. In 1780 he returned there to convince a number of men he knew to invest in Kentucky land he had located across from Fort Boonesborough, north of the Kentucky River. With the aid of his father-in-law, Thomas Burrus, a prominent Orange County landowner, he lined up eight men to purchase Virginia Treasury Warrants entitling them to nearly 18,000 acres of land. With the warrants acquired at Richmond in March, Bush hurried back to Kentucky to enter his claims at the surveyor's office in May.

The next step in completing land titles in Kentucky involved having the claims surveyed. For this task, Captain Billy enlisted his friend Daniel Boone. In fact, the first eleven surveys ever run by Daniel Boone made were for Billy Bush and his investors in January of 1783. Since Bush had located all these tracts, he accompanied Boone on the surveys as the "Land marker & pilot." The lands were situated between Lower Howard's Creek and Twomile Creek.

The original owner of my property was Andrew Tribble, one of Bush's investors. On January 10, 1783, Daniel Boone surveyed 500 acres of land for Tribble. The tract extended from Twomile Creek on the east to Lower Howard's Creek on the west. The northern boundary was near present-day Flanagan Station Road, and the southern boundary ran parallel to it about one-half mile to the south. Tribble received a patent for his 500 acres from Virginia governor Benjamin Harrison in May 1784.

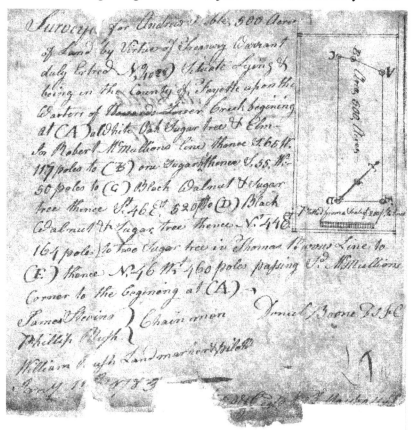

Andrew Tribble's Survey with Daniel Boone's Signature

Andrew Tribble (1741-1822) married Sarah Ann Burrus and was Billy Bush's brother-in-law. Tribble became a Baptist minister in Virginia. He pastored a small church in Albemarle County where, it is said, Thomas Jefferson attended his services. By January 1786, when he was accepted as a member of Howard's Creek Baptist Church, he had probably moved onto his 500-acre plantation. The term "plantation" was carried here from Virginia and signified a large farm.

In 1790 Howard's Creek Church members divided over some unspecified issue of doctrine. Their pastor, Robert Elkin, led one faction, Tribble led the other. That August, some of the latter members "Came forward and assumed the Constitution, Received Andrew Tribble & the part with him and threatened Elkin and the part with him with Excommunication." Baptist ministers were called in from other churches to seek a reconciliation but their efforts failed. In the end, they agreed to divide the congregation. They constituted Reverend Elkin as pastor of a church to be called "Providence" and constituted Reverend Tribble as pastor of a church, ironically, called "Unity." Tribble moved his congregation a mile upstream on Lower Howard's Creek and erected a church in the creek bottom near the present waterworks. Reverend Tribble also had strong ties in Madison County, where he established Tates Creek Baptist Church and was minister there until his retirement.

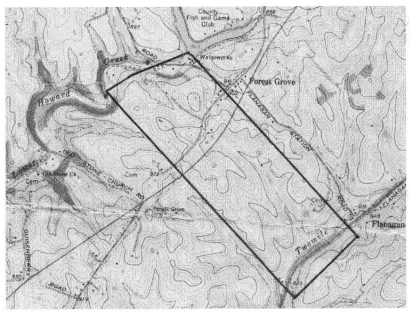

Map of Andrew Tribble's Patent

Tribble moved to Madison and began selling off his 500-acre tract in Clark. In 1794, James Ragland (1743-1818) paid him 100 pounds for 108 acres on the Lower Howard's Creek end of the tract. Ragland was born in Albemarle County, married Sarah Rowland, and the couple brought two sons—Nathaniel and James Jr.—with them to Clark County. James and Sarah joined Providence Church. Their two-story log home survived as a residence until 1943. It stood about fifty yards from my house. Their family graveyard, long since destroyed, was nearby.

Several years ago, two paintings of the Ragland sons were identified. The portraits were made by an itinerate painter known only as the "Guilford Limner," best known for his work in Guilford County, North Carolina. These paintings have become the subject of an extensive investigation by Sally Gant of the Museum of Early Southern Decorative Arts in Winston-Salem, North Carolina.

James Ragland Jr. & Wife Frances, 1820

In 1830, James Ragland Jr. sold his deceased father's 108 acres to John Lisle for $1,500. John E. Lisle (1795-1868) was born in Clark County, a son of John Lisle Sr. and married Mary George in 1821. He was one of several well-to-do farmers in the neighborhood.

John Lisle kept the property only three years before selling to his neighbor Tandy Quisenberry for $2,000. Tandy Quisenberry (1792-1869) was the son of Rev. James

Quisenberry, an Orange County native and another brother-in-law of Billy Bush. Tandy married Margaret "Peggy" Bush, and they joined Providence Church. The couple raised nineteen children who all lived to adulthood. He was a prosperous farmer with substantial land holdings in the Bush Settlement. Tandy and Peggy are buried in a small graveyard near the intersection of Old Stone Church Road with Route 627.

4
History of a Clark County Plantation
Part 2

July 8, 2016

In 1872, Tandy Quisenberry's heirs sold his 108 acres plus an attached 114 acres to Philip P. Nunnelley (1830-1909) for the sum of $11,000. The location of the additional acreage is uncertain, as the deed did not have survey metes and bounds. Philip lived on the place with his family for seven years and then apparently was forced to sell.

According to an article in the *Winchester Democrat* in 1878, "Messrs. P. P. Nunnelley, L. B. Nunnelley, R. M. Nunnelley and J. C. Nunnelley are four brothers who have been living in Clark several years, and who have commended themselves to our people by their industry, steadiness and general good conduct." The article went on to say that two of the brothers, P. P. and L. B., had to sell property to satisfy creditors. The Nunnelleys, who came to Clark from Pulaski County, were all farmers except Richmond M. who was a physician. Philip, in debt to Rodney Haggard, had his farm sold at auction. The buyer was his brother Richmond's wife Mary for the sum of $7,853.

Richmond M. Nunnelley (1829-1904) married Mary Calmes (1843-1914) in Clark County. A notice in the *Winchester Sun-Sentinel* (1880) stated that "Dr. R. M. Nunnelley has moved to the place on the Boonesboro pike recently occupied by C. G. Bush and which Dr. Nunnelley purchased several months ago." The census for that year listed the couple with four children aged 4 to 12; Richmond gave his occupation then as "farmer."

The Nunnelleys lived there until 1903, when Richmond's failing health caused the couple to sell the farm and move to Winchester. He died the following year "at his home on Hickman Street...after a long illness." Mary lived on there until her death in 1914.

In 1903, the Richmond and Mary conveyed their 133-acre farm to "A. H. Hampton, as trustee for Henry G. Bush" for the sum of $9,364. The conditions of this sale were more complicated than stated in the deed. The farm was purchased for the benefit of Henry G. Bush and Leila Bush Woodford according to the terms of their grandfather Henry Grant's will. Henry and Leila were children of V. W. Bush and his first wife Prudence Grant. A. H. Hampton made the purchase for them as executor of Henry Grant's will.

Henry G. Bush (1856-1932) farmed this land for more than 30 years and died while still residing there. He never married, and his grandfather's will only left him a life interest in the farm. When Henry died, the land passed to his sister Leila.

Leila Bush (1858-1937) grew up in Winchester and attended Daughters College at Harrodsburg. She married Henry M. Woodford of Mt. Sterling and spent most of her married life in Montgomery County. Leila lived only five more years after inheriting the farm at Forest Grove. The farm then fell to her three daughters Margaret, Elizabeth and Mary.

In 1938, two of the Woodford sisters, Margaret Marsh and Elizabeth Cott, conveyed the farm to Mary Woodford Hamilton for "One Dollar and other good and valuable

considerations." Mary Woodford (1883-1952) was born in Mt. Sterling. She married James Carroll Hamilton and they lived in Sharpsburg where he was a farmer. He died in 1925 and Mary moved to Lexington with her children and aged mother (Leila). She died at her Lexington home in 1952.

Mary never lived on the Forest Grove farm. Her son, James Carroll Hamilton Jr. (1916-2003), ran the farm and occupied the old Ragland homeplace. He was

Mary Woodford Hamilton (1883-1952)

living there, unmarried, when the home burned in 1943. The fire was reported in the *Winchester Sun*:

"A Clark county landmark—the Carroll Hamilton home on the Boonesboro Road—lay in ruins today after a fire early Saturday night reduced to ashes a home whose history went back to the first settlers.... On Sunday old logs in the dwelling still were burning. According to S. J. Conkwright, historian, a part of the Hamilton homestead was constructed by James Ragland, pioneer, who lived on the farm, six miles south of Winchester, in the 1780s."

J. Carroll Hamilton on the farm at Forest Grove.

That year (1943) Carroll married Bettie Gay. He continued to farm at Forest Grove, but he never owned the property which remained in his mother's name. She died in 1952, and her will devised the farm jointly to her five children—Sarah, Leila, Archibald, Carroll and Buckner. In the 1960s, the heirs subdivided the farm, which became Hamilton Acres, and began selling off lots.

In 1969 the surviving heirs sold 11 acres to Glenn Wilson and his wife Frieda. Their lot on Goldwings Road was bordered by Forest Grove Christian Church, Waterworks Road and Lower Howard's Creek. Glenn "Red" Wilson (1916-2004) was born in Owsley County, graduated from Berea College, became a career naval aviator serving during World War II, the Korean Conflict and Vietnam War, and retired to Clark County. The couple built a two-story frame house on their lot in 1971. Mr. Wilson spent years planting native trees, shrubs and wildflowers on the land which had long been farm pasture. His wife's failing health led him to put the house up for sale in 1999.

Glenn "Red" Wilson on his place in 1990.

That was the year Brenda and I began looking for "a place in the country." One of my dreams was to find a house with a few acres of mature trees. The properties where I had lived in Lexington only had very young trees and not many of those. One day Brenda called me at UK and said I needed to come see this place in Clark County. She and her sister Judy had been out looking at houses for sale and stumbled onto the Wilsons'. "It has trees," she said, "lots of them." I drove over after work and was immediately infatuated. The place seemed a woodland paradise to me—and still does.

We closed on the 11-acre property in November 1999 and moved in. We got to spend a little over six years living together here in the forest. Brenda passed away in February 2006, and these woods and I grieved for her. I have now remarried, and I believe it will take dynamite to blast me off this place.

* * *

Researching the history of your property can be a rewarding experience. The process involves establishing a chain of successive owners by chasing deeds back in time as far as possible. Deed books and indexes are found at the courthouse and are easy to use. To gain addition knowledge about the property owners, you can gather biographical data for each. Excellent sources for this information are the Clark County Public Library and Bluegrass Heritage Museum.

Photos of Mary Woodford Hamilton and J. Carroll Hamilton, courtesy of Sarah Hamilton, and Glenn Wilson, courtesy of the Lexington Herald-Leader.

Sources

Harry G. Enoch, *Captain Billy Bush and the Bush Settlement, Clark County, Kentucky, A Family History* (Winchester, KY, 2015); Andrew Tribble's survey and patent, Kentucky Land Office, online at http://apps.sos. ky.gov/land/nonmilitary/patentseries/vaandokpatents/; George F. Doyle, *First Record Book of Providence Church, Clark County, Kentucky* (Winchester, KY, 1924), pp. 3, 5, 12-13, 148; Clark County Deed Book 1:343, 24:304, 26:283, 45:97, 48:162, 71:191, 116:460, 189:133, 367:571; *Clark County Democrat*, October 9, 1878; *Winchester Semi-Weekly Sun,* February 20, 1880; *Winchester Sun-Sentinel*, September 22, 1904; Clark County Will Book 2:151; *Winchester Sun*, January 19, 1914, "25 Years Ago," 1968 clipping describing the Ragland home fire, Ragland file, Clark County Public Library; *Lexington Herald-Leader* May 15, 1990.

5
Ann Sphar, alias Ann Smith

July 15, 2016

Several months ago we started what was intended to be a series of articles on Winchester residents in 1810. There are 48 names on the list, and we have only covered two of them: Henry Clampet and Mordecai Gist. We now take up the strange case of Ann Smith.

"Ann Smith" appears in the 1810 census for Winchester. She was over 45 years old and head of a household of one white male 10 to 16 years old and one slave. The previous November, Clark County Court had awarded her a "license to retail liquor & as a tavern keeper." These licenses had to be renewed each year. She owned two parcels of land in the county—just north of Washington Street, then outside the city limits—and three city lots numbered 46, 47 and 48. The lots were located on the west side of Highland Street beginning at Main Cross (Broadway) and running north to the middle of the block. All her property was acquired under the name "Ann Sphar"—"and thereby hangs a tale."

The story begins with the patriarch John Ulrich Sphar who brought his family from Germany and settled in what is now Berkeley County, West Virginia. His son Theodorous married Ann, maiden name unknown, and the couple had six children. Theodorous' two brothers, Jacob and Matthias, were among the first residents of Strode's Station in the fall of 1779. Theodorous joined them there soon after with his family, including his wife, Ann Sphar.

In early 1780, Theodorous staked a claim to 400 acres of land about two miles south of Strode's Station. He had the land surveyed in 1783 and was awarded a patent signed by Governor Patrick Henry. As these were unsafe times, however, Theodorous and family probably still resided at the station.

In March 1781, Strode's Station was attacked by Indians, said to number one hundred. Jacob Sphar, outside the fort at the time, was shot and scalped. In September 1784, Matthias Sphar in company with Joshua Bennett and Michael Cassidy were camped on Plum Lick Creek in now Bourbon County when they were attacked by Indians during the night. Matthias and Bennett were killed, Cassidy somehow managed to escape. Sometime after these family disasters, Theodorous returned to Berkeley County. His wife stayed behind. According to a Sphar family history, Theodorous' wife Ann "ran off with a man named Jacob Smith, Winchester, Kentucky. Theodorous traded 200 acres of land for a horse and returned to Virginia."

We can verify that Ann stayed behind, and she began using the names Sphar and Smith interchangeably. In March 1803 the Clark Court paid Ann Smith $4 for "two days & one Night sitting by william Stewart" and providing him with "whisky & Candles." Stewart died while in her care, and the coroner held an inquest on his death "on the 10th day of March in the house of Anna Sphar." The coroner's jury found "no marks of any violence" suggesting a natural death. No record of a divorce from Theodorous Sphar or marriage to Jacob Smith could be found. The incident at her house suggests she was operating a tavern at that time.

From information in a lawsuit, we learn she was still keeping a tavern in 1805. John Herrington sued three practical jokers—Orson Martin, Daniel Coleman and Alexander Kelley— for burning him with hot bricks while he was passed out drunk. Testimony indicated the pranks began at William Adams tavern and continued later at "Ann Smiths in Winchester."

Goff Bedford in his book *The Proud Land* states that "Ann Smith and her sister Mary had a rather long record for bootlegging and the oldest profession. It was a tolerant community." This may be true, but I have tried and so far failed to verify these claims.

When Ann Sphar wrote her will in September 1814, she was living in a house at the corner of Main and Broadway she had purchased from her son-in-law John Gosney. Her son "William Sphar alias William Smith" was executor of her will, probated in January 1815. She named her children by Theodorous: John, Nancy, Catherine, Betsy and a granddaughter Marthy, the child of deceased daughter Rebecca. Theodorous Jr., who had also died but left no heirs, was not listed. She also named sons Jacob and William, her children by Jacob Smith. Her children with Theodorous must have stayed behind or returned after Theodorous went back to Berkeley County. They were all living in Clark County when they sold their deceased mother's property. Since she signed all her official documents—deeds and will—as Ann Sphar, it seems unlikely she and Jacob Smith ever married.

Jacob Smith, who is listed as a Winchester resident in 1810, was in Clark County by 1793 and possibly before. He owned over 600 hundred acres of land east of Winchester. In 1795 he was licensed to keep an ordinary (tavern). Little additional information about him was found. Jacob died in 1838 and left a very detailed will. After directing "my Body to be buried in a good christian manner," he stated, "I Desire all my slaves shall be Freed amediately after my Death & all costs of their emansopation shall be paid out of my estate." Seven were named and three received additional generous bequests. For example, to "David my Faithful slave" he left "one Horse worth Fifty Dollars, two milch cows, one Sow and pigs, a how plough & axe & his beding & Household Furnature." The remainder of his estate he left to "my Two Sons whom I dearly Love, Jacob who is commonly Called Jacob Spaw & William who is generally cald William Smith." Ann's and Jacob's wills confirm that they had two children together, Jacob Jr. and William. From the little evidence available, Jacob Sr. seems to have been a decent man. There is no doubt much of this story still left untold.

As for Theodorous Sphar, after leaving Ann and returning to Berkeley County, he settled on land near Martinsburg. He also owned a lot in Bath, now Berkeley Springs, a popular resort then and now. In 1794, he sold 250 acres of his Clark County land to nephews Daniel and James Sphar, sons of Matthias. Theodorous married Dorothy Davis and they had seven children. He died in 1808 and left a will naming his surviving children from both marriages. In 1811, his heirs sold off the 150 acres of land he still owned in Clark County. There was no mention of a "horse" in any of the land sales.

Sources

Herman G. Spahr, *Spahr Family History* (Lafayette, IN, 1994); Theodorous Sphar warrant, survey and patent, Kentucky Land Office, http://apps.sos.ky.gov/land/nonmilitary/patentseries/vaandokpatents/; William Clinkenbeard and Daniel Sphar interviews, in Harry G. Enoch, *Pioneer Voices* (Winchester, KY, 2012), pp. 27-28, 93; Clark County Deed Book 1:306, 421, 6:340, 431, 7:161, 425, 8:264, 9:378, 543, 10:291, 11:89, 12:247, 15:398, 20:423, 24:226; Ann Smith tavern license and William Stewart receipt and inquest, loose papers in the Clark County Courthouse attic; *John Herrington v. Orson Martin et al.*, Clark County Complete Records Book, 1806, pp. 149-151; A. Goff Bedford, *The Proud Land* (Mt. Sterling, KY, 1983), pp. 233, 281, 340; Clark County Will Book 3:365, 418, 424, 4:13, 9:216; Clark County Order Book 1:164; Berkeley County (VA) Will Book 4:192.

6
Three Notable Winchester Residents

July 22, 2016

We continue this series on Winchester residents of 1810 by considering three you may not have heard of, who went on to achieve some notoriety after they left Clark County.

Silas Webster Robbins (1785-1871) was born in Connecticut, graduated Yale College then attended Tapping Reeves' celebrated Litchfield Law School. We first learn of Robbins when he announced in December 1809 that he planned to open a school on Water Street (now Maple). His notice in the *Kentucky Gazette* set tuition at $3.50 per quarter for reading, writing and arithmetic; $5 for English grammar; $6 for bookkeeping; $8 for Greek and Latin; $9 for trigonometry, surveying, natural and moral philosophy.

In 1811, Robbins hung out his shingle and announced in the *Gazette* that he "will punctually attend the circuit courts of Fayette, Madison, and Clarke, and will faithfully discharge any business in his profession." The following year he returned to Connecticut to marry Caroline, the daughter of U.S. Senator Uriah Tracy.

Like many other Winchester attorneys, Robbins invested his earnings in local property. In 1816, he acquired 224 acres just north of town from Joseph Foreman. Robbins was residing in a brick home on the place in 1824, when financial problems forced him to cede his interest to his brother Moses.

Robbins served as a circuit judge and, according to one source, "was appointed Judge of the Supreme Court of his adopted State." I have been unable to verify the latter. "Due to the strong prejudice in the state against Yankees," Robbins moved to Springfield, Illinois, in 1841 and took up the practice of law there. It was inevitable, perhaps, that he would cross paths with a rising young attorney named Abraham Lincoln. To give but a few examples, in 1845 *Lockridge v. Foster et al.* was argued before the Illinois Supreme Court. Silas Robbins represented the plaintiff and Abraham Lincoln the defendant. Then in 1847, Robbins and Lincoln worked together as a legal team for the defendants in *Hill v. Masters and Goodpasture.*

Court document in *Hill v. Masters and Goodpasture*. Last line reads "Robbins & Lincoln f.d. [for defendants]." (Papers of Abraham Lincoln, Springfield, Illinois)

* * *

James Dunnica was a carpenter and builder in Winchester. He married Philadelphia Thomas in 1812. Dunnica built a brick house at the southeast corner of Main and what is now Hickman Street on land he purchased from David Dodge for $280. In 1814, he sold the house and lot to Chilton Allan for $1,375. The next year, when James and Philadelphia sold the last of their Winchester property, they were residents of Woodford County. They moved to Cole County, Missouri, along with many other Kentuckians. In 1825, Dunnica was named one of the first trustees of Jefferson City, which became the capital of Missouri. From 1827 till 1834 he served as a justice for Cole County. Dunnica received a contract to erect the brick State House for $25,000. The legislature assembled in the new capitol in 1826. He then superintended construction of the Cole County courthouse. Dunnica, "a master stonemason," also built the Missouri State Penitentiary in Jefferson City. This massive limestone prison complex operated from 1833 until 2004 and is now a historic landmark and tourist attraction. An early Missouri gazetteer stated, "The citizens of Cole are much indebted to Mr. James Dunnica for the tasteful architecture at Jefferson [City]."

Missouri State Penitentiary
(Courtesy of Missouri State Archives)

* * *

William Vaughn (1785-1877) was born in Westmoreland County, Pennsylvania, and came to Kentucky with his parents at an early age. At 18 he apprenticed to Lawson McCullough, a tailor in Lexington. After his apprenticeship he married Lydia Wing Allen and moved to Winchester, where he established himself as a tailor. He purchased a lot from Jesse Garner at the northwest corner of Main and now Hickman Street and built a house there. He joined "an infidel club" in town, but soon had a change of heart. In October 1810 he was baptized by Rev. James Quisenberry at Friendship Baptist Church (where Winchester Cemetery is today). He was licensed to preach at Friendship in 1811, was ordained at Lulbegrud Church in 1812, and began a storied career as a Baptist minister.

Vaughn's first church was in Montgomery County, his second in Mason. He established a church at Augusta where he preached and taught school, then moved to Fleming where he bought a farm and preached at several churches. In 1829, he debated the renowned Alexander Campbell, a founder of the Disciples of Christ. After a brief stint with the American Bible Society, Vaughn moved to Bloomfield in 1836. He preached there until 1868, when he became disabled from a fall.

At some point in life he adopted "Vaughan" as the spelling of his surname. His biographers have been enthusiastic in their praise. "No other man in Kentucky ever became so great a preacher as he [and] suffice it to say that all accord to Wm. Vaughan the first place as a great preacher of all who lived during the first half of the nineteenth century. Others have risen up who have perhaps been as great, but none equaled him in his day."

William Vaughan

Sources

Robbins: *Kentucky Gazette*, December 25, 1810, February 19, 1811; Clark County Deed Book 10:181, 12:358, 25:12; Obituary Record of Graduates of Yale College, 1808, http://mssa.library.yale.edu/obituary_record/1859_1924/1871-72.pdf; Lee H. Hoffman, *Historical Documents about Montgomery County, Kentucky* (Mt. Sterling, KY, 2006), p. 19; *Lexington Observer Reporter*, February 3, 1836; John M. Palmer, *Bench and Bar of Illinois, Vol. 1* (Chicago, IL, 1899), p. 180; The Lincoln Log, www.thelincolnlog.org/Results.aspx?type=CalendarMonth&year=1845&month=2; Abraham Lincoln's Cases, History of the Illinois Supreme Court, www.illinoiscourts.gov/supremecourt/historical/Lincoln.asp; Roger Billings, *Abraham Lincoln, Esq., The Legal Career of America's Greatest President* (Lexington, KY, 2012 edition), pp. 93-96; Sangamon County (IL) Probate Records, Book 5:438. **Dunnica**: Louise P. du Bellet et al., *Some Prominent Virginia Families, Vol. 4* (Lynchburg, VA, 1907), p. 240; George F. Doyle, *Marriage Bonds* of *Clark County* (Winchester, KY, 1933); Clark County Deed Book 10:342, 11:141; Goodspeed Publishing, *History of Cole, Moniteau, Morgan, Benton, Miller, Maries, and Osage Counties, Missouri* (Chicago, IL, 1889); Cole County, Missouri, www.livingplaces.com/MO/Cole_County.html; Jefferson City Correctional Center, www.jeffcitymo.org; Jamie P. Rasmussen, *Missouri State Penitentiary: 170 Years Inside The Walls* (Columbia, MO, 2012), pp. 10-11; Alphonso Wetmore, *Gazetteer of the State of Missouri* (St. Louis, MO, 1837), p. 63. **Vaughn**: J. H. Spencer, *History of Kentucky Baptists, Vol. 1* (Cincinnati, OH, 1885), pp. 204, 219-229; Ben M. Bogard, *Pillars of Orthodoxy, or Defenders of the Faith* (Louisville, KY, 1900), pp. 64-69; Clark County Deed Book 9:235, 10:359.

7
Early Winchester Physicians

August 5, 2016

In 1814, Clark County's local newspaper, the *Winchester Advertiser*, announced: "Doctors Barbee, Mills and Taliaferro have entered into co-partnership in the practice of Medicine, Surgery, &c. They have on hand a complete assortment of Drugs & Medicines, which they offer for sale on good terms in their apothecary way. Winchester" These doctors were Thomas Barbee, John Mills and Robert Taliaferro.

* * *

Thomas Barbee, though erroneously referred to as "General Barbee" in some local histories, was in fact a physician. We learned in a previous column that Thomas Barbee built what is now called the "Ogden House," which stands at the corner of Main and Ogden Alley and is one of Winchester's oldest houses.

Doctor Barbee also entered Winchester's business community. In the 1816 *Advertiser*, he and James Bristoe announced they had gone into the wool-carding trade "in the house formerly occupied as a Cotton Factory by [John] Coons." That same year "Doctors Barbee, Mills & Taliaferro offered "to purchase a quantity of Palma Christi seed." They were paying "$2 per bushel for good clean seed." Palma Christi was an early name for the castor bean plant (*Ricinus communis*). Its seed is the source of castor oil, whose medicinal uses go back to 17th century in America.

By 1820, Doctor Barbee had moved to Paris, where he became a ruling elder in the Presbyterian Church. He seems to have been more involved there in church-related activities than in the practice of medicine. Thomas Barbee died in Paris in 1821. His estate inventory reveals he owned more than 60 books of a religious nature and none on medicine.

* * *

Robert Taliaferro came to Kentucky from Caroline County, Virginia. (The name is pronounced "Tolliver.")

According to a family history, Robert was the brother of Winchester's Hay Taliaferro, who ran the Indian Queen tavern and hotel on the site of the later Rees House and present-day Brown-Proctor.   In 1812, Robert married Hubbard Taylor's daughter Nancy in Clark County.   She reportedly died in childbirth the following year. In 1816, Robert married America Arnold of Bourbon County.

According to an 1819 notice in the *Advertiser*, "Doctor Talliaferro has removed to town and will diligently continue the practice of Medicine. He occupies the Old Stand of Mills and Talliaferro." A second notice in the same issue states, "All those indebted to the firm of Mills & Taliaferro are requested to call and settle their accounts by note or otherwise." Evidently, the partnership of doctors had broken up. Barbee had moved to Paris by then, and Mills and Taliaferro may have been going their separate ways.

In the following year's census (1820), we find "Dr. Robt. Talliferro" residing in Paris. He practiced medicine there until his death in 1836. He is buried in Paris Cemetery beside his wife America, who died in 1832. Her stone lists the names of their six children.

*   *   *

Dr. John Mills

John Mills was born in Maryland, trained as a physician, married Lucy Rice, and immigrated to Winchester, where he joined the partnership of Barbee and Taliaferro. He resided on a 30-foot lot on Main Street between Barbee's house and the Winchester Branch of the Commonwealth Bank.

After Taliaferro and Barbee moved away, Mills entered into medical practice with his son, Augustus W. Mills. Both distinguished themselves during the cholera epidemic of 1833. Augustus' son, John A. Mills, also became a physician.

At some point, John Mills gave up medicine for the law and became a respected member of the Winchester bar. He was so well thought of that the county court commissioned A. C. Smith to paint his portrait in 1852. The painting still hangs at the courthouse in the second-floor court room.

* * *

Samuel D. Martin (1791-1881) was one of Clark County's most noted physicians. He was the son of the "Basin Springs" John Martin, Revolutionary War veteran and first sheriff of the county. Samuel was born in Clark County and studied medicine at Transylvania University. He married Jonathan Taylor's daughter Elizabeth in 1812. The 1816 *Advertiser* announced, "Doctor Samuel D. Martin has removed to Winchester and tenders his services to the public in the practice of Medicine & Surgery. His shop is on Main Street between the stores of George G. Taylor & Co. and Wm. N. Lane & Co." In the same issue, he placed an advertisement for "Fresh Medicines": "Dr. S. D. Martin has on hand and intends keeping at this shop on main street...a constant supply of Medicines and Paints, which he pledges himself to sell as low as they are sold by any merchant in Winchester, among which are the following articles...." Here he listed 113 items he planned to stock, which included some dangerous—muriatic acid, quicksilver, opium— and some mysterious—Godfrey's cordial, Quassia bitters, and nutgalls.

In 1825, after practicing in Winchester for ten years, Doctor Martin moved back to the Basin Springs farm where he resided until his death. His plan to give up medicine failed as he was continually called upon to treat sick neighbors. He did manage to become a prominent breeder of shorthorn cattle and frequently contributed articles to agricultural journals of the day. Doctor Martin was a long-time diarist, kept detailed daily weather records for years, and at age 75 was still making medical rounds on horseback. In 1879, when the Clark County Medical Society was formed, he was elected the first president. He was at that time the oldest physician in the county. Samuel D. Martin is buried beside his wife Elizabeth in the family graveyard on Basin Springs Road.

* * *

Dr. Andrew Hood

Andrew Hood (1796-1859) had a distinguished Clark County lineage. His grandfather of the same name was an early settler who established Hood's Station north of Winchester. His father, Lucas Hood, a well-known military figure, raised three sons who became physicians: Andrew, John and William. (Dr. John Hood was the father of Confederate Civil War general, John Bell Hood.)

Andrew Hood was one of the most prominent doctors of the county. His fine home and office on French Avenue were outside the town limits at that time. In addition to statewide recognition in his profession, Doctor Hood was chosen as a delegate to the Kentucky Constitutional Convention of 1849. Three of his children also became physicians: James, Joseph, Richard. Andrew is buried in Winchester Cemetery. The county court commissioned his portrait, and the painting hangs in the same court room as Dr. John Mills'. Andrew Hood's home on French Avenue is listed on the National Register of Historic Places.

Sources

Barbee: *Winchester Advertiser*, September 23, 1814; *Kentucky Advertiser*, August 10, 1816; *Paris Western Citizen*, October 1821; Clark County Deed Book 11:168, 12:161, 445; H. E. Everman, *History of Bourbon County, 1785-1865* (Paris, KY, 1977), pp. 64-65, 185-186; Bourbon County Will Book G:1.

Taliaferro: James T. Taliaferro, *Taliaferro Family History, 1635-1899* (Reno, NV, 1995); George F. Doyle, *Marriage Bonds of Clark County* (Winchester, KY, 1933); Bourbon County Marriage Returns 2:55; *Kentucky Advertiser and Farmer's Magazine*, October 30, 1819; findagrave.com.

Mills: Clark County Deed Book 15:309; Lucille G. Clark, *Biographies of Portrait Subjects of the Clark County Circuit Court Room* (Winchester, KY, 1958), p. 7; Edna T. Whitley, *Kentucky Ante-Bellum Portraiture* (n.p., 1956), pp. 86-87.

Martin: Samuel D. Martin, *Genealogical Record of the Martin Family*, copy of Bobbie Newell, Winchester, KY; Clark County Deed Book 10:251, 15:313, 573; *Kentucky Advertiser*, August 10, 1816; Clark County Chronicles, *Winchester Sun*, May 6, 1926.

Hood: Lucille G. Clark, *Biographies of Portrait Subjects of the Clark County Circuit Court Room* (Winchester, KY, 1958), pp. 1-3; Edna T. Whitley, *Kentucky Ante-Bellum Portraiture* (n.p., 1956), pp. 78-79.

8

Jonathan Swift and His Lost Silver Mines

August 12, 2016

Few things stir the imagination more than tales of lost treasure and indescribable quantities of gold or silver or rare jewels, which helps explain why Jonathan Swift's lost silver mines still excite treasure hunters in Kentucky today. Although the legend is now more than two centuries old, interest in the mines has dimmed little over time. Scores of adventurers still actively pursue the elusive prize.

The outline of the story goes like this: A Jonathan (or John) Swift came into Kentucky with George Munday and others in 1760—well before Daniel Boone—and discovered several silver mines. They carried loads of treasure back to Virginia, returning periodically for more. They set up furnaces to smelt the metal and form it into silver bars and coins. Years later, Swift, who had gone blind, was unable to find his mines. There are many, many variations on the basic story. Supposed copies of Swift's journal and maps have been in circulation for years. The journal gives detailed but practically useless directions for finding the mines and furnaces:

"The furnace that I built is on the left hand side of a long rocky branch that heads southwest and flows northeast in a very remote place in the west. There is a very large rockhouse that faces the east, a hundred yards above the rockhouse the furnace is in. You can stand at the furnace and facing the east you can see two monument rocks—one 25 feet high and one 15 feet high."

Versions of Swift's map, such as the one shown here, are similarly unhelpful.

In spite of geologists' claims that large silver deposits do not occur in Kentucky, strong interest in the subject persists to this day. A Google search for Swift's lost silver mines returned nearly 700,000 hits.

One of the most surprising findings is how early the search for Swift's mines began. Companies of men from central Kentucky were going out on organized hunts before we achieved statehood. In February 1792, Col. James Harrod, the founder of Kentucky's first permanent settlement, went out with a group looking for the silver mine. Harrod did not return and was never heard from again. (His wife accused James Bridges of murdering him.)

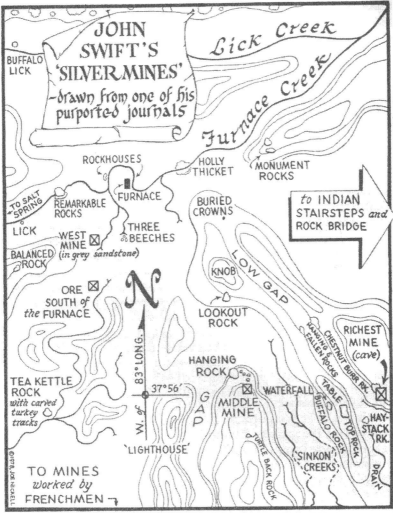

One of Many Purported Maps to Swift's Silver Mines

Rev. John Dabney Shane interviewed many of the old pioneers in the 1840s. One of them told Shane that Capt. Billy Bush knew Swift personally and had his confidence.

"Bush was the principal one to get out Swift's family [to Kentucky]. That was after Swift had gone blind. He with James Young, James Bridges and Michael Stoner were the original party, each to share equally. These were the first persons to go after Swift had revealed the particulars to them. Each was sworn not to disclose the directions while he lived."

Billy Bush continued his pursuit of the mines into his old age. Writing about her great-uncle, Julia Ann Tevis stated, "He spent his later years in the visionary pursuit of silver mines, which he never found. Like the mirage of the desert they eluded his grasp, forever and forever vanishing as the spot was neared."

Many other pioneers interviewed by Reverend Shane recited some piece of the tale or told about others who searched for the lost mines. In Clark and Montgomery alone, we have accounts by Samuel Tribble, James Wade, Septimus Scholl, William Risk, Jesse Daniel, William Calmes, Nancy Goff, Samuel Gibson, Richard French and William Barrow. Clark County men searching for the mines included Thomas Burrus, John Martin, Peter Daniel, William Eubank, Jacob Embree, Maples Hardwick, John Johnson, Thomas Lackey, Aaron Crosthwaite, James Jackson, William Hanks, Micajah Clark, Martin Johnston, and William McMillan. McMillan persisted in his quest for many years. To find the mines, he organized a company composed of John Bush, John Bruner, Elijah Crosthwaite, Zachariah Field, James McMillan, John McClure, and others.

The pioneers also spoke of certain Shawnee Indians who, on several occasions, passed through the county into the knobs of present-day Powell County and returned with bags of silver. Several enterprising souls in the Indian Old Fields area cooked up schemes to bilk investors by claiming they had found the Indians' source of silver ore.

History detective and skeptic, Joe Nickell, claims there is no evidence that Swift's silver mines ever existed. Nickell suggests the scheme was a hoax perpetrated by John Filson to promote his land sales. According to his research, the first historical record of the "silver mines" may be Filson's 1788 land entry in Fayette County:

"Robert Breckenridge and John Filson as Tenants in Common Enters 1000 acres of land...about Sixty or Seventy miles North Eastwardly from Martins Cabbins in powells Valley to Include a silver mine which was Improved about 17 years ago by a Certain man named Swift. At said mine the said Swift Reports he has extracted from the oar a Considerable quantity of Silver, some of which he made into Dollars and left at or near the mine, together with the apperatus for making the same."

This entry was made at a time when Filson was being harassed by creditors. He disappeared later that year while trying to establish a town at present-day Cincinnati. After Filson's death, Nickell points to another scoundrel, Eli Cleveland, who composed another fiction to spring on an unsuspecting public:

"April 1791. Eli Cleveland and John Morton enters 1483 acres of land...on a branch of Red River to Include an Old Camp in the Center where there is some old troughs at said Camp by the branch side. The said Camp is a place difficult of access Supposed to be Swift's Old Camp and others including a mine said to be occupied formerly by said Swift and others."

Neither historical evidence nor geologists' expert opinions has stopped the search for the lost mines or the outpouring of books on the subject. The Red River Gorge remains a prime location for modern treasure hunters. We have landmarks in Wolfe County named Silvermine Arch and Swift Camp Creek. ("Swift got hurt and lay sick for a good while out on Swift's Camp Creek.") Campton has an annual Swift Silver Mine Festival on Labor Day weekend. Not to be outdone, there are enthusiasts who believe the lost mines are located in Ohio, Tennessee, Virginia, West Virginia, North Carolina, Georgia and Alabama.

Sources

Thomas D. Clark, *The Kentucky* (Lexington, KY, 1942), pp. 30-41; Charles Kerr, editor, *History of Kentucky, Vol. 1* (Chicago, IL, 1922), pp. 110-133; Joe Nickell, "Uncovered—The Fabulous Silver Mines of Swift and Filson," *Filson Club History Quarterly* (1980) 54:325; Lincoln County Entry Book

2:299; Warren H. Anderson, *Rocks and Minerals of Kentucky* (Lexington, KY, 1994), p. 50; Robert H. Ruchhoft, *Kentucky's Land of the Arches* (Cincinnati, OH, 1976), p. 20; Michael S. Steely, *Swift's Silver Mines and Related Appalachian Treasures* (Johnson City, TN, 1995), p. viii; Harry G. Enoch, *Captain Billy Bush and the Bush Settlement* (Winchester, KY, 2015), pp. 117-122; Draper MSS 11CC 53, 89-90, 98, 12CC 41, 43-44, 125, 203, 211; Clark County Chronicles, *Winchester Sun*, April 10, 1924. Swift's Map was taken from the *Filson Club History Quarterly*, October 1980.

9
James Clark
"A Man for All Seasons"

August 19, 2016

James Clark (1779-1839) is well known locally as Kentucky's thirteenth governor and the builder of Holly Rood, also called the Clark Mansion. I must confess that until gathering material for this article, I was scarcely aware of the breadth of his remarkable career.

To gain an appreciation for his accomplishments, a little background is in order. Kentucky has three branches of government: executive, legislative and judicial. James Clark served in all three branches, one of only three persons ever to do so. But there is more, which no one has matched. The highest offices of the executive branch are governor and lieutenant governor. Clark served as both. The legislature has two chambers, the Senate and House of Representatives. Clark served in both. The state judiciary in his day had two courts, the Circuit Court and the Court of Appeals. Clark served in both. (The Court of Appeals was then the state's highest court. The Kentucky Supreme Court was not created until 1975.) To top this off, Clark also served several terms in Congress.

James Clark was born near the Peaks of Otter in Bedford County, Virginia, the son of Robert Clark and Susannah Henderson. James is said to have begun his law practice in Winchester in 1797. He was elected to the Kentucky House of Representatives in 1807 and served until 1808. In 1810 he built a house on a lot purchased from James Sympson. The lot was located just outside the town boundary, on the east side of Main Street between now Ogden Alley and Hickman Street. That year Clark was appointed to the Kentucky Court of Appeals. He served until 1813, when he was elected to the U.S. House of Representatives, the same year he began building Holly Rood. He resigned that office in 1816 to accept an appointment as circuit court judge for Clark and Bourbon Counties. He left that office to run for Congress and in 1825 was again elected to the U.S. House of Representatives, filling Henry Clay's seat when Clay was appointed Secretary of State.

Governor James Clark
(Portrait by Sophia Gray at the Kentucky Historical Society)

Clark served in Congress until 1831, when he was elected to the Kentucky Senate. That body made him President of the Senate. In 1834, Gov. John Breathitt died in office and was succeeded by Lieutenant Governor James T. Morehead. As President of the Senate, Clark succeeded to the office of lieutenant governor (acting). Clark was elected governor by a large majority in 1836. He may truly be called Kentucky's first "education governor." At his initiative the legislature created a state board of education, the office of state superintendent, and a county school commissioner in every county. Clark died in office on September 27, 1839. His remains were brought home and buried on the grounds at Holly Rood.

James Clark was honored with a handsome granite monument erected by the state, which recognizes all the offices he held: "Representative, Senator, Congressman, Circuit Judge, Judge of the Court of Appeals, President of the Senate, Acting Lieutenant Governor, Governor." One of his contemporaries penned this description:

"He was of fine personal appearance, of cheerful and social disposition. An easy address and fascinating manner made him the life of every circle in which he mingled. He was full of fun, fond of anecdotes, and could tell a story with inimitable grace. He possessed those qualities well calculated to display the amiable traits of his character in their best light, and those stern and manly virtues which inspire confidence and command respect."

I now understand Frank Vermillion's long time fascination with James Clark. For many years Mr. Vermillion, a retired Clark County educator, gave regular presentations on Governor Clark, often in costume.

The foregoing digression is really an aside from the article I intended to write, which concerns James Clark's role in one of Kentucky's most famous and most dangerous controversies: the Old Court-New Court struggle. According to Lowell Harrison and James Klotter, authors of the *New History of Kentucky*, it was during this battle that "the commonwealth came close to civil war as the result of some of the most vicious politicking that Kentucky has ever endured."

The general prosperity of the post-War of 1812 period ended with the nationwide Panic of 1819. Commodity prices fell, credit dried up as banks failed, and creditors refused to accept depreciated bank notes in payment. As a result, a host of Kentuckians found themselves hopelessly in debt. The legislature responded with a series of "relief laws" that allowed debtors to delay payment on contracts and "replevin laws" that provided a legal means to recover property said to have been wrongly taken. Creditors, not surprisingly, cried foul, and it was not long before the laws were contested in court.

As it happened, the first challenge—*Williams v. Blair*—came to the Bourbon Circuit Court before Judge James Clark in 1822. Judge Clark found the replevin law unconstitutional due to the fact that *ex post facto* (retroactive) laws regarding contracts were prohibited by the U.S. and Kentucky constitutions.

Since debtors far outnumbered creditors in Kentucky, Clark's ruling created a firestorm. He was hauled before the legislature to defend his ruling, which he did in a masterful response. The House of Representatives then attempted to remove him from office but the vote, 59-35, failed to achieve the required two-thirds majority. Next, they tried to outlaw "judicial review," a ruling that declared an act of the legislature unconstitutional. (Such rulings were rare.) The legislature failed in this effort as well. In 1823, the Court of Appeals heard the case and upheld Judge Clark's decision. The legislature then tried to unseat the Court of Appeals judges but again failed to obtain a two-thirds majority.

Representative George Robertson, of the Anti-relief Party, later wrote that "no popular controversy, waged without bloodshed, was ever more absorbing and acrimonious than that which raged like a hurricane over Kentucky for about three years." In 1824, the Relief Party succeeded in electing the governor, Joseph Desha, and obtained a majority in both houses of the legislature. They immediately moved to abolish the Court of Appeals, replaced it with a new Court of Appeals, and appointed four new judges sympathetic to the plight of debtors.[*]

The Old Court refused to recognize the New Court, and for the next two years both held regular sessions, placing litigants in the nearly impossible position of having to determine which one was legitimate. Finally, in 1826 the Old Court Party obtained

---

[*] One of the new judges was John Trimble, son of Clark County pioneer William Trimble and brother of U.S. Supreme Court Justice Robert Trimble.

enough seats in the legislature to abolish the New Court and reinstate the Old Court—and the crisis ended. The fact that the state's economy had begun to recover by then helped restore sanity.

James Clark fits the description of "one who remains true to himself and his beliefs while adapting to all circumstances and times, despite external pressure or influence," thus earning him the sobriquet "a man for all seasons."

Sources

William B. Allen, *History of Kentucky* (Louisville, KY, 1872), pp. 96-97; Biographical Dictionary of the United States Congress, http://bioguide. congress.gov/biosearch/biosearch.asp; Lowell H. Harrison and James C. Klotter, *New History of Kentucky* (Lexington, KY, 1997), pp. 109-112; Thomas B. Jones, New Thoughts On An Old Theme," Register of the Kentucky Historical Society (1971) 69:293-312; Clark County Deed Book 7:587, 10:160.

10

John G. Stuart's
New Orleans Flatboat Journal

August 26, 2016

In 1806 John G. Stuart worked as a hand on a flatboat trip to New Orleans. Stuart kept a diary during his journey down the Kentucky, Ohio and Mississippi Rivers. In 1952 the diary, then in private hands, was transcribed and published in the *Register of the Kentucky Historical Society.* Several years ago the diary, now archived at the Historical Society, was adapted for a stage production put on at the KHS Museum Theatre. Who was this John G. Stuart?

John Gaitskill Stuart (c1782-1853) was born in Culpeper County, Virginia, the eldest son of Revolutionary War veteran James Stuart and Elizabeth Gaitskill. John grew up on his father's farm in the Wade's Mill area of Clark County. When he was 36 years old, he married a neighborhood girl, Sarah "Sallie" Gaitskill, sixteen years his junior. James divided his land among his adult sons, and John resided on 200 acres where he farmed and raised a family. He died of pneumonia in 1853 and is buried in the Stuart family graveyard.

All four of James Stuart's sons—John, Roy, James Jr. and Robert—served in the War of 1812. Capt. John Stuart commanded two of the eleven companies sent from Clark County. One of his messmates during the war, as well as lifelong companion, was Samuel Williams. Samuel named his famous son—John Stuart Williams—after his friend and neighbor. John S. "Cerro Gordo" Williams distinguished himself in the Mexican War and served as a Confederate general during the Civil War.

John G. Stuart served as a county justice from 1818 until 1834. He then held the office of sheriff in 1835 and 1836. In 1830 Clark County voters sent Stuart to the Kentucky House of Representatives for one term.

Stuart died March 25, 1853, without leaving a will.[*] Estate inventories usually contain a fairly common list of household goods and farm implements. Stuart's inventory, however, was anything but typical. The first two pages recorded his books; 31 were listed by title and an unknown number were divided into 18 separate lots. Other unusual items included a prism, a pocket compass, flower vases, and two violins. Household items claimed by his widow included 4 counterpanes, 7 coverlets, 7 quilts, 11 blankets, 36 sheets, and 14 tablecloths.

Sallie died in 1891 at age 93. Her obituary, which appeared in the *Richmond Climax*, stated that she was the "last survivor in Clark County of the widows of the veterans of 1812 drawing a pension, except Mrs. James Chism."

John G. Stuart began his flatboat diary on February 22, 1806: "Started from my father's with my brother Roy for Cleveland landing." Eli Cleveland's landing was on the Kentucky River at the mouth of Boone Creek. Here Stuart joined George Halley, whose boat was tied up at the landing, and his deckhand, E. Clark.[†] George was the son of Clark County pioneer Richard Halley. Richard was the brother of John Halley, who was among the earliest to take flatboats to New Orleans—in 1789 and 1791—and kept a diary of his journeys.[‡]

George Halley's boat carried "flour & a little whiskey & tobacco," 315 barrels in all. After loading the boat, they waited at the landing for the rise of the river known as the "spring tide." The wait proved nearly interminable—54 days in all—as the rains were exceptionally late to come in 1806. During the interval, John went sightseeing, dined and partied at homes along the river, and visited other boats in the same predicament, including one belonging to John Baker (probably the son of Winchester's founder of the same name). Stuart stated that "there are said to be at this time about 100 Boats lying in the Kentucky waiting for water to carry them out." Of one of the boats, he

---

[*] Gravestone says March 25; county death record says March 5.

[†] E. Clark could not be identified.

[‡] Harry G. Enoch, *Bound for New Orleans! Original Journal of John Halley of His Trips to New Orleans Performed in the Years 1789 & 1791* (Winchester, KY, 2005).

commented, "The crew are a specimen of what I may expect to see in my voyage, drinking swearing & kicking."

Stuart pronounced their boat one of the finest on the river in terms of accommodations. "We have a very good fireplace and a comfortable little room in her." He would later learn that "Our boat, tho' in other respects one of the best, has a very bad roof. Last night it let the rain in prodigiously."

Three weeks into his wait, Stuart noted that "Mr. Halley...brought me three newspapers, the first Literary amusement I have enjoyed since here. A luxury I considered them." A week later he mentioned reading a novel, "the Beggar Girl," and a little later "Saunders Journal."[*]

Flatboat on the River
(Alfred R. Waud engraving, Historic New Orleans Collection)

Finally, after several days of heavy rains, they prepared to leave. On April 16, he noted, "By 10 o'clock [the river] had

---

[*] *The Beggar Girl and Her Benefactors* (1797) by Mrs. Agnes Marie Bennett; *A Journal of the Travels and Sufferings of Daniel Saunders, Jun. : a Mariner on Board the Ship Commerce, of Boston, Samuel Johnson, Commander, which was cast away near Cape Morebet, on the coast of Arabia, July 10, 1792* (1805).

risen 12 or 15 feet at which time we hove off." They made 40 miles the first day, then had to stop because the river had reached a dangerous level. "It has now risen above 30 [feet]. We judged it too high this morning to proceed." While tied up, they watched "the Wreck of a large new produce Boat," four tobacco barrels, several canoes, and a cow "flying past."

They spent several days there at a place he called "the Vineyard." This was Kentucky's first winery, established by Swiss native John James Dufour in Jessamine County in 1799. (The winery, re-established in 2006 by Tom Beall, was recently listed on the National Register of Historic Places.) Stuart borrowed some tools at the vineyard then "passed some hours in conversing with an amiable Swiss Girl." He returned the next morning and "spent some agreeable hours in the company of the amiable Maria Dufore." Downriver two days later, he wrote, "Maria still runs in my mind."

Their boat reached the Ohio River on April 23 and Louisville on the 25th. They hired a pilot to take to them through the "Indian shute" at the falls of the Ohio. They made it to the Mississippi on May 5, where "the Misquitoes began on us." He described meeting two Cherokees "dress't in stile," swimming in the river, and catching a 30-pound catfish. They docked at Natchez on May 25, unloaded the produce, and from there Stuart accompanied Joshua Baker on his boat to New Orleans, which they reached on June 3. "My greates expectations are gratified.... 150 Ships & upwards of 300 Flats.... Some Grand buildings.... Frequent disturbances between different parties.... an American was stabbed here today by a Spaniard.... very hot. misquetoes very bad. Fine Girls."

They started home on foot on June 9. He complained much of the way with sore feet and swollen legs then, later on the journey, of dysentery and high fever. His last entry was on July 22: "This morning we cross't Dix River."

Sources

Stuart's Journal, *Register of the Kentucky Historical Society* (1952) 50:5-25; Clark County Order Book 6:57, 10:263, 321; Clark County Deed Book 2:21, 8:326, 9:1; *Mt. Sterling Advocate*, July 19, 1898; *Richmond Climax*, March 18, 1891; Clark County Death Records, 1853, ancestry.com; Kathryn Owen,

Old Graveyards of Clark County, Kentucky (Winchester, KY, 1975), p. 122; loose papers in the attic of Clark County Courthouse; Clark County Chronicles, *Winchester Sun*, May 13, 1926; Richard H. Collins, *History of Kentucky, Vol. 2* (Covington, KY, 1874), p. 774.

11
Famous Landowners of Early Clark County

September 2, 2016

For many years, whenever I heard "the West" or "out West," my mind conjured visions of places on the other side of the Mississippi River. You know what I'm talking about: cowboys and Indians, wagon trains and gunfights, Tombstone, Deadwood and Dodge City. Most of our westward expansion was driven by people in search of land, a quest epitomized by the great land rush in Oklahoma territory (and the Sooners who jumped the gun and crossed the border before the official opening).

Historians argue that Kentucky should rightly be considered the "first West." The story unfolds something like this: For nearly 150 years, settlement in the American colonies spread slowly and none breached the continental divide, the Allegheny Mountains. Pressure for new lands eventually grew so strong that even King George's edicts could not hold back hunters and traders who crossed the mountains and began exploring the wilderness that later become Kentucky. The 1750s saw visits by traders like John Findley and land company explorers like Dr. Thomas Walker and Christopher Gist. The 1760s brought the "long hunters" whose number included Daniel Boone. Things developed rapidly in the next decade. Virginia created Fincastle County in 1772, and two years later the highest ranking county official, Col. William Preston, sent a group of surveyors out to locate lands for veterans of the French and Indian War. Kentucky's first two permanent settlements— Boonesborough and Harrodsburg in 1775—opened the floodgates for migrants from Virginia, North Carolina and elsewhere. They all came to the frontier seeking land. Their ranks swelled as visitors returning east described Kentucky's abundant game and fertile soils as a kind of new Eden. By 1780, over four million acres had been claimed. By 1800, Kentucky's population topped 220,000.

Acquiring land in early Kentucky could be a dicey process. Four steps were involved.

—**Warrant**. One had first to obtain a land warrant, which was a general entitlement to a specific quantity (acres) of land. Military warrants were issued for service in the French and Indian War and Revolutionary War.* Treasury warrants could be purchased from the state of Virginia.

—**Entry**. After a specific tract of unoccupied land was located, an entry had to be made in the surveyor's office giving a precise description of the property. The entry, which reserved the property for the claimant, could be sold or assigned to someone else.

—**Survey**. One of the officially appointed surveyors had to go to the property and measure all the angles and distances ("metes and bounds") that enclosed the tract. From that information a map ("plat") was prepared and returned to the surveyor's office. Surveys, like entries, could be bought and sold.

—**Patent (or grant)**. The warrant and survey were sent to the governor's office for final approval. A patent signed by the governor gave one fee simple (complete and unconditional) ownership of the property.

At this point I can address the topic really intended for this column: famous persons who acquired land in Clark County prior to 1793, when it was still part of Fayette County. It should surprise no one that many early landowners obtained property with an eye to profit rather than settlement. Some of these speculators acquired their land through a third party without leaving Virginia. In fact, these first three did so without ever setting foot in Kentucky.

John Marshall (1755-1835). Yes, this is the same John Marshall who served as Chief Justice of the U.S. Supreme Court.

---

* Military warrants for Revolutionary War service could only be used to acquire land "south of the Green River." I continue to encounter family researchers who claim, incorrectly, that their ancestor received land in the Bluegrass Region for service in the Revolutionary War.

Chief Justice John Marshall
(Henry Inman, 1832)

His father, Col. Thomas Marshall, was appointed the first surveyor of Fayette County in 1780; he moved his family to Kentucky soon after and resided in what is now Woodford County. Three surveys totaling 4800 acres were run for John Marshall in Clark County. These were made on treasury warrants and were probably entered by his father. The tracts were located immediately north and west of what later became Winchester. John Marshall assigned two of the surveys to his father and kept one of 1640 acres for himself. His land acquisition occurred at the time (1782-1785) Marshall was practicing law in Fauquier County and serving in the Virginia House of Delegates.

Daniel Morgan (1736-1802). A survey of 1532 acres was made for "the Honourable Brigadier General Morgan"—one of the heroes of the Revolutionary War—in 1783. This was about the time Morgan built a house near Winchester, Virginia, which he named "Saratoga" after his successes in New York. Morgan's land speculation eventually resulted in his owning over 250,000 acres. His Clark County land, acquired on a treasury warrant, was located in the extreme northeast corner and lay partly in Montgomery and partly in Bourbon.

Gen. Daniel Morgan
(Charles Willson Peale, c1794)

Patrick Henry (1736-1799). Patrick Henry, attorney, orator and first governor of Virginia, had two 1000 acres land claims in Clark County. The land was bounded, approximately, by present-day Colby Road on the north, Becknerville Road on the east, and Combs Ferry Road on the south and west. The surveys were run by John Floyd on a military warrant that Henry acquired from James Robinson, awarded for Robinson's service

in the French and Indian War. Henry assigned both surveys to Thomas Madison, who had married Henry's sister Susannah.

Other prominent figures who held land in early Kentucky include two famous pioneers, **Daniel Boone** (1400 acres near Schollsville) and **Simon Kenton** (1000 acres near US 60 at the Clark-Montgomery line); military figures, **Gen. Marquis Calmes** (1400 acres in Indian Old Fields),

Gov. Patrick Henry
(George B. Matthews, c1891)

Gen. Benjamin Harrison (1000 acres on Stoner Creek and Mt. Sterling Road), **Gen. Isaac Shelby**, Kentucky's first governor, and his brother **Col. Evan Shelby** (500 acres each, on Colby Road near Patrick Henry's land); politician **James Speed**, judge, trustee of Transylvania University and grandfather of Joshua Speed, the friend of Abraham Lincoln, and James Speed, U.S. Attorney General (1000 acres adjoining Patrick Henry and 8200 acres on Stoner Creek northeast of Winchester).

Sources

Kandie Adkinson, "Kentucky Land Grant System," www.sos.ky.gov/admin/land/resources/articles/Documents/SaddlebagNotes.pdf; Joan E. Brookes-Smith, *Master Index, Virginia Surveys and Grants, 1774-1791* (Frankfort, KY, 1976); Philip F. Taylor, *Calendar of the Warrants for Land in Kentucky, Granted for Service in the French and Indian War* (Baltimore, MD, 1917, 2001 edition). Surveys were downloaded from the Kentucky Land Office at http://apps.sos.ky.gov/land/nonmilitary/patentseries/vaandokpatents/ and mapped using DeedMapper 4.2 software.

12
Winchester Advertiser and Its Successors

October 7, 2016

On Monday, the *Winchester Sun* named Mike Caldwell the new publisher of the newspaper. We wish him every success here. Long live the *Sun*! This seems an appropriate time to talk about our town's first newspaper—the *Winchester Advertiser*—started in 1814, with William W. Martin and Nathaniel Patten Jr. jointly serving as the publishers and editors.

William W. Martin (1781-1850) was born in Bedford County, Pennsylvania and, according to his biography, in the spring of 1794, his parents sought a home "in the wilds of Kentucky." They settled in Paris, where Martin joined the Presbyterian Church. He married Susan Depew of Paris in 1810 and studied for the ministry there under Rev. Samuel Rannels. In 1813 he moved to Winchester, was ordained that fall then assumed the pastorate of Sugar Ridge Presbyterian Church. To augment his salary he formed a business partnership with Nathaniel Patten.

Nathaniel Patten Jr. (1793-1837), was born in Roxbury, Massachusetts, where his family had been prominent for several generations. In 1808, the family moved west and settled in Mt. Sterling. Patten cast his lot with Martin in Winchester to begin the town's first newspaper.

Several documents preserved at the Wisconsin Historical Society attest to the paper's beginning. (1) In June 1814 George Gibson Taylor of Winchester wrote to Lexington businessman and fellow Presbyterian, James Maccoun, soliciting his influence to procure subscribers to the new paper and adding, "I would not be wrong in saying that Mr. Martin will be the Most able Editor in the State." (2) Taylor enclosed a broadside announcing "To the Public, William W. Martin & Co. propose publishing a weekly newspaper in the town of Winchester, Clarke County, Kentucky, as soon as a sufficient number of subscribers shall be obtained to justify such a measure. The paper is to be entitled The Winchester Advertiser, and its character to be decidedly republican. It shall contain intelligence *cujusque veri*, foreign and domestic, poetry, &c printed on a super-royal sheet and a new and elegant type. All possible means shall be used to please and inform the public."

WINCHESTER ADVERTISER.

NUM. 1.]   WINCHESTER, (KEN.) FRIDAY, AUGUST 5, 1814.   VOL. 1.]

The *Winchester Advertiser* commenced publication on Friday, August 5, 1814. Copies of the paper can be viewed today on microfilm at the University of Kentucky's William T. Young Library. While the first issue is missing, they have the next 18 issues. A subscription website, GenealogyBank.com, has many issues (1814-1819) including the first. The University of Chicago houses the Robert T. Durrett (founder of the Filson Club) Collection, which includes a large number of original *Advertisers*.

The annual cost of the paper was $2.50 if paid at the end of three months, $3 if paid at the end of the year. (This pay-later policy was a constant sorrow for the firm.) Advertisements cost fifty cents per "square" (presumably, the height and width of one column) the first time and twenty-five cents thereafter. Letters to the editor were required to be post-paid.

The newspaper consisted of four pages that were five columns wide and 13 x 21 inches in size. The content was almost entirely national and international news. Events of statewide interest received attention (e.g., Kentucky's role in the War of 1812 was reported on extensively), but local events were rarely mentioned. Reading these papers today, ones finds the advertisements and legal notices provide most of the local content—more on this later.

In the first issue the editors included a notice for apprentices: "Wanted immediately, at the Office of the Winchester Advertiser, two or three Boys, who can come well recommended, as apprentices to the printing business." They also hired a young printer from Virginia, Thomas T. Dillard. In addition to his printing duties, Dillard was responsible for delivering the paper to city and county residents, a duty he carried out on horseback.

The firm wanted other printing business in the community and announced in the paper: "Handbills, Cards, and all kinds of job printing done at the shortest notice and on the most reasonable terms."

The *Advertiser* received its national and foreign news from Eastern newspapers and had to await their delivery to Winchester. That news, by the time it was printed, might seem quite stale to us, but back then it was relished as "the latest." Additional delays were frequent. The editors complained on August 26, "We have not received any papers containing official accounts [of the war] this week. Our readers will attribute the barrenness of this week's paper to negligence, if not perfidy, of those engaged in forwarding the Marietta mail."

In the same issue they announced, "The office of the Winchester Advertiser is removed to the brick building nearly opposite the Post Office." This was followed by an ad: "For rent, small building lately occupied by the Winchester Advertiser."

In July 1815 the original publishing firm was succeeded by Patten and Finnell, after Reverend Martin left to devote more time to his ministry. He moved to Indiana in 1818 in order to escape from "the shadow of slavery." He pastored a number of churches there on his way to becoming one of the most noted "pioneer ministers" in the northwest. Martin established a famous school near his home, long known as "the Log College." Three of his sons became ministers and five of his daughters married ministers.

Nimrod L. Finnell (1799-1850) came to Winchester from Orange County, Virginia, where he learned the printer's art. Patten and Finnell changed the name of the paper to the *Kentucky Advertiser* and put out their first issue in July 1815. Finnell married Elizabeth Rielly that August. He left the paper in August 1816, and Patten carried on alone until July 1817, when he removed to Missouri and settled in a region known as the "Boon's Lick Country." There he published the first newspaper west of St. Louis or north of the Missouri River, the *Missouri*

Intelligencer established in 1819, which he published for 17 years. After suffering many years of bad health, Patten died at age 44.

Finnell returned to Winchester and took over the *Advertiser* in 1817, which he published until 1819.

That July the *Kentucky Gazette* reported that James Armstrong, a former partner in that paper, had purchased the *Advertiser*. "It seems to be his intention to render it a somewhat agricultural paper. As a printer and conductor of a newspaper, we believe Mr. Armstrong will give general satisfaction." The editors wished him success and then published an extract from Armstrong's paper.

EXTRACT.

"The commercial world is in a highly embarrassed situation. Europe complains heavily of pressure—and the constant cry in America is *"hard times."* To alleviate our distresses, the editor is decidedly of opinion that a rigid system of economy *must* be adopted and pursued. Domestic manufactures *must* be resorted to—and agricultural employments *must* be encouraged. It is thus the whole system of the body politic ought to be medicated. Temporary and partial relief might be, perhaps, otherwise obtained. But no permanent pecuniary happiness can be looked for, until the great radical cure is effected. It will, therefore, be with peculiar pride that the editor will turn much of his attention to *agricultural* and *manufacturing* topics. Several works, exclusively devoted to subjects of this kind, have been established eastwardly. In obtaining these, the editor will have great additional aid to the resources which his own country may afford."

Kentucky Gazette, July 30, 1819

Armstrong soon changed the name to *Kentucky Advertiser and Farmer's Magazine*. It is uncertain how long his newspaper continued.

We know that Finnell was publishing the *Republican Sentinel* in Winchester in 1821, but no issues have yet been found. There is some evidence that the *Republican Sentinel* was succeeded by the *Winchester Republican* in 1830. He continued his publishing career in 1832, when he joined Edwin Bryant to purchase the *Lexington Reporter*. Finnell later published Lexington's first daily paper, the *Lexington Intelligencer*.

Little further has been learned about James Armstrong. In September 1819 he married Mrs. Jane Price Ridgely, a daughter of Rev. John Price of Lexington. The nuptials were performed in Lexington by Dr. Rev. Cloud.

Next week we will examine tidbits of early Winchester history taken from advertisements and notices in the newspaper.

Sources
Clarence S. Brigham, *Bibliography of American Newspapers, 1690-1820, Part 2* (Worchester, MA, 1914), pp. 401-403; A. C. Quisenberry, "Brief Historical Sketch of the Newspapers of Winchester," 1894, copy at M. I. King Library, University of Kentucky; "Old Winchester newspapers," *Mt. Sterling Advocate*, April 29, 1908; Richard H. Collins, *History of Kentucky, Vol. 2* (Covington, KY, 1874), pp. 180, 437-438; F. F. Stephens, "Nathaniel Patten, Pioneer Editor," *Missouri Historical Review* (1915) 9:139-155; Winchester Advertiser broadside: "Documents from the Shane Collection," *Journal of the Department of History of the Presbyterian Church in the U.S.A.* (1931) 14:282-283; Robert S. Sanders, *Presbyterianism in Paris and Bourbon County, Kentucky, 1786-1961* (Louisville, KY, 1961), p. 42; Hanford A. Edson, *Contributions to the Early History of the Presbyterian Church in Indiana* (Cincinnati, OH, 1898), p. 102-107; A. Goff Bedford, *Land of Our Fathers, History of Clark County, Kentucky* (Winchester, KY, 1958), p. 404; *Kentucky Gazette*, July 30 and September 24, 1819.

13
Winchester History in the
Advertiser, 1814-1819

October 14, 2016

The *Winchester Advertiser's* news focus included approximately three pages of stories from the nation's capital, Canada and Europe. There were occasional items of happenings in Kentucky, usually from Frankfort, but no local news at all. The publishers of newspapers at that time assumed readers already knew what was going on in their communities. The coverage of local news versus national and international was almost the reverse of today's *Winchester Sun*.

The Kentucky Advertiser.

WINCHESTER, (Kentucky)—Printed by PATTEN & FINNELL.

NUM. 100.]   SATURDAY MORNING, JUNE 29, 1816.   VOL. II.

Paid notices in the *Advertiser* provide a window for viewing Winchester in the early 19th century. I have copies of the paper from 1814 through 1817 and one issue of 1819. The town was evidently a prosperous place during and immediately after the War of 1812. Keeping in mind that there were only six streets then—Washington, Main Cross, Fairfax, Water, Main, Highland—a surprising number of businesses show up in the paper.

The stores advertising in the few surviving issues of 1814 alone included William and Mathew Alexander, George G. Taylor, Clark & Pelham, Samuel Poston, William Poston, James Anderson & Co., James Ritchie, James L. Hickman, C. K. Duncan, Edward McGuire & Co., Coons, Collins & Crosthwait, Walter Karrick, E. G. Browning & Co., and Cast & Holley. All of these carried general merchandize.

Other concerns combined manufacturing and sales at their business locations. Examples are Benjamin Doggett, shoe and boot making; Linville Brinegar, shoe and boot making; James and Thomas Barr, tanning; John Bruner, tanning; James and Philip Pool, tailors. Thomas Jones, Edmund Callaway and Hay Taliaferro kept tavern. Taliaferro had the Winchester Hotel (southwest corner of Main and Lexington Ave.), and Joshua Lampton kept a livery stable next door. The doctors were Thomas Barbee, John Mills and Robert Taliaferro.

Another surprise was how often businesses formed and broke up partnerships. George G. Taylor & Co. dissolved his business with an unknown associate and formed a new store with William N. Lane. Browning & Co. broke up with E. G. Browning and Samuel Poston each going on their own, and the same for Robert Clark and Jesse W. Garner, and a long list of others.

Ads also indicate that businesses frequently changed locations. Alexander & Co. moved to Samuel Poston's old place, while Poston moved to "the frame house at the north end of Colonel John Martin's Tavern." Martin ran a tavern on the site where the Clark County National Bank Building stands today (present offices of Ludwig Blair & Bush). Achilles Eubank & Son "removed their store to the building occupied by Peter Flanagan. James Ritchie moved his store "to the room lately occupied by William R. Massie just below the Hotel." And many more. Even the *Advertiser* moved three times in four years.

There was still a shortage of specie (cash money) in Kentucky during these years and many businesses were forced to resort to barter. For example, William Poston offered merchandise "which will be sold cheap for cash, feathers, good linen, or saltpetre." James Ritchie took payment in country linen, linsey, feathers, hog's lard, whiskey, and country sugar. The *Advertiser*, desperate for payment from delinquent subscribers, accepted "most of the productions of husbandry at the market prices, viz.: flour, meal, corn, wheat, rye, pork, beef, hams, pickled pork, poultry, potatoes, lard, tallow, wood, &c."

Curiously, in 1814-15, Winchester sported four hat makers. An ad to purchase flaxseed announced that deliveries would be accepted at "the house formerly occupied by Benjamin Webb, hatter." Frederick Merckley informed the public that he had moved his "Hat Manufactory" from Mt. Sterling to Winchester. In the same issue of the paper, William R. Massie "informs his friends and the public generally that he still continues to carry on his hat manufactory in Winchester, at his former stand, three doors below the Hotel, where he has on hand a real good assortment of hats." Later that year, Fritzlen & Decret advertised for "two apprentices to the hatting business."

The papers carried ads for property sales. "For public sale on December 1, the late dwelling of Mary Strode, deceased, near Winchester and all the estate consisting of horses, cattle, sheep, hogs, corn, hay, farming utensils, wagon, &c. (1814)" Mary was the widow of John Strode who established Strode's Station in 1779.

William Jamison offered for sale a corner lot, where Dan's Discount Jewelry now stands, "containing a full quarter of an acre under good fence, having on it a hewed Log House, 18 x 24, with a shingled roof and brick chimney, also a convenient Log Kitchen."

There were regular notices for schools in town. Most were for the Winchester Academy, on the site of the later Hickman Street School, which stood at the corner of Highland and Hickman. A notice of December 1814 is typical:

"Mr. Amzi Lewis, late of New York, will commence his first session in the Winchester Academy on the 11th of December. He will teach Spelling, Reading, Writing, Arithmetic, English Grammar, the Latin & Greek Languages and the various branches of Mathematics. It is hoped parents and guardians will avail themselves of this advantage of having their children and wards well educated. By the order of the Board, James Sympson, President."

In 1816, a Mr. Green of Lexington informed "the ladies and gentlemen of Winchester that he wishes to undertake a school for teaching the Piano Forte."

One of the few items the paper carried from time to time that could be called local news was marriages. An example from October 15, 1814:

"Married: On Thursday evening last by Rev. Augustin Easton, Hubbard Taylor, Jr. of this place to the amiable and accomplished Miss Mary Ann T. Arnold of Paris. Also John H. Hickman of this place to the amiable Miss Eliza Burnau of Mercer."

Military announcements also appeared regularly. "We have heard that Governor Howard has required 1000 men from Kentucky to check the insolence of the savages, and guard some defenceless parts of our frontier. (1814)" That was Benjamin Howard, governor of the Missouri Territory and son of Clark County pioneer, John Howard.

"The men composing Captain Robert Scobee's company of detached militia are requested to meet at Winchester on Monday, the 16th of January, at 12 o'clock to fix upon a suitable uniform. (1815)"

"Volunteers wanted. Another opportunity offers for the militia of Kentucky to shew their patriotism. Gen. McArthur leading an expedition, Kentucky volunteers to meet at Urbana, Ohio, on the 20th of this month [September 1814]."

Sources

The *Winchester Advertiser* can be accessed in several places. Microfilm copies of various issues are available at the W. T. Young Library, University of Kentucky, Lexington, KY. Additional issues may be accessed through GenealogyBank.com (available from Ancestry.com). The 1814 issues of the *Advertiser* may be viewed at the Clark County Public Library; check with the Reference Desk.

14
Clark County History in the *Advertiser*

October 21, 2016

As was the case for Winchester, most of what can be learned about Clark County from the pages of the *Advertiser* comes from notices placed by subscribers and businesses. Only one county store ran regular ads—Lindsay & Bush at "Boonsborough":

"Lindsay & Bush inform their friends and the public that they have just received a neat and elegant assortment of New Goods, which they are determined to sell at the most reduced prices for Cash or Tobacco...."

The subscriber, N. L. Lindsay, asked "all those indebted to him to call and settle their accounts." This was Nimrod Long Lindsay, who came to Clark County from Culpeper County, Virginia, with his father Thomas. It is uncertain if the store was in Clark or Madison, as both sides of the river were referred to then as "Boonesborough." His Bush partner cannot be identified—too many Bushes.

Regular ads were placed for various mills in the county. In 1814, Henry Parrish declared he was taking the place of William Taylor, who had operated a fulling mill on Lower Howard's Creek and had died that year:

"The subscriber returns his thanks to his friends and the public for a generous share of their custom since the death of Mr. Taylor, and wishes to inform them that he will carry on the Weaving and Fulling business in all its branches this winter, and will receive and deliver clothes the first day of every Court in Winchester at Mr. William Poston's store. Henry Parrish, Clark County, Lower Howard's Creek."

Two years later, the fulling mill had a new operator:

"The subscriber informs his friends and the public that he intends carrying on the Fulling Business in Clarke county, Lower Howard's creek, at the mill formerly occupied by William Taylor, deceased. His Works being entirely new, he flatters himself that he will be enabled to do their work as good and as cheap as any other person. Stephen Miller"

There were numerous gristmills in the county, though none advertised in the paper. There were ads for millstones, however, which were manufactured at a quarry near Pilot Knob:

"James Daniel has for sale mill-stones of a superior quality made at the Red River quarry by himself and Spencer Adams."

Land sales were frequently listed, such as the following in 1814:

"For sale, tract of land 120 to 270 acres, lying on the road from Combs Ferry to Paris, and between Strode and Todd's roads leading from Winchester to Lexington, and adjoining Hubbard Taylor Esq., Maj. Brassfield and Capt. Colby H. Taylor. Lays well, tolerable water, good title, apple and peach orchards, pastures and meadow, 60 or 70 acres cleared. John W. Hinde, Clark County" Hinde was the son of Dr. Thomas Hinde, who achieved fame in Virginia—served as personal physician to Patrick Henry; treated the dying General Wolfe at Quebec during the French and Indian War—before moving to Clark County at an early date.

"To be sold at public auction on Saturday, October 8, a tract of land where Henry Hieronamus now lives, containing 120 acres, including warehouse and ferry owned by said Hieronamus, on Kentucky River between Combs' warehouse and the mouth of Boon's creek. John Wilkerson" Warehouses along the Kentucky River were important storage and loading points for goods destined for shipment to New Orleans.

"J. R. and Jesse Hampton give notice that they have purchased the tobacco warehouse lately owned by Thomas W.

Shepard, and that it is about three miles nearer to Winchester and the neighborhood of Four Mile than any tobacco warehouse on the Kentucky river."

Horses were essential for transportation as well as farming operations in early Clark County. As the animals frequently strayed, there were laws dealing with how strays were to be treated when found, an event so frequent that the county had a stray pen near the courthouse in Winchester. As indicated in the notices below, some suspected their horses were stolen rather than strayed:

"Taken up by Elijah Crosthwaith, living near Winchester, an iron grey colt, two years old next spring, branded with the letter S on its off shoulder, has a star on his forehead, his near hind foot white. Appraised to $15."

"$50 reward for a horse stolen out of my stable on Monday night the 10th, a dark bay horse. Mathew Anderson, 2 miles northeast of Winchester"

Jeremiah Bush reported that he found "between Upper and Lower Sandusky [Ohio], a bay horse with a star and snip, four years old, near 15 hands high...thought to be left by some of the mounted men under Gen. McArthur. The owner can get him by applying to me in Clark County, near Boonsborough." Duncan McArthur led a regiment of Kentucky volunteers during the War of 1812.

The paper served as the place to post all kinds of lost and found notices:

"Lost, on Monday evening after sunset near Hornback's mill, perhaps between the mill and the parting of the Winchester and Mount Sterling roads, a pair of saddle bags, of a reddish cast and furnished with an elegant lock, in which were between 75 and 100 dollars in silver. Ten dollars reward. James Shortridge"

"Found, about a mile and a half from Winchester, on the great road leading from this place to the Iron Works, a lady's outside dress of Stuff and a pair of kidskin Gloves. Samuel Morton"

"Lost, on the 27th of November, a new Saddle and a plated kirb [curb] Bridle; also a Shirt, Overalls, workman's apron and a wallet of Clothes. Benjamin Rankins" A curb chain is a piece of horse tack required for proper use on any type of curb bit.

"Found, on Sunday last, at Friendship Meeting House, a Great Coat. The owner may have the same by applying at this office and paying for this advertisement." Presumably inserted by one of the editors.

Another type of notice was often run by husbands seeking to avoid paying debts run up by their estranged wives:

"Whereas my wife Nancy has left my bed and board without any just cause, this is to forewarn all persons from trusting her on my account, as I am determined to pay no debts of her contracting after this date. Orson Martin" Martin was not as innocent as he made out. His promising career dissolved as he succumbed to alcoholism. Nancy sued for divorce and provided numerous witnesses to his physical abuse. She left him and moved to Missouri with her family.

Rev. William W. Martin, one of the editors, occasionally announced the time and place where he would be preaching:

"William W. Martin will preach at Sugar Ridge on Sunday the 16th [October 1814] at 11 o'clock and in Winchester at 4 o'clock." Sugar Ridge Presbyterian Church was located between Mt. Sterling Road and Ecton Road and between Stoner and Little Stoner Creeks.

Sources
Margaret I. Lindsay, *Lindsays of America* (Baltimore, MD, 1979), p. 253; Charles D. Hockensmith, *Millstone Quarries of Powell County, Kentucky* (Jefferson, NC, 2009); Albert H. Redford, *Life and Times of H. H. Kavanaugh* (Nashville, TN, 1884); Harry G. Enoch, *Rise and Fall of Orson Martin, Blacksmith* (Winchester, KY, 2013).

15
The Rodney Haggard House

October 28, 2016

Back in April of this year, Bobbi Newell sent me an email with the subject "A house for us to find!" She attached a newspaper clipping copied from Boo Baldwin's scrapbook. The article pertained to Rodney Haggard's funeral, which was held at his residence, and contained this paragraph:

"This is a historic house. It is an old-fashioned house, situated on a high hill in the northwestern suburbs of the city. It was built by Col. Thomas Moore seventy years ago; in it have resided Governor Hawes, Colonel Moore, Charles Eginton and other well known citizens."

Rodney Haggard resided on West Broadway when he died in 1901. After making numerous trips out that street, the "historic house" could not be found, and I filed the project away as unfinished business. Cogitating on it for six months provided no insights, so last week I decided to search for the house using the "brute force method": deed research. This involved looking up deeds of the residents listed in the newspaper article—Moore, Hawes, Eginton, Haggard—and connecting one or more of them with a property description that would identify the location of the house. After multiple trips to the courthouse, the sequence of owners was determined, and the location of the house pinpointed. The search was prolonged due to the fact that I began by examining more than fifty of Rodney Haggard's deeds before determining that he never owned the house.

As it turns out, the house is no longer standing. No surprise there. The home site is now covered by the salvage yard of Paul & Sons Auto Recyclers. I have been unable to find out when the house was razed.

The remainder of this article provides a history of the house through its various owners, many of whom were indeed "well known citizens" of Winchester. We will take up the story beginning with the last known occupant, Rodney Haggard, who must have rented the house where he lived on West Broadway

Rodney Haggard (*Winchester Handbook*, 1889)

from the actual owner, Dixie Green.

Rodney Haggard (1844-1901) had a remarkable career in Clark County where he was born and raised. He was the son of Judge Augustus L. Haggard and great-great-grandson of the pioneer Nathaniel Haggard, who came to Kentucky from Albemarle County, Virginia. Rodney graduated from high school in Winchester and began teaching. When the Civil War broke out, he joined the Buckner Guards under Gen. Kirby Smith in 1862 at age seventeen. He left to raise a company for Col. David Waller Chenault's regiment, the 11th Kentucky Cavalry, and was elected lieutenant. The regiment served under John Hunt Morgan. Haggard fought in battles at Mill Springs, Richmond, Lebanon and Green River Bridge in Kentucky and Hartsville, Tennessee. He accompanied Morgan on the Great Ohio Raid in 1863 and at one point was in command of the regiment as all of his superior officers had been killed, wounded or captured. Haggard himself was captured at Salineville, Ohio, and imprisoned on Johnson's Island until the end of the war.

After the war, Haggard returned to teaching until August 1866, when he was elected sheriff of Clark County and became the youngest man in Kentucky to ever hold that office. He was re-elected in 1870 and began studying law under Chief Justice James Simpson of Winchester. Haggard subsequently graduated from the Louisville Law School and was admitted to the bar in 1873. He built a lucrative practice in Winchester and was said to have been "engaged upon one side or the other in all the important cases in the county." He served as an attorney for the C&O Railroad for fifteen years and for the Kentucky Central Division of the L&N Railroad for twelve years.

In 1880, Haggard was elected to the Kentucky Senate and served four years. He was the author of "one of the most noted laws of the period," an act creating the State Board of Equalization, which dealt with the role of county attorneys and commonwealth attorneys. In 1893, he was elected county judge to fill an unexpired term, and in 1894 was re-elected to a full term. According to his biography, Haggard was "an able judge and an upright, trustworthy citizen in whom the community places unbounded confidence. He is a public speaker of much ability and his time and means have been freely given in the interest of his party." He left the Democratic Party in 1896, refusing to support the William Jennings Bryan ticket. The following year Haggard formed a fusion party of Republicans and gold-standard Democrats that was badly defeated in local elections, whereupon he abandoned politics altogether.

Judge Haggard married Mary Eliza Baldwin in 1868. She was a daughter of Lt. W. W. Baldwin, one of Morgan's men killed at the disastrous battle of Green River Bridge. A friend related the following story of his marriage: "There was a romance about it which was very sweet. When he was scarcely more than a lad he happened to see his wife, then a girl about ten years of age and instantly announced that that girl was to be his wife. The war intervened, years elapsed and finally the young lawyer succeeded in winning the hand of the fatherless girl."

The couple had seven children, one of whom, Rodney Jr., became a prominent Winchester attorney. The family home at 117 Boone Avenue is still standing. A Winchester directory shows the family residing there in 1892, but at the time of the 1900 census they were living at the West Broadway residence. Then, in September 1901, the *Winchester Democrat* broke the dreadful news:

"The community was doubly shocked Saturday morning. To the verified news of President McKinley's death, which was not unexpected, was added the tiding that sent a thrill of horror to the hearers, that Judge Rodney Haggard had died by his own hand."

Rodney Haggard
(*Notable Men of Kentucky*, 1902)

Judge Haggard wrote his will on Friday, September 13, leaving "my beloved wife all my property of every kind." He returned home, but could not sleep, then arose before daylight and according to the paper's shockingly vivid account, "He went to a fence in the rear yard of his home on West Broadway; he placed a pistol in his mouth and pulled the trigger, the ball passing through the brain and out near the top of his head." His wife found the body Saturday morning. By way of explanation, the paper noted that "for some time business and domestic troubles had preyed upon him and his mind had evidently become unbalanced and in this condition he took his own life."

According to the paper, "The funeral was probably more

largely attended than any funeral ever held in this city." It was said that "the hearse reached the burying place [Winchester Cemetery] before the rear carriage had left the yard."

Tributes and memorials poured in, from the United Confederate Veterans, the Elks Lodge, Haggard's good friend from Lexington, Col. W. C. P. Breckinridge and many others. The circuit court issued Resolutions of Respect then adjourned for a day in his honor; they also commissioned a portrait of Judge Haggard to hang in the courtroom.[*]

Sources

Winchester Democrat, March 30, 1900, September 17, 24 and 27, 1901; John M. Gresham Co., *Biographical Cyclopedia of the Commonwealth of Kentucky* (Chicago, IL, 1896), p. 594; Thornton & Sherlock, *1892 Winchester City Directory* (Midway, KY, 1892); Ben LaBree, *Notable Men of Kentucky* (Louisville, KY, 1902), p. 76.

---

[*] The painting was removed at some point and cannot be located.

16
Owners of the Haggard House on West Broadway

November 4, 2016

This is a continuation of last week's column about the house on West Broadway where Rodney Haggard died. The newspaper article concerning Haggard's funeral (1901) stated that his home "was built by Col. Thomas Moore seventy years ago," suggesting a construction date of 1831.

Thomas Ransdell Moore (1785-1844) was born in Fauquier County, Virginia, and came to Kentucky with his parents at an early age. They settled near Lexington at Poplar Hill—now part of Dixiana Farm—in the Russell Cave neighborhood, where Moore received a "country education." He then taught school for a time and had as one of his pupils Robert J. Breckinridge. Moore studied law under John Breckinridge, patriarch of that noted Kentucky family. Moore volunteered to serve in the War of 1812. He was engaged in the disastrous Battle of the River Raisin and survived the horrific massacre of the surrendered army that followed.

After the war, he entered the mercantile business in Winchester (ca. 1814) with his brother Charles Chilton Moore. Their store, at the corner of Cleveland and Main, prospered. Thomas rode horseback to Philadelphia to purchase goods, which were hauled by wagon to the Ohio River and by flatboat down the river to Kentucky. In 1817, their notice for "New Goods" appeared in the Winchester newspaper.

"T. R. & C. C. Moore have just received from Philadelphia and are now opening at their store in Winchester an elegant assortment of Merchandize, suitable for the season, which they offer low for Cash, Tobacco, Linnen, Linsey or such articles of country produce as may suit them."

During his Winchester period, Thomas was elected to the Kentucky General Assembly; he served one term but did not stand for re-election. According to his biography, he "continued the mercantile business for about fifteen years, when he and his brother dissolved their partnership and he [Thomas] retired to the country."[*]

Thomas R. Moore
Painting by Robert Moore (Whitley's *Ante-bellum*
***Portraiture of Kentucky*)**

In 1825, Thomas purchased 431 acres of prime farmland in the Van Meter Road area from the Goffs. His homeplace there, called "Welcome Hall," is said to have been erected in 1833. Thomas and his wife, Evaline Hockaday, were the parents of nine children. Thomas and Evaline are buried in a graveyard on their

---

[*] C. C. Moore moved back to Fayette County to the Russell Cave area and married Mary Anne Stone, a daughter of Rev. Barton Stone, who was one of the leaders of the Cane Ridge Revival (1801) and helped to establish the Christian Church (Disciples of Christ). A son of C. C. and Mary Anne, Charles Chilton Moore Jr. (1837-1906) was the editor of the *Blue Grass Blade*, one of the United States' first newspapers promoting atheism. Moore spent time in prison for his outspoken opposition to religion and the Bible. John Sparks, *Kentucky's Most Hated Man, Chares Chilton Moore & The Bluegrass Blade* (Nicholasville, KY, 2009).

farm.

It is difficult to reconcile Thomas Moore building the West Broadway home in 1831 and Welcome Hall in 1833. An 1819 deed confirms that Moore purchased the West Broadway property from Joseph Coulter for $7,445. The purchase price indicates that the property already had a substantial structure when Moore bought it. Further complicating this question—who built the house and when?—is the fact that the sale from Moore to the next owner, Richard Hawes, cannot be found in the deed books.

Gov. Richard Hawes
Painting by Harold Collins (Kentucky Historical Society)

"Governor Hawes"—Richard Hawes Jr. (1797-1877)— was born in Caroline County, Virginia, and came to Kentucky with his parents in 1810. He attended Transylvania University, read law under Robert Wickliffe in Lexington and was admitted to the bar in 1818. That same year, he became a law partner of Wickliffe and married a daughter, Hetty, of the noted George Nicholas. In 1824 Hawes came to Winchester where he resided until 1843.

While a practicing attorney there, Hawes began a long political career. He was elected to the Kentucky General Assembly in 1828, 1829 and 1836. In 1838 he was elected to Congress where he served for four years representing Henry Clay's "Ashland district." He also served in the Black Hawk War of 1832.

Hawes and partner Benjamin H. Buckner[*] owned and operated the rope walk and bagging factory in Winchester that had been established by David Dodge. Hawes lived in a house on the property until about 1833 when he sold out to Buckner. (The rope walk was located in the area framed by Highland, Hickman, Main Street, and Valentine Court. The house was moved to 19 Alabama Street when the First Christian Church was built in 1908.)

About that time (1833), Hawes must have moved to the West Broadway house. He lived there until 1843 when he sold Charles Eginton the property "where the said Hawes has for many years resided," it being "the same Lott conveyed by Thomas R. Moore & Eveline W. Moore his wife to the said Hawes."

That year, 1843, Hawes moved his law practice to Paris. He would play a significant role in events that preceded Kentucky's entrance into the Civil War. He and Beriah Magoffin were the Southern Rights representatives to a commission appointed to decide the state's position on the war and secession. Hawes advocated for peace based upon recognition of independence for the Southern Confederacy. When Kentucky's neutrality ended in September 1861, Hawes fled to the Confederate lines in Tennessee. He was appointed a commissary officer for Gen. Humphrey Marshall's command in eastern Kentucky. While recovering from typhoid fever in April 1862,

---

[*] Benjamin Hawes Buckner's mother was Elizabeth Hawes. He was a cousin of Richard Hawes.

Hawes learned he had been elected Kentucky's second Confederate Governor by the Provisional Government following the death of George W. Johnson.

During the Kentucky invasion in the fall of 1862, Hawes followed Gen. Braxton Bragg's army to Frankfort. The Union government had fled and Bragg installed the new governor in the capital. Hawes' tenure there would be measured in hours. After an elaborate ceremony at the Capitol, the official party retired to dinner. While eating, Bragg received a note that federal forces were approaching the town. Union shelling forced Hawes to abandon Frankfort, and after Bragg's defeat at Perryville he had to withdraw with the army to Tennessee. Hawes and his absentee government accomplished little from then until the war's end.

When the Confederacy collapsed in the spring of 1865, the Provisional Government vanished, and Hawes hurried back to Bourbon County to resume his law practice. The community, apparently harboring little animosity, elected Hawes county judge in 1866 and re-elected him in 1870 and 1874. Following his death in 1877 he was interred in Paris Cemetery.

Sources
James C. Klotter, *Breckinridges of Kentucky, 1760-1981* (Lexington, KY, 1986); Benjamin F. Van Meter, *Genealogies and Sketches of Some Old Families* (Louisville, KY, 1901), pp. 124-130; Kathryn Owen, *Old Homes and Landmarks of Clark County, Kentucky* (Winchester, KY, 1967), p. 45; Edna T. Whitley, *Kentucky Ante-bellum Portraiture* (n.p., 1956), p. 89; Clark County Deed Book 14:35, 16:242, 21:61, 26:213, 30:589; Kentucky Advertiser, January 11, 1817; Richard H. Collins, *History of Kentucky, Vol. 2* (Covington, KY, 1874), p. 774; Lowell H. Harrison, "George W. Johnson and Richard Hawes: The Governors of Confederate Kentucky," *Register of the Kentucky Historical Society* (1981) 79:3; *Biographical Encyclopedia of Kentucky* (Cincinnati, OH, 1878), p. 142; Robert M. Polsgrove, *Survey of Historic Sites in Kentucky: Clark County* (Frankfort, KY, 1979), pp. 117, 145; Biographical Directory of the U.S. Congress, http://bioguide.congress.gov/.

17

More Owners of the Rodney Haggard House

November 11, 2016

This column continues the series of biographical sketches of those who owned the house on West Broadway where Rodney Haggard died. We begin with Charles Eginton, who purchased the house from Richard Hawes.

Charles Eginton (1814-1890) was born in Philadelphia, came to Kentucky in 1833 and taught school at Matthew Hume's in Clark County. Eginton studied law under Judge James Simpson and was admitted to the bar in 1836. His biography states, "He soon took a front rank among such legal giants as Judge Simpson, Samuel Hanson, Gen. [John B.] Huston and others who made the Winchester bar of that time the strongest in the State."

Eginton married Sarah Louise Taylor, a daughter of Reuben T. Taylor. He was an active Mason and, in a rare honor, was twice elected Grand Master of the Grand Lodge of Kentucky. Eginton was also an officer in the Order of the Sons of Temperance. About 1870 he moved to Covington and became a prominent attorney and judge in Kenton County. He died in 1890 and is buried in Linden Grove Cemetery in Covington.

Eginton purchased the West Broadway house from Richard Hawes in 1843 and sold it to William Buckner in 1850. The deed states that the property "had been in the possession of Hawes as a family residence and since the conveyance has been so used by Eginton."

William Buckner (1801-1876) was born in Caroline County, Virginia, the son of Henry Buckner and Elizabeth Catlett. William, who never married, was a wealthy Clark County farmer. He is buried beside his parents in Winchester Cemetery. Buckner kept the West Broadway house for seven years then sold to Elizabeth Hedges in 1857.

Elizabeth Hedges (circa 1798-1868) was a daughter of

Ennis Sutherland of Clark County. She married a cousin, Thomas Sutherland, in 1819. After his death, she married John Hedges in 1850. No further record is found for John, so he may have died soon after. On the 1861 map of Winchester the house, owned by "Mrs. Hedges," is accessed from an unnamed street off Lexington Road. Elizabeth sold the house to William H. Spencer in 1867. She died soon after and, although she had purchased a lot in Winchester Cemetery, her grave has not been located.

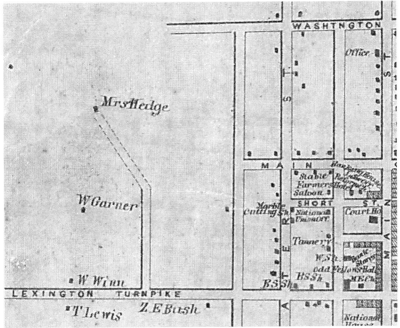

Mrs. Hedges' home on the 1861 map of Winchester

William H. Spencer (1807-1901) was a wealthy Clark County farmer residing in the Colby Road area. He married Rebecca Brooking in 1846. Sometime in the 1870s they moved to Fort Scott, Kansas. They died and are buried there in Evergreen Cemetery. In 1869, Spencer sold the West Broadway house to Thomas H. Moore for $5,000, it "being the house now occupied by the said Moore."

Thomas H. Moore (1826-1879) was the eldest son of Thomas Ransdell Moore, who had owned this same house some thirty years before. Thomas H., the son, married Maria Bright, a daughter of Tennessee congressman, John Bright.   Thomas served in the Union army in the Civil War, first as a provost marshal and later promoted to the rank of major.[*] He was still residing in the West Broadway house in 1875, when he sold the place to L. M. Green in exchange for a farm on the Kentucky River. The farm, known as the Jackson Place, included Jackson Ferry, which had been established by Josiah Jackson in 1795. Thomas lived there until his death in 1879, and his wife continued on the place until her death 18 years later. Both are interred in Winchester Cemetery.

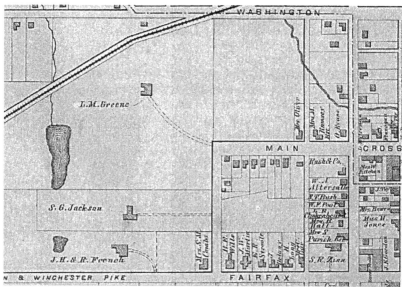

Lafayette M. Green's home on the 1877 Winchester map

Lafayette M. Green (1830-1898) was a native of Bath County, grew up in Montgomery and was a lifelong farmer. Lafayette married first Susan Daniel, by whom he had a daughter, May. After Susan's death he moved to Winchester, where he married Lucy Jackson. Following her death in 1880, he married Dixie Kennedy, who was the same age as his daughter May. Lafayette and Dixie resided in the West Broadway house from 1875 until his death in 1898. The house is shown on the Beers

---

[*] A later newspaper article stated that Thomas H. Moore was a colonel in the Civil War. *Winchester Democrat*, June 10, 1902.

map of Winchester (1877).

Lafayette's heirs, widow Dixie and daughter May, made an amicable division of his property. Dixie was deeded the West Broadway house, which she sold to Elizabeth Hunt in 1902. This concluded my search for the Rodney Haggard house. Dixie Green is identified as the owner of the house where Rodney died in 1901. He must have been renting from her. Little is known about Dixie. A street near the house was named for her: Dixie Street runs parallel to Broadway between Burns Avenue and Wainscott Avenue.

There are, doubtless, other properties in Winchester that have had as fascinating a series of owners as the "Haggard House"—we will keep an eye out for them.

Sources

Richard H. Collins, *History of Kentucky, Vol. 1* (Covington, KY, 1874), p. 525; William D. Buckner, *The Buckners of Virginia* (New York, NY, 1907), pp. 183, 185; E. A. and G. W. Hewitt, "Topographical Map of the Counties of Bourbon, Fayette, Clark, Jessamine and Woodford, Kentucky" (New York, 1861); Clark County Deed Book 30:589, 35:298, 38:371, 43:40, 501, 45:622, 64:321, 70:16; Clark County Order Book 1:182; Clark County Will Book (red) 1:185; www.findagrave.com; Benjamin F. Van Meter, *Genealogies and Sketches of Some Old Families* (Louisville, KY, 1901), pp. 124-125; *Winchester Semi-Weekly Sun*, March 21 and April 21, 1879; *Winchester Democrat*, September 15, 1880, October 1, 1890; April 16, 1897, February 18, 1898, and June 10, 1902, February 7, 1908; Winchester map in D. G. Beers & Co., *Atlas of Bourbon, Clark, Fayette, Jessamine and Woodford Counties, Kentucky* (Philadelphia, PA, 1877).

18
Poynterville
Origins of a Black Community

November 27, 2016

Following the Civil War, in December 1865, ratification of the 13th Amendment abolished slavery in the United States. Free blacks would experience difficult times in post-war Clark County: The majority of men worked for wages as farm laborers, the women in domestic service, and most families lived in extreme poverty. Enterprising individuals and those with a skilled trade fared better than others, and a few were able to acquire property in one of the black communities that sprang up in Clark County—Lisletown, Hootentown, Poynterville and others.

Poynterville has a long and interesting history. In this article, however, we only have space to explore its formative years, beginning with the man who gave the community its name.

Wiley Taul Poynter (1838-1896) was born in Montgomery County, grew up near Frankfort and came to Winchester while still young. At age 17 he was the principal and a teacher at the Winchester Academy. He married Pattie Poston in 1857. Poynter served with the Union army during the Civil War as regimental quartermaster for the 16th Kentucky Infantry. Returning to Winchester, he worked as a bookkeeper for his father-in-law, Henry Poston, and in 1865 became the first cashier of the Clark County National Bank.

According to his biography, Poynter, an ardent Methodist, entered the ministry in 1867 and "at once took front rank." He pastored the church in Winchester for four years, then preached at Millersburg and Paris. In 1879 he purchased the Science Hill Female College in Shelbyville. The school had been established in 1825 by Clark County native Julia Ann Tevis. Reverend Poynter hired 16 well-qualified faculty members to teach 125 or so students and achieved a national reputation for the school. (The school closed in 1939, and the buildings are now occupied by the Wakefield-Scearce Galleries.)

Bringing our story back to Winchester, we find from deed records that Poynter purchased 65 acres of land adjoining the west side of Winchester from William H. Winn. In July 1867 Poynter had the tract laid out in 52 lots and platted as "Poynterville." The new subdivision was bordered on the north by Walnut Street, on the east by First Street, on the south by an extension of Washington Street, and on the west by Elm Street, which was then called "the old Paris Road." Poynterville was the first of many suburbs created in Winchester's history.

Wiley Poynter left behind no explanation of his purpose for creating Poynterville but after examining his lot sales, his intentions seem clear. From July 1867 through the end of the year he sold 19 lots, all to African Americans. He continued the practice after leaving Winchester. Between 1867 and 1890, he made 54 deeds conferring 66 lots in Poynterville; all the sales but one[*] were to African-American men or women whose names are shown in the table below.

Purchasers of Poynterville Lots

Richard Rupard	Moses Green	David Embry
John Allen	Shelton Jones	Mat Taylor
Xantippe Ecton	Joseph Price	Lizzie Vivion
David Smith	Sally Bush	Willis Bean
Daniel Davis	Aaron Taylor	James A. Robinson
Mason Fry	Aaron Downey	Thomas Webb
Albert Smith	Louisa Allen	Jesse Jackson
Winston Rankin	Burgess Ramsey	Rachel McDaniel
William Rowe	Jane, Mary & John Wills	Eli Carey
Jerry Stephenson	Gibson "Gip" Taylor	Clarissa & Cricket Barnes
Ann Nicholas	Ann Nicholas	Rachel Malone
George Miller	Anthony Miller	Sophia Buckner
Daniel Wheeler	Robert Wilkerson	Mildred C. Haggard
Jacob Carey	Agnes Combs	Margaret Brown
Eliza Burch	James S. Berry	Andrew Buckner
Reuben Ragland	Press Woodford	Henry C. Hart (white)

The lots sold exceeded the number laid out in the plat. Some of the sales were for "half lots." Poynter also sold some of the lots on credit—an unusual practice for selling to blacks at that

---

[*] The exception was a sale to Henry C. Hart, grandson of Josiah Hart and Judith Tanner. Josiah was the original owner of an 800-acre tract of land on the north side of Washington Street that included all of Poynterville.

time—and a few of the purchasers lost their lots by not paying the full amount.

Reverend Poynter must have intended his suburb to become a community for black families. This notion is supported by his article, "The Church and the Black Man," published in the *Methodist Review*, which begins, "I risk nothing in saying that among the imperative and pressing duties of the American Church, and especially of the Church in the Southern States, none is more important than the duty to the colored people in our midst." He stated that "the home, the school and the Church" were critical factors, and that first they "must be housed in homes of their own.... There can be no true progress without this."

Few of the purchasers of lots in Poynterville had an occupation other than farm laborer.* John Allen was a house painter, Mason Fry a distillery worker, Jerry Stephenson a grocer, George Miller a butcher, Aaron Taylor a post and railer (fence builder), Gip Taylor a railroad worker, Samuel Brown (husband of Margaret) a harness maker, and Thomas Webb a blacksmith. Laborers who purchased lots must have carefully saved their wages.

At least six of the buyers were Civil War veterans (Mason Fry, Joseph Price, Reuben Ragland, Burgess Ramsey, Gip Taylor, Thomas Webb), who could have used their military pay to buy lots.

Thirteen of the buyers were women; their reported occupations were housekeeping and domestic service.

John Allen, Reuben Ragland and Shelton Jones were trustees of the CME Church on Broadway. This was the first black church in Winchester.

Thirteen of the lot owners had been married while enslaved: John and Louisa Allen, Aaron and Catherine Downey, David and Milly Embry, Moses and Anna Green, Shelton and Mary Ann Jones, Anthony and Joan Miller, George and Betty Miller, Joe and Mary Hannah Price, Reuben and Nancy Ragland, Richard and Nancy Ragland, Jerry and Kate Stephenson, Aaron

---

* Occupations of blacks were reported in the censuses of 1870 and later; of the 47 lot purchasers, only 24 could be found recorded in the censuses.

and Mandy Taylor, Gip and Manda Taylor. Their unions were not legally recognized before the Civil War. After the law was changed, black couples paid scarce money to formalize their marriage ties.

Eliza Burch purchased a lot in 1869; she died in 1876. By will, she left her house and lot in Poynterville to her son, Samuel, who "has for the last four years cared for me during my sickness"; it was to be "compensation for his kind treatment of me and his loving care and protection." She could leave sons Philip and Ames only "a mother's affection." She added, "My other children were sold during slavery and I do not now know whether they are still living or not. I can only leave for them a mother's prayer that they meet me in heaven."

More research needs to be done to gather information about the first men and women of Poynterville.

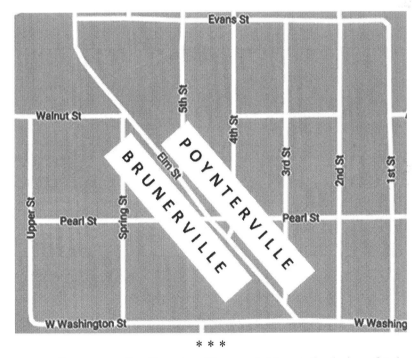

* * *

One year after Poynterville was laid out, the heirs of John Bruner established an adjoining suburb: Brunerville (1868). Brunerville lay on the west side of Elm Street and was framed by

Walnut, Upper and Washington. Brunerville persisted until sometime in the 20th century, after which the area was assumed to be part of Poynterville.

* * *

The *Kentucky African American Encyclopedia* has an entry for "Bucktown," which it states is officially part of Poynterville. The origin of the name is uncertain. Some credit it to Buck Clay, a some-time grocer who resided on Upper Street. Locally, Bucktown is most closely associated with the area of West Washington Street that was once the center of black businesses in Winchester. The area was recognized in 2008 with the dedication of Heritage Park at the corner of Washington and Maple Streets.

Sources

Winchester Democrat, July 31, 1896; Jonathan K. T. Smith, *Genealogical Abstracts from Reported Deaths, The Nashville Christian Advocate, 1894-1896* (Jackson, TN, 1896), pp. 72-73; National Education Association, *Journal of Proceedings and Addresses of the 37th Annual Meeting* (Chicago, IL, 1898), p. 294; Thomas Speed, *Union Regiments of Kentucky* (Louisville, KY, 1897), pp. 436-437, 442; *Report of the Adjutant General of the State of Kentucky, 1861-1865* (Frankfort, KY, 1866), p. 926; W. T. Poynter, "The Church and the Black Man," *Methodist Review* (March-April 1896), p. 76; Clark County Deed Book 42:243, 43:19, 156:415, the many deeds for lot sales are too long to list, they may be found in the deed index at the Clark County Courthouse; Clark County Declarations of Marriages of Negros and Mulattos; Clark County Colored Will Book 1:9; Gerald L. Smith, et al., *Kentucky African American Encyclopedia* (Lexington, KY, 2015), p. 73.

19
Chalybeate Spring and Other Lost Places

December 2, 2016

Today our running water and indoor plumbing are things we take for granted. It was not always so. Before rural electrification and rural water districts, county residents had to supply their own water with wells and cisterns. Our first settlers relied on springs and creeks and had to spend part of each day hauling water. Once upon a time there were dozens of named springs in Clark County, as well as hundreds more unnamed. Some provided pure drinking water. Others provided mineral water which attracted wild game (salt licks such as Log Lick on Lulbegrud Creek) or were tapped for medicinal uses (resort spas such as the Oil Springs, also on Lulbegrud).

An example of the latter is the Chalybeate Spring. The exact location is now lost, but court records (1829) state that it was immediately across the Kentucky River from the mouth of Otter Creek. This places the spring in the Ford area, before there was a community of Ford. The spring would have been on the site of East Kentucky Power's William C. Dale Power Station. Very near the north ash pond, a small drainage is visible on Google Maps, directly opposite the mouth of Otter Creek. This may have been the outlet of the spring. The spring itself would have been destroyed by construction of the power plant.

Chalybeate (*kuh'-libby-it*) is not a single mineral. The term is used to denote waters containing salts of iron, magnesium, manganese and calcium. Chalybeate springs have been noted for their health-giving properties since the early 17th century. One of the most famous was Tunbridge Wells in England, discovered in 1606. Its waters were said to cure "the colic, the melancholy, and the vapours; it made the lean fat, the fat lean; it killed flat worms in the belly, loosened the clammy humours of the body, and dried the over-moist brain." Princess Victoria (the later Queen) drank the waters every day during her visit to Tunbridge Wells.

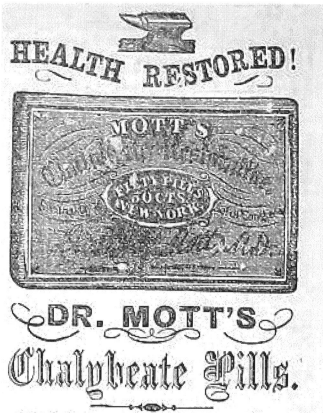

1860 Advertisement
(Frank Leslie's Illustrated Newspaper)

Chalybeate springs were found all across Europe and were especially abundant in the British Isles. Many were found in the United States; some of the better known include Saratoga Springs in New York, Brandywine Springs in Delaware, Chalybeate Springs in Indiana and dozens more. In Kentucky, there were resorts at chalybeate springs in Russell and Union Counties. There is a village in Edmonson County called "Chalybeate Springs," where people went to "take the waters"; the springs were discovered in the early 1800s and were famous for their supposed healing powers. The hotel there had dancing, dining, horse racing, golf, tennis, and fox hunting. It was a popular resort for more than 100 years and closed during World War II.

It is uncertain when the Chalybeate Spring in Clark County was discovered. In 1839 a road was opened "from the Boonsborough ferry on the Kentucky River up to the ford at the Chalebiate spring." The route began at the ferry and ran "up the River on the bank of the river through the Land of Thomas C. Barr [a tanner], a short distance through the Land of Landon Bush, thence through the land of William Hooton, thence through the Land of Henry Lysle. Said route is marked by us[*] up to the spring at the ford[†] opposite Barns or Halleys Road leading to Richmond, a distance of one and a half to Two Miles."

Other noted Clark County springs little known today and possibly gone are Bramblett's Lick in the Wades Mill area, William Trimble's spring near Factory Bottom on Lower Howard's Creek, Stone Lick on the Stone Lick Fork of Upper Howard's Creek, Logan's Lick on a branch of Fourmile Creek near Logan Lick Road, Bybee Lick on Stoner Branch of Fourmile, Cold Spring near Pinchem on Fourmile, Buffalo Spring on a branch of Lower Howard's Creek on the Farris farm, Cave Spring west of Stoner Creek near the intersection of I-64 and US 60, and many more. One of the most important locations

---

[*] The road report was prepared by Jonathan Bush, Armistead Blackwell and Benjamin R. Waller.
[†] The assumption that Ford took its name from this ford in mistaken. The community was named for Thomas M. Ford, a large property owner and lumber mill operator here in the late 1800s.

in early Winchester was the "Publick Spring," where residents obtained water for many years. It was on the west side of Water (now Maple) Street near the Beverly White Towers. To protect the water supply, town trustees approved numerous ordinances aimed at preventing a host of unseemly practices, such as disposing of animal carcasses, watering livestock, washing dirty laundry and dishes, and so on. The spring flowed into Town Branch, both now relocated underground.

McMillan's Spring, later known as Calmes' Spring, was well known until the early 20th century. It was a stopping place for a cold drink of water for travelers along the road from Winchester to the Old Stone Church and Boonesborough. The spring, located on the property of the new county high school, still flows. In fact, in recent weeks the fork of Lower Howard's Creek from Winchester has been dry until the point where the spring waters enter the creek (near the bridge on Old Boonesboro Road).

John Martin Springhouse

There are two strong flowing springs within the Lower Howard's Creek Nature & Heritage Preserve. Both are marked stops on the John Holder Trail that begins at Hall's Restaurant and feature dry-laid stone wall enclosures. There are numerous other wet weather springs in the Preserve.

These old springhouses are still fairly common in Clark County. Examples with stone or brick walls may be found at the Walter Preston House on Basin Springs Road, the Gaitskill House on Wades Mill Road, the Zachariah Elkin House and the old John Martin farm on Boonesboro Road, the old Dudley Wade farm on Donaldson Road, and the Vaughn place on Twomile Creek off Elkin Station Road.

Sources
Clark County Order Book 8:239; "Chalybeate" at wikipedia.org; Dianne Wells, editor, *Roadside History; A Guide to Kentucky Highway Markers* (Frankfort, KY, 2002), pp. 126, 182; *The Edmonson Voice*, June 7, 2016; road report in loose papers in the attic of the Clark County Courthouse; Harry G. Enoch and Larry G. Meadows, *Clark County Road Book, 1793-1876* (Clay City, KY, 2005), pp. 2, 4, 12, 27; Harry G. Enoch and Diane Rogers, *Deposition Book, Clark County, Kentucky, Court Depositions, 1795-1814* (Winchester, KY, 2005), pp. 9-10, 56-57, 109-110, 198; Winchester Trustees Minute Book, pp. 39, 43-44; Harry G. Enoch, "Calmes Spring," *Winchester Sun*, August 27, 2011.

20

What Was That Name Again?

December 9, 2016

I have a fascination with unusual names and thought it might be amusing to share some of them. I once wrote an article entitled, "Peter Goosey's Plantation," because his name struck my fancy.* Many early Clark County residents had uncommon given names or surnames or both. Here are a few that I picked out.

Septimus Scholl (1789-1849) bears a name that dates back to Roman times: Septimus is Latin for "seventh." Septimus was the second child of Joseph Scholl and Lavina Boone, a daughter of Daniel Boone. There is an amusing story in the Clark County Chronicles about Septimus and his grandfather.

"When Boone came back to Kentucky in 1801, he visited his daughter, Mrs. Scholl. He went from Scholl's home to Winchester one day, taking with him his grandson, Septimus Scholl. Septimus was told by his mother to get some coffee while in town; but Septimus was so engrossed with the strange and interesting sights that he saw in town that he forgot it. Returning home that evening they had gotten as far as the place where the C&O Railroad now crosses the Iron Works Pike, when Boone said to his grandson, 'Septy, did you get that coffee for your mother?' Septimus exclaimed, 'Oh! Grandpa, I forgot it. You sit here in the shade while I go back after it.' Boone rested until his grandson went to town and returned."

Original Young gets points for originality. Original, who went by "Rig," lived on the Mt. Sterling Road and served as a magistrate on the Clark County Court.

Barzilla Abbott's name has a biblical origin: Barzillai was a wealthy Gileadite who showed hospitality to David when he fled from Absalom (2 Samuel 17:27). Barzilla Abbott operated Abbott's Mill on Lulbegrud Creek in the 1830s and

---

* See *Where In The World? Historic Places in Clark County, Kentucky* (Winchester, KY, 2007), p. 34.

'40s. The only other Barzilla I have come across is my great-great-grandfather, Barzilla Shaw.

Lamentation Bush is another favorite. He was a son of Ambrose Bush Jr. and along with his brother, James, was accused of murdering Samuel R. Combs on the courthouse steps in Winchester in 1833. The brothers were prosecuted and both were acquitted.

Wildy McKinney has a nice ring to it. Wildy (1784-1852) was born in Augusta County, Virginia, came to Winchester with his father, John McKinney, and later moved to Estill County, where he raised a large family. The family held the 91st "Wildy McKinney Reunion" this year at Spout Springs. Their recorded genealogy lists 2,676 descendants of Wildy's sons and daughters.

General Davis served in the Union army during the Civil War. He was a 45-year-old slave belonging to William Cole, when he enlisted at Camp Nelson in December 1864. General was a private in the 115th Infantry Regiment, United States Colored Infantry.

Branch Tanner (1782-1870) is a fine appellation. He was a brother of Judith Tanner who married Josiah Hart, Joel Tanner Hart's parents. Branch married Hanna Cooper; they are buried in the Tanner Graveyard on Morris Road. His father was Archelaus Tanner. Another biblical name, Archelaus is the Latinized version of the Greek name meaning "master of the people."

Prince Snow is a great name, but we know very little about him. He is mentioned several times in Clark County records between 1797 and 1802, and then he disappears. I've always wondered if Snow Creek in now Powell County could have been named for him.

Pretty Mary Shepherd was christened Mary Jane Shepherd and widely known for her great beauty. She was born to Augustine Shepherd in Amherst County, Virginia in 1754, married John Haggard in Albemarle County, and died in Clark County in 1846 at age 92.

Hay Taliaferro had two unusual names. The surname came from Tagliaferro, which was Italian for "iron cutter." The Taliaferros were a prominent Virginia family who pronounced their name "Toliver" and sometimes spelled it that way.

We could say the same about Mourning Quisenberry. Mourning sounds like a Puritan name. She was one of Rev. James Quisenberry's 24 children by two wives. Some of the early Quisenberrys pronounced their name "Cushenberry."

Waddy Tate (1798-1875) was a son of William Tate and Martha Winn. Waddy was born in Clark County, married Ruthie Miles, and died in Macon, Missouri. He takes his given name from a venerable English surname. The Waddys were a well-known family in Northumberland County, Virginia. Giving children a first name from the mother's family name is an old Virginia custom, and once used the name often reappears for generations. Waddy was named for his grandfather, Waddy Tate, who was the son of John Tate and Mary Waddy.

Other Clark County favorites of mine may follow the same naming pattern: Beverly Daniel, Ransom Tinsley, Flavel Vivion, Sharshall Jordan, Smallwood Acton (Ecton), and Shastain (or Shasteen) Watkins.

There are a few nice surnames too. John Sidebottom was the owner and operator of the Boonesborough Ferry in the early 1800s. John Halfpenny was born in New Hampshire, served in the Revolutionary War in the Connecticut Line, and received a disability pension for wounds received in the Battle of Long Island. The pension was awarded in 1818 while Halfpenny was residing in Clark County.

John Ronimus was a son of Johann Franz Hieronymus, an Austrian immigrant who died in Clark County in 1819. Hieronymus has been spelled in dozens of imaginative ways. One wonders if family members or county clerks are responsible for the version shortened to "Ronimus."

Reuben Blades, "of color," died of smallpox in Clark County in 1873. His name is special to me because it happens to be the same as the actor who played in one of my favorite movies: "The Milagro Beanfield War."

I will close with my all-time weird name: North East, who appears on the 1797 Montgomery County tax list. Mr. East came west from Louisa County, Virginia, and was commissioned a lieutenant in the Madison County militia. North East married in Lincoln County in 1786. His wife was Karenhappuch Peyton—not a bad name either.

Sources

Scholl: *Winchester Sun*, June 14, 1923; **Young**: Harry G. Enoch and Diane Rogers, *Deposition Book, Clark County, Kentucky, Court Depositions, 1795-1814* (Winchester, KY, 2005), p. 241; **Abbott**: Clark County Will Book 11:243; **Bush**: Harry G. Enoch, *Colonel John Holder, Boonesborough Defender and Kentucky Entrepreneur* (Winchester, KY, 2009), pp. 240-244; **McKinney**: *Citizen Voice & Times*, July 24, 2015; **Davis**: Civil War enlistment rolls at the Kentucky Military History Museum in Frankfort; **Tanner**: Kathryn Owen, *Old Graveyards of Clark County, Kentucky* (Winchester, KY, 1975), p. 127; Enoch, *Where In The World?*, p. 43; **Snow**: Clark County Order Book 2:479, 491; *Kentucky Gazette*, October 25, 1797; **Shepherd**: Martha S. Fox, *Stuart-Quisenberry Kith and Kin* (Winchester, KY, 1986), p. 67; **Taliaferro**: Anthony Wagner and F. S. Andrus, "Origin of the Family of Taliaferro," *Virginia Magazine of History and Biography* (January 1969), 77:22-25; **Quisenberry**: Fox, *Stuart-Quisenberry Kith and Kin*, p. 116; **Tate**: Simpson Family History, http://simpsonhistory.com/; **Sidebottom**: Harry G. Enoch, "Kentucky River Blue Water Trail Guide," http://www.bgheritage.com/html/on_line_documents.html; **Halfpenny**: Revolutionary War pension application, S. 35,387 NH; **Rominus/Hieronymous**: Ben T. Hieronymus and R. Dean Heironimus, *The Hieronymus Story, 1985* (Baltimore, MD, 1985), p. 101; Clark County Deed Book 1:502, 5:69; **Blades**: Clark County Order Book 10:451; **East**: 1797 Montgomery County tax list; Shirley Dunn, *Marriages, 1780-1850 & Tombstone Inscriptions* (1977), p. 11.

21

Women on the Frontier

December 16, 2016

   Fort Boonesborough Foundation holds an annual event at the fort called "Women on the Frontier." It was conceived as a way to honor those pioneers who seldom get recognized for their contribution to the settlement of Kentucky. In the male-dominated society of the time, it was rare for a woman's name to make it into the written records, so sources of information about women are sparse. Several years ago, Dr. Randolph Hollingsworth of the UK History Department spoke at the Women on the Frontier celebration. In her talk, she referred to the 1787 Fayette County tax list. The roll had the names of 31 women listed as the head of a household. They were almost all widows who had lost husbands on the frontier and had not remarried. Knowing that a woman's lot in the Kentucky wilderness called for a large measure of courage and unending hard work, imagine how much more challenging that role would have been for a single woman raising a family on her own.

   My interest in the 1787 tax roll peaked when I recognized the names of seven of the women who were living in what would become Clark County. Anyone with an interest in the beginnings of our county should know a little about these exceptional individuals.

   Sarah Bush—Sarah (possibly Lewis) married Josiah Bush, the eldest brother of Capt. Billy Bush. Sarah and Josiah resided in Albemarle County until 1781, when they departed for Kentucky. They joined a group of Bush family members on the Holston River near present-day Abingdon, Virginia, where Josiah took sick and died. Sarah continued on to Kentucky with the Bush colony and settled on Twomile Creek in Clark County. Like many other family members in the Bush Settlement, she belonged to Providence Baptist Church. In 1794 "Sary Bush" gave consent for her daughter Frankey to marry John Hooton, and in 1797, she gave consent for daughter Sally to marry John

Duncan. The latter is the last positive record we have for Sarah. She did have several adult children living nearby. Son Philip was mentioned in his grandfather's will, and there is circumstantial evidence for sons Lewis, James, Joseph, Joshua, John and William.

Elizabeth Clements—We know very little about Elizabeth. She was married to John Clements, and the couple resided at McGee's Station on Jouett Creek. John was killed at the Battle of Upper Blue Licks, or "Holder's Defeat," on August 14, 1782. According to accounts of the battle, Clements was one of four killed and "left on the ground," while two others later died from their wounds. Elizabeth received 26 pounds in compensation for the loss of "a Rone mare, a Bay Mare, one Saddle & Blanket." She was listed on the tax rolls as a single woman until 1792; after that date, no further record could be found.

Margaret Drake (1755-1827)—Margaret was a daughter of John Buchanan, a wealthy landowner of Botetourt County, Virginia. She married an adventurer, Joseph Drake, one of the Long Hunters of Kentucky. Joseph and Margaret came to Boonesborough with their two young children in the spring of 1778. That August Joseph was killed by Indians near the fort. Margaret remained at the fort, unmarried, and had a liaison with Capt. John Holder that resulted in a daughter, Rhoda Drake. When Holder moved across the river and established Holder's Station, Margaret came too. Holder married Fanny Callaway and took Rhoda Drake into his household to raise. Evidence indicates that Margaret had two more children by Holder—Sabrina and Euphemia—but since he was married at that time, he did not acknowledge these daughters. Margaret remained single until at least 1791, and sometime after married William Jones. They later moved to Franklin County, Tennessee, and Margaret died there in 1827.

Rebecca Hunter—Rebecca was a daughter of Michael Dumford, who came to Kentucky from North Carolina. Michael patented 400 acres of land on the Kentucky River between Boone Creek and Jouett Creek. Rebecca was married to Charles Hunter, also of North Carolina. In August 1782, an army of Shawnee laid siege to Bryan's Station. Hearing the news, William Hays, son-in-law of Daniel Boone, raised a company of twelve men who rode to the aid of the besieged inhabitants. When nearing the station, the company came down a lane where Indians had set an ambush. According to one account, "Charles Hunter was wounded through the body & died that night." In 1791, the widowed Rebecca purchased a 100-acre tract of land adjoining her father's near Boone Creek. Rebecca remained single and the head of her own household until 1795, when she married Daniel Burch.

Margaret McGuire—Margaret and her husband James McGuire came to Kentucky in 1779, first to Boonesborough then to McGee's Station. On August 19, 1782, James, a lieutenant in the Fayette County militia, was killed at the Battle of Blue Licks. Margaret was still single and the head of her own household on the 1787 tax roll. Her son John was listed as a tithable (between age 16 and 20). What happened to Margaret after that is not known.

Mary Sphar—Mary was married to Matthais Sphar, the son of a German immigrant, Hans Ulrich Sphar. They resided in Berkeley County, Virginia, until Mary and her husband came to Kentucky. They occupied one of the cabins at Strode's Station in 1779. In 1784 Matthais went out on a hunting trip with Michael Cassidy and Joshua Bennett. While they were camped a little east of present-day North Middletown, Indians crept up and shot Sphar and Bennett; Cassidy escaped. William Clinkenbeard stated, "Cassidy lived with Spohr. Expected him to marry the widow Spohr but he didn't. Wells took her." According to Matthais' son, Daniel, "September 1784 my father was killed, about the 20th. Cassidy staid till 1786 or 1787 with my mother, then formed the station [Cassidy's Station in Fleming County]." Nothing further has been learned of Mary and her presumed second husband, Wells. Her son Daniel left a line of prominent descendants in Clark County, including Asa Rogers Sphar (1851-1929), William R. Sphar Sr. (1880-1963) and William R. Sphar Jr. (1914-2005).

Jane Wilson—We have little information about Jane. Her husband, John Wilson, was killed at the Battle of Blue Licks,

August 19, 1782. Jane was listed on the tax roll of 1787 (Fayette County) and continued to be listed until 1794 (Clark County). On the latter she appears as the head of a household with seven males over 21; she was taxed for two horses, seven cattle and no land or slaves. Her son James claimed the land of his father in an 1803 lawsuit against David McGee, but the suit was eventually dismissed.

Sources

Bush—Harry G. Enoch, *Captain Billy Bush and the Bush Settlement* (Winchester, KY, 2015), pp. 216-218; **Clements**; Harry G. Enoch, *Colonel John Holder, Boonesborough Defender and Kentucky Entrepreneur* (Winchester, KY, 2009), pp. 114-116; **Drake**—Enoch, *Colonel John Holder*, pp. 68-89; **Hunter**—Draper Manuscripts 22C10, 60; **McGuire**—Ruth E. Moran, "Three John McGuires of Early Kentucky," *Kentucky Ancestors* (1994) 30:2-4; **Sphar**—Harry G. Enoch, *Pioneer Voices, Interviews with Early Settlers of Clark County, Kentucky* (Winchester, KY, 2012), pp. 27-28, 93-95; Herman G. Sphar, *Sphar Family History* (Lafayette, IN, 1994); **Wilson**—*James Wilson v. David McGee*, 1806, Fayette County Complete Record Book B, p. 338.

22
Winchester's Remarkable Year: 1906

December 23, 2016

The coming of the railroads brought profound changes to Winchester. The town was fortunate to attract three major lines: Elizabethtown, Lexington & Big Sandy (later C&O) in 1872; Kentucky Central (later L&N) in 1883; and Lexington & Eastern (later L&N) in 1889. The town became a destination for mountain residents and a jumping off place for drummers plying their trade in Eastern Kentucky. This earned Winchester the cognomen of "Gateway City to the Mountains." The tracks were soon lined with a series of railway warehouses, where proprietors could purchase and store local products and ship them off to distant markets.

The railroads likely propelled Winchester's transformation from rural county seat to fourth-class city, which the Kentucky General Assembly approved in 1882. This resulted in a change in governance from town trustees to an elected mayor and city council. Other changes followed in rapid succession: a gas plant and electric generating plant in 1887, and telephone service in 1890.

Lucien Beckner, then publisher and editor of the *Winchester Sun-Sentinel* (forerunner of the *Sun*), authored a 16-page pamphlet entitled, "Winchester, Its Remarkable Growth During The Past Twelve Months And A Few Reasons Therefor." In the introductory paragraph, Beckner stated, "The year 1906 will be counted by the future historian of this community the most remarkable one for growth that Winchester has known" He added that growth "has lunged forward by leaps and bounds that have startled the most optimistic prophets." To prove his point, Beckner went on to describe each of the year's new additions.

Union Depot—"The first thing a traveler to Winchester over the Louisville & Nashville or Chesapeake & Ohio railways sees is the new Union Passenger Depot put up by these two roads." The "modern" new facility replaced the old depot which residents had complained about for years. It served eight passenger trains a day on the L&N and ten a day on the C&O, remarkable numbers in themselves.

Union Depot, Winchester, Ky.

Union Depot (Clark County Public Library)

Street Railway System—The city granted a franchise to Central Kentucky Traction Company to operate the streetcar line that ran from the railroad station down Main Street all the way to the fairgrounds. The company removed the wooden rails, laid two miles of steel track and replaced the old mule-drawn cars with electric trolleys.

Brown-Proctoria—"The Brown-Proctoria, the largest and best equipped and furnished hotel in Kentucky outside of Louisville, was opened January 1." The hotel had two elevators and one hundred rooms "with electric light, gas and telephone service in every room."

Kentucky Wesleyan—The old college building was destroyed by a spectacular fire in February 1905. Its replacement, opened in April 1906, contained 21 rooms, a chapel, chemistry and physics laboratories, a gymnasium and baths.

Gas Company—"On January 19, 1906, the Central

Kentucky Natural Gas Company turned on natural gas, piping it from Menifee county, about thirty miles away." The company later became Columbia Gas of Kentucky. Customers paid 25 cents per thousand cubic feet. Natural gas service resulted in four new plumbing establishments in Winchester.

Brown Proctoria Hotel (above) and Kentucky Wesleyan College.
(Clark County Public Library)

Water Works—The Winchester Water Works Company "added to the dam at the old reservoir...and built a new reservoir." The improvements increased their storage capacity from 50 million gallons to 210 million gallons. WMU still operates a reservoir at that location.

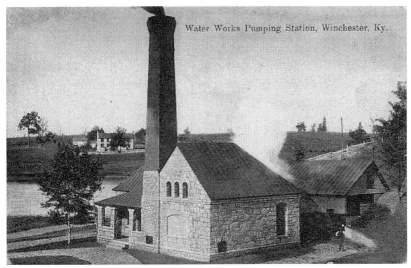

**Water Works (above) and Hagan Engine Factory.
(Clark County Public Library)**

Dental Burr Factory—"The Northrop Dental Burr factory is one of only two [in the country] that make a machine finished burr." Northrop's machines produced dental drill bits with a precision of one ten thousandth of an inch.

Overall Factory—"The D. B. Young Manufacturing Company, a $10,000 corporation, came here the past spring and are now turning out about 150 dozen pairs of overalls a day, which they will increase to 300 dozen shortly." Their factory was on East Broadway at Church Alley.

Engine Factory—"The Hagan Gas Engine Company...added a three-story brick building, 60 by 125 feet in size" that "will double their output of thirty engines a month." The factory was on East Washington Street, just east of the railroad. The company made gas and gasoline engines that are prized as collector's items today.

Creamery—The creamery "opened July 1 by Mr. B. A. Ogden & Son has a dairy in connection, in which they milk about fifty cows. The fresh milk comes into town, is aerated, bottle or separated, then sold or stored or churned."

Flour Mill—"R. C. Mansfield & Son opened their new steam flouring mill on March 12 and are now making one hundred barrels of Best Patent, Mountain Lily and Good Luck flour and about 500 bushels of meal a day." The 4-story brick mill stood on Pendleton Street, just north of the L&E Railroad.

Grass Seed Cleaning Plant—"Mr. David S. Gay has during the past year added a new grass seed cleaning plant to his large warehouse business that will clean 1,000 bushels a day" of bluegrass seed. Gay's warehouse was at the intersection of Main Street and Winn Avenue.

Steam Bakery—"The Baer-Douglas Imperial Steam Bakery began business last May and...has a capacity of 5,000 loaves a day and a growing wholesale business throughout Central Kentucky." The bakery was located at 102 North Main Street.

Lumber Mill—"The Winchester Lumber and Manufacturing Company, incorporated for $15,000, which opened here last March is already shipping its products from Philadelphia to Dacotah." The business was situated between Main and Maple Streets, just south of the L&N Railroad. The two mills at Ford and three in Winchester made Clark County one of the leaders in the lumber industry in Kentucky.

Granite Brick Plant—The Winchester Granite Brick Company began operation in 1906 and "they are now turning out about 18,000 a day of the prettiest and best brick made in the United States." The plant also turned out builder's sand, "which on account of its fine grade, they are selling as far East as New Jersey." The First Christian Church on Hickman Street is faced with their white granite brick.

People's State Bank—"Last but not least amongst the new enterprises is the People's State Bank with a capital stock of $100,000, established in the new Brown-Proctoria building" with Joe L. Brown, president, Laban Cockrell, vice president, and John M. Hodgkin, cashier.

Beckner concluded by listing "our most important manufactories besides those already mentioned." These included "two large mills at Ford; three large dressed lumber plants in this city; the flouring mills of McEldowney, Matlack & Woolcott (formerly S. P. Kerr); Wainscott's Pop and Candy Factory; the Winchester Novelty Manufacturing Company, makers of the King Lunch Box; and the Scobee-Williams Spoke Factory."

A number of the businesses Beckner wrote about are still with us today.

Sources

Thomas D. Clark, *Clark County, Kentucky: A History* (Winchester, KY, 1995), pp. 279-307; Sanborn Map Co., 1907 Sanborn Fire Insurance Maps, Winchester, KY; Inter-State Directory Co., *Directory of Winchester and Clark County Gazetteer* (Marion, IN, 1908); "Prosperity in Kentucky," *Rock Products* (Dec. 22, 1909) 9:36, (Feb. 22, 1910) 10:36.

23
Captain Leeland Hathaway's Grand Adventure

January 6, 2017

Leeland Hathaway (1834-1909) was born in Montgomery County. He was a student at the Kentucky Military Institute, then located on the outskirts of Louisville, and Transylvania University, where he studied law. In September 1862, Hathaway made his way to Tennessee, enlisted in John Hunt Morgan's command and was made adjutant of the 9th Kentucky Cavalry. He campaigned with Morgan until the summer of 1863, when he was captured at Buffington Island during Morgan's Indiana-Ohio raid.

Imprisoned at Allegheny, Pennsylvania, Lieutenant Hathaway was exchanged in April 1865. Having been reassigned before his capture to the 14th Kentucky Cavalry, he tried to make his way back to the regiment in company with two companions, Winder Monroe and Jack Messick. On their way south they encountered Lee's troops retreating from near Richmond. They continued on to Danville, Virginia, where they met Gen. John C. Breckinridge, who supplied them with boots and horses. They made their way farther south, dodging federal patrols, without finding any sign of their unit.

Winder Monroe suggested they head for Abbeville, South Carolina, where his grandfather was a judge. They arrived there near the end of April. Two days later they learned that President Jefferson Davis' wife, fleeing Richmond, had just reached the town and was in need of assistance. Varina Davis was travelling with her four children, her sister, and the president's secretary, Burton Harrison. Hathaway later wrote about his attempt to escort Mrs. Davis to safety.

She wanted to start for the Florida coast where she could board a ship and take her children to safety. Hathaway "suggested that we might be of service to Mrs. Davis," and she gladly accepted. Together with Monroe and Messick they got her voluminous baggage loaded on two ambulances and set out on the 30th.

Leeland Hathaway
(Hathaway Family Collection, University of Kentucky)

The caravan reached Washington in northeast Georgia on May 2. "After leaving Washington, our trip for several days was only a march of a score or more of miles during the day and the incidents of camp-life during the night. Mrs. Davis...bore the fatigues of travel and the rude fare of the camp with a spirit that was contagious, and veterans learned a new lesson of heroism from this gentle woman."

They were stopped several times by "parties of disbanded troops, who mistook our train for quartermaster stores or the Confederate Treasury." A wagon hidden in the woods was discovered that same month—May 1865—and found to contain $180,000 in coin and four million dollars in Confederate paper money. Even so, for years after the war lurid stories were published about the fate of the Confederate treasury that some estimated to be worth from two to thirty million dollars.

Jefferson Davis and wife Varina
(Museum of the Confederacy)

Around midnight on May 6, "we were aroused by the sound of horses' feet [and] to our great surprise it was the President with his staff and escort." On May 9, they went into camp about a mile from Irwinsville, Georgia, "the President occupying a tent with his wife and smaller children."

At daylight, a regiment of Michigan troops appeared at the camp and "startled us with their shouts, 'Where is the

President?'" Davis was soon recognized and surrendered to a federal officer. "The absurd story of his being in woman's clothing has been so thoroughly contradicted and put to rest that it is not necessary to mention it further."

Davis and his wife, Hathaway and companions along with the rest of the company were taken by wagon to Macon, by train to Augusta then by boat to Savannah. There they boarded a government vessel, "which without delay steamed away for—we did not know where." Hathaway and his friends were so exhausted that "the uncertainty which veiled our fate could scarcely disturb our rest."

"We awoke one morning to see the casemates of Fortress Monroe frowning upon us." (Casemates are fortified gun emplacements.) "Mr. Davis...at once predicted that this was to be his gaol." After Davis' family was released, he was imprisoned at Fort Monroe in Hampton, Virginia and remained there for two years.

Hathaway, Monroe and Messick were taken to Fort McHenry and locked in separate cells in an old brick stable. Two months later Hathaway had still not learned why they were there. He decided to risk using a $20 gold piece Varina Davis had given him to bribe a guard into mailing a letter addressed to his father in Kentucky.

Hathaway's father, after being denied entrance to Fort McHenry, went directly to President Andrew Johnson explaining the boys' predicament. Johnson soon learned from the Secretary of War, Edwin Stanton, that the boys were suspected of being involved in Lincoln's assassination, in a plot supposedly cooked up by President Davis himself. When Stanton could produce no evidence of his suspicions, President Johnson ordered the boys' release.

That August Hathaway was invited to attend the Clark County Fair by Levi Wheeler, whom Hathaway had served with during the war. At the fair, Hathaway met Levi's sister, Mattie Wheeler. In her diary she recorded, "I made a great many acquaintances, among the rest was Mr. Leland Hathaway, one of the most interesting and fascinating gentlemen I ever met." They would marry the following April.

Hathaway settled in Clark County, where he established a successful law practice with James French. Their office was on Court Street. Leeland and Mattie lived at 253 South Main Street (a few doors south of the Bluegrass Heritage Museum). Mattie died in 1893, Leeland in 1909. They are buried in Winchester Cemetery.

Sources

An Eyewitness [Leeland Hathaway], "The Capture of President Jefferson Davis," *Register of the Kentucky Historical Society* (1966) 64:270-276, originally published in 1875 in the *Winchester Democrat*; Dee Alexander Brown, *Morgan's Raiders* (New York, NY, 1959), pp. 301-321; Harry G. Enoch, *Where In The World? Historic Places in Clark County, Kentucky* (Winchester, KY, 2007), pp. 91-95; *Winchester Democrat*, August 9, 1893, November 19, 1909.

24
The Strange Case of Peter Evans

January 20, 2017

The title may be a bit too dramatic, but the story of Peter Evans' Revolutionary War pension is certainly an unusual case. Let's begin at the beginning.

Peter Evans (1758-1814) was born in Prince William County in northern Virginia. He married Ann Newman in the same county in December 1777. She was a daughter of Capt. John Newman and Hannah Posey.

In February 1776, before his eighteenth birthday, Peter enlisted as a private in the Virginia Light Horse Troop commanded by Henry Lee. Lee, a captain at that time, fought with distinction throughout the war earning the nickname "Light Horse Harry Lee." He was the father of Robert E. Lee.

Peter was engaged in the battle of Princeton in January 1777 then went into winter quarters with General Washington's army in Morristown, New Jersey. He was commissioned a 1st lieutenant (1779) and a captain (1780) by Gov. Thomas Jefferson. Peter commanded a company throughout the entire siege of Yorktown that ended with the surrender of Lord Cornwallis (1783). His children could not recall the "many other hard fought Battles" he was in.

Like many Virginians, Peter immigrated to Kentucky after the war. He was listed as a taxpayer of Madison County in 1787 and resided there for many years before moving to Clark County sometime before his death, which occurred on February 12, 1814. One record describes his home being located "near the Red River Ironworks in Estill County." Although the statement implies he lived in Estill, he was a resident of Clark where his will was probated. An 1811 road order suggests his home was near where present-day Ironworks Road (Route 15) crosses Red River at Clay City. Peter died before passage of the pension laws for Revolutionary War veterans.

Peter's widow, Ann, died in 1836 at the age of 81. She was attended in her last illness by her grandson, Dr. Peter Evans (son of Peter Evans Jr.). The cause of death was said to be "ovarian dropsy," an antiquated term used to describe fluid buildup in the abdomen caused by ovarian cancer. She was then living with her son, Paul, who inherited the home place of Peter Sr. A law passed in 1832 made Ann eligible for a pension based on Peter's Revolutionary War service, but she did not apply.

Six years later, her son Belain Posey Evans applied for a pension on behalf of the heirs of Peter Evans Sr. In doing so he took advantage of an obscure provision in the pension law amendments of 1836, stating that "the right of the widow [to a pension] under the act is to be regarded as a vested interest...and not defeated by the omission to apply for it; and it goes as such, on her death, to her personal representatives, that is, her children."

In 1842 Belain, as administrator of Ann's estate, applied for a Revolutionary War pension on behalf of her surviving children. They were awarded a pension in the amount of $43.33 per year. In addition to Belain, her children still living at that time were Catherine Amelia Augustus Evans, Paul Jones Evans, and Silas Evans.

What marked this as a "strange case"? This Revolutionary War pension was issued 61 years after Peter Evans was discharged from the service, 28 years after his death, and 6 years after his widow's death. It is the only pension I have come across where the first application was made by the veteran's and widow's surviving children.

Peter and Ann raised an interesting family with a long history in Clark County.

Paul, their youngest son, was born in Madison County. He was interviewed by Rev. John D. Shane in the late 1840s. "Paul Evans, on Red river, house about one-half mile from the forge, up the river and on or nearly on the Clarke and Montgomery line, he in Clarke." Depositions in the pension application indicate that both his parents were buried on the place. Paul married Polly Combs, a daughter of Benjamin Combs.

Silas married Sally Combs, a daughter of Cuthbert Combs.

Peter Jr. married a widow, Polly Combs Baker, another daughter of Cuthbert Combs and the third wife of Winchester's founder, John Baker. Peter Jr. was very active buying and selling property in Winchester. He resided on Ironworks Road near the County Farm. He died in 1842; Polly died in 1863 at the age of 87. She was buried in Winchester Cemetery; according to the Evans-Baker family bible, he was buried there also. Their son, Dr. Peter Evans, studied "at the medical school in Lexington [Transylvania]." Doctor Evans married Letitia Quisenberry, a daughter of James and Chloe Quisenberry. Chloe Shipp was the second wife of Reverend Quisenberry.

Belain Posey Evans, eldest son of Peter Sr., received his unusual name from his maternal grandmother's family. He married Lucy Hickman, a daughter of Rev. Henry Hickman of Fayette County. Belain died in Jessamine County in 1843, one year after obtaining a Revolutionary War pension for the benefit of the children of Peter Evans Sr.

Thanks to Lanny Evans for suggesting this topic.

Sources

Pension Application of Peter Evans, W. 14695, VA; Clark County Order Book 4:474, 11:155, 159, 170; Clark County Deed Book 6:220, 221; Clark County Will Book 3:332; Evans-Baker Bible, transcription courtesy of the Clark County Historical Society, http:/ancestry.com; Harry G. Enoch, *Pioneer Voices, Interviews with Early Settlers of Clark County, Kentucky* (Winchester, KY, 2012), p. 53.

25
The Inspiring Career of
William Webb Banks

February 3, 2017

Over the past two centuries, our community has produced many noteworthy citizens. Though he is little known today, William Webb Banks (1862-1928) deserves a place in that pantheon. Banks, born into slavery in Clark County, acquired a college education and achieved statewide acclaim as a journalist and churchman. His death was marked by an unusually lengthy obituary in the *Winchester Sun*, from which we are able to glean many items of his personal history.

William Webb Banks (from the *Golden Jubilee of the General Association of Colored Baptists in Kentucky*, 1915)

Webb was the son of Paducah Banks and Catherine Martin. His father, though named for the famous Chickasaw chief "Paduke," usually went by Patrick; he was raised by the Webb family in southwest Clark County. His mother, also known as "Kitty," was said to have been raised by the Bush family, but records uncovered by researcher Lyndon Comstock indicate she was owned by Elizabeth Baber Field Martin, wife of Robert E. Martin. Sometime after the Civil War, Patrick moved the family to Winchester where he was a carpenter. In 1868, Patrick and Catherine came to court to declare that they had been married for 14 years. This step was necessary since slaves could not legally marry.

In Winchester Webb "became a pupil of the famous Carey [sadly unidentified]. The desire for a higher Education was planted in his heart under this pioneer instructor." Webb then worked his way through State Colored Baptist University in Louisville. The school, founded by a convention of black Baptist churches in Kentucky, later became Simmons University. Webb graduated in 1886. That year he was selected to head the colored schools of Winchester, but decided he was unsuited to the job. He then went into the grocery and mercantile business for many years.

In 1879 Webb joined the First Baptist Church in Winchester. He headed a movement in 1889 to organize the Broadway Baptist Church and was their first Sunday School superintendent. About that time, he became president of the largest Sunday School convention in the state of Kentucky and served five years as recording secretary for the Consolidated Baptist Association.

In 1891 he successfully launched his career in journalism and founded the *National Chronicle*. He sold the paper the following year and went to Indianapolis for four years to continue his editorship.

Webb returned to Winchester in 1896 and married Annie Simms (1862-1923), a school teacher in Louisville. She had the distinction of being the first African American female delegate to the Kentucky Republican Convention, where she served on the Rules Committee. Annie and Webb had no children.

He continued his journalism career in Winchester, contributing articles to black journals and newspapers. He wrote the "Colored News" column in the *Winchester News* for a number of years.

Webb enjoyed numerous honors during his career. Gov. J. C. W. Beckham appointed him as one of Kentucky's special representatives to the 1907 Jamestown Exposition. Webb was active in Kentucky's Republican Party and was their candidate for U.S. Land Office Recorder in 1891. He was part of the "anti-separate coach movement" and made a formal protest before the Kentucky General Assembly on a proposed state law that would require racial segregation of train passengers. He was a commissioner at the Inter-State Exposition in Raleigh, North Carolina (1908), commissioner to the Emancipation Exhibition in New York (1913), and a delegate to the Half-Century Anniversary Celebration of Negro Freedom in Chicago (1915).

Employment for blacks was extremely limited in Winchester in his day. Census data indicate that Webb worked as custodian for the Elks Club and Citizen's National Bank for nearly thirty years. He lived on West Broadway where his parents had preceded him. Webb died of cancer at a local hospital in 1928 and was buried beside his wife in Winchester Cemetery.

Accolades poured in following his death. Examples include "honored citizen, well beloved by all," "Winchester suffers the loss of a most distinguished character," and "his place in this community cannot be easily filled." The editor of the "Colored News" in the *Winchester Sun* headed his column "A King in Israel Has Fallen."

Following his death, Webb delivered a final surprise: He left an estate of about $10,000. Having no children of siblings, his will designated $200 to Winchester Cemetery for the upkeep of his family lot; the remainder he left to his alma mater to establish the "Banks Ministerial Relief Fund" in order to perpetuate the memory of his father and mother.

Sources

Winchester Sun, September 15, 19, 21, 24, October 1, December 12, 1928; Notable Kentucky African Americans Database, http://nkaa.uky.edu/; Gerald L. Smith et al., *Kentucky African American Encyclopedia* (Lexington, KY, 2015), p. 33; C. H. Parrish, editor, *Golden Jubilee of the General Association of Colored Baptists in Kentucky*, (Louisville, KY, 1915), p. 163; Frank L Mather, *Who's Who of the Colored Race, Vol. 1* (Chicago, IL, 1915), p. 18; Clark County Colored Will Book 1:168.

26
Notable African Americans of Winchester

February 17, 2017

Although the subject of black history languished for many years in the popular press, significant progress has been made over the last few decades.   An especially important contribution close to home is the *Kentucky African American Encyclopedia*. That 2015 publication runs 600 plus pages and features more than 150 contributors. This article focuses on some of the men and women mentioned in the *Encyclopedia* who have Winchester connections.   The biographies that follow were supplemented by information from other sources.

George Ecton

George French Ecton (1846-1929) was born in Winchester, the son of Antonio Ecton and Martha George. At the close of the Civil, in June 1865, "George and a friend determined to 'make way for liberty,' having received a set of 'free papers,' which even at that late date were necessary to every traveling Negro to insure recognition of freedom." They made their way to Cincinnati and found work as deck hands on an Ohio River steamboat. George soon returned to Cincinnati and found employment at the Burnett House and several other hotels. After recovering from smallpox, he began his education in night school. In 1873 he moved to Chicago and was given charge of the dining room at the Hotel Woodruff. He married Patti Allen from Winchester in 1877. "Their union is childless, but their home is thronged by a brilliant set of intelligent people, and both he and his wife take a great interest in passing events."

George established ties to the Republican Party in Chicago and, in 1886, was elected to represent Chicago's Third Senatorial District. He was the first African American elected to the Illinois General Assembly.   After serving one term he returned to Chicago to resume his career as one of the city's preeminent caterers. He remained active in Republican politics until his death in 1929. He is buried in Chicago's Lincoln Cemetery.

Mary Spradling

Mary Elizabeth Mace Spradling (1911-2009) was born in Winchester, a daughter of Ella Nora Travis, a teacher, and Mynor J. Mace, a minister. She obtained a degree in English from Kentucky State University and a library science degree from Atlanta University. Mary Elizabeth began her career teaching French in Lynch, Kentucky. She was the school librarian there in the 1930s and then a teacher-librarian in Shelbyville in the 1940s.

In 1936, she married Louis Spradling, a teacher and elementary school principal. From 1948 until 1957, she served as branch librarian for Louisville Public Library. Spradling left Kentucky to become the first African American librarian at Kalamazoo Public Library in Michigan. She served as head of the Young Adult Department until her retirement in 1976.

Spradling accumulated a large collection of works by and about African Americans and used them to write a number of books. Her reference book, *In Black and White: Afro-Americans in Print*, mentioned nearly 2,000 authors. The book went through three editions and her 1985 "supplement" lists more than 6,700 black writers. Spradling donated her book collection of 20,000 volumes to the Kalamazoo Valley Community College.

Dr. Joseph Laine

Joseph Fields Laine (1881-1967) was born in Winchester and educated at Berea College. Joseph completed his medical training at Meharry Medical College in Nashville. He followed that with postgraduate work at Meharry, Tuskegee Institute and Talladega College, the latter two in Alabama. He was an active physician for over sixty years, mostly spent in Kentucky.

Laine established an office in Lexington and practiced there for about 18 years. In the late 1920s he moved to Louisville where he founded the Laine Medical Clinic on Walnut Street (now Muhammad Ali Boulevard). He was instrumental in bringing other African American doctors to Kentucky. Laine served as president of the Falls City Medical Society and the Bluegrass State Medical Association. He was also an active member of the Louisville Urban League and the NAACP. He is buried in Louisville Cemetery.

Stanley Williams

Stanley R. Williams (1894-1975) was born in Danville and studied music at Tuskegee Institute. Williams taught school in Winchester where he earned the nickname "Fess," short for professor. He played many different instruments but performed most often on the clarinet and alto saxophone. The 1920 census for Winchester lists his occupation as "writer of music." He organized a number of orchestras and worked his way from Cincinnati to Chicago then to New York where, in 1926, his Royal Flush Orchestra opened at the Savoy Ballroom. The following year he left to become the front man for Dave Peyton's band playing at Chicago's Regal Theatre. His group became known as the Fess Williams' Joy Boys and played to sold out audiences.

Fess Williams on clarinet at a New York office party, ca. 1948
(William P. Gottlieb Collection, Library of Congress)

A bandleader known for his magnetic personality, Williams played "jazz high class as well as low down." He performed in a top hat and diamond-studded tuxedo, and when he yelled to the crowd, "Hello folks," they responded, "Hello Fess."

His orchestras made over fifty recordings which included the hit song "Hot Town." In 1933, he signed a contract with Columbia Broadcasting System. In the 1940s he played less as he got into the real estate business. In the 60s he worked as mail room supervisor at New York's Musicians' Union headquarters. He died in New York at the age of 81.

Elaine Farris

We could not end this article without including Elaine Farris, who was born and raised in Clark County. She obtained her Bachelor's and Master's degrees from Eastern Kentucky University then taught physical education in Clark County for seven years. To quote from the *Encyclopedia*, "she began her meteoric rise in 1993 when she was appointed assistant principal at George Rogers Clark High School." Then she served as principal at Shearer Elementary School before being named "elementary director" for Fayette County Schools.

In 2004 Farris became the first African American superintendent in Kentucky. She was selected for that position by the Shelby County School Board. Following her tenure there, she served successively as deputy commissioner of the Kentucky Department of Education (2007), interim education commissioner for the Kentucky Board of Education (2009) and, later that year, superintendent of the Clark County School System. Few persons in our community have matched her historic accomplishments.

Sources

Except where otherwise noted, information was taken from Gerald L. Smith, et al., editors, *Kentucky African American Encyclopedia* (Lexington, KY, 2015) and Notable Kentucky African Americans Database, http://nkaa.uky.edu/. **Ecton:** William J. Simmons, *Men of Note* (Cleveland, OH, 1887), p. 358. **Spradling:** *Kalamazoo Gazette*, January 30, 2009. **Laine:** John E. Kleber, editor, *Kentucky Encyclopedia* (Lexington, KY, 1992), p. 530. **Williams:** *New York Times*, December 20, 1975. **Farris:** *Lexington Herald-Leader*, June 30, 2007.

27
Early Winchester Businesses

March 3, 2017

Our town was established by an act of the General Assembly on December 19, 1793. Turn-of-the-century Winchester still reflected the wilderness character of the surrounding area. Pioneers recalled that the streets were cut out through thick canebrakes.

There were only six streets in the original town plan. Running generally north-south were Water, Main and Highland; those running east-west were Washington, Main Cross and Fairfax. None were paved. Dirt streets were crisscrossed by forks of Town Branch, which caused problems for years. Bridges had to be built and maintained to allow passage of wagons. This stream still flows but has been channeled underground.

The first courthouse, completed in 1794, was a log cabin. It was replaced in 1797 by a two-story brick structure. Other public facilities included a jail, market house, stray pen and public spring.

By 1809-1810, Winchester had six taverns licensed by the county court: John Martin, Ann Smith, Edmund Callaway, Peter Flanagan, Mordecai Gist and Amon Cast. There was plenty to drink—the county had 44 distilleries in 1810. Anyone could make whiskey; however, one could be fined for "retailing spirituous liquor without a license."

At this time, the town had a post office, hotel (National House), Masonic lodge, school (Winchester Academy, usually called the "Seminary"), a state-chartered library company and a branch of the Bank of Kentucky. Businesses identified from early deeds include a ropewalk, brickyard, slaughterhouse, livery stable, saddler shop, two cabinet shops, two tanneries, two tailors, several bootmakers, several doctors and attorneys, a wool-carding factory and a blue dyer. In the 1812-1815 timeframe, John Ridgway, Philip B. Winn, William N. Lane, George Kennedy, Joseph Coulter, George Webb, James Dunnica, Thomas Barbee, William Hickman and Thomas R. Moore had brick houses, which were combination businesses and residences.

A local newspaper, the *Winchester Advertiser*, made its debut in 1814. Its office was in "the brick building nearly opposite the Post Office." Advertisers used the pages to hawk their wares. There were nearly two dozen merchants who sold a surprising variety of goods. Most of the merchandise came from back East and required a grueling journey to transport to Kentucky. Most Winchester merchants made at least two trips each year to Philadelphia to acquire their goods. James Anderson used the newspaper to cajole his customers to pay their bills: "Please settle accounts, as we wish to start to Philadelphia in February for a fresh stock of goods."

New Goods at Cast & Holly, 1814

Superfine cloths	Black worsted hose	Silk & tabby velvets
Fine cloths, various colors	Bombazett	Tape
Cassimeers & cassinets	India & domestic check	Hat linings and binding
Velvets and corduroys	Calicoes	Hatters jack cards
Coatings	Furniture calicoes	Shaving boxes & strops
Blankets	Dimity	Green's ware
Flannels	Domestic cottons	GROCERIES, viz:
Toilinet & swansdown vesting	Plaid, snip and chambray	Imperial and hyson tea
Fancy vesting	N. England shirtings	Coffee
Superfine marseills	Sewing silk	Madeira wine
Black florence	Cotton balls	Brandy
Mantua	Ladies' shoes, a great variety	Rum
Levinthine	Morocco hats	Bounce
Lutestring & satins	Cotton shawls, assortment	Indigo and madder
Leno, jackinet & cambric muslins	Silk, assortment	Allum
Coarse muslin	Tortoise shell combs	Alspice
Linen cambric	Combs of various kinds	Pepper
Pocket handkerchiefs	Brushes of different kinds	Ginger
Cotton sleeves	Glass ware	Arronita
Pinknot sleeves	Cotton and wool cards	Chocolate
White kid gloves	Hard ware	Rosin
Beaver gloves	Best playing cards	Copperas
Long silk gloves	Shaving soap	Coffee mills
Short silk gloves	Pocket books	Spanish & domestic cigars
Ribbands	Pencils	Chewing tobacco
Silk & cotton laces	Books & stationary	Iron, steel & castings
Silk cords and chintz	Silk and cotton umbrellas	Lead
Ridicules	An assortment of hats	Cotton
Suspenders	Tin ware	Whiskey, barrel or gallon
Irish linen	Shirting cambric	Also, a variety of other articles, too
Cotton hose	Black cambric	tedious to mention

A merchant first had to travel to Pittsburgh, by land or water, over the mountains then east to Philadelphia. Buyers purchased goods from wholesalers, packed them onto wagons and drove them over the mountains to near Pittsburgh. Goods were put onto flatboats, usually at Redstone (now Brownsville) on the Monongahela River. Boats floated down the Ohio River to Limestone (now Maysville), where merchandise was again loaded on wagons. The last part of the journey was along the road from Maysville to Lexington on the old buffalo trace (now US 68). A few miles past Lower Blue Licks, they turned off onto Strode's Road, which ran south to near Winchester.

As mentioned above, Winchester merchants stocked a wide array of goods. The sample shown here is from Cast & Holly's 1814 advertisement: "New Goods, Cast & Holly. Have just received and are now opening in the house formerly occupied by Amon Cast, a large and elegant assortment of Merchandise, consisting in part of the following articles, viz...." (see the list above).

My first impression after looking over the list was "Wow! What an amazing assortment of items for such a small town." Winchester at that time had fewer than 50 families. The store carried an especially wide selection of fabrics and other materials for homemakers to fashion into clothing.

On closer inspection, there were numerous items that I had no idea of their meaning. I have heard of "dimity," for example, but could not describe it. According to Wikipedia, dimity is "a lightweight, sheer cotton fabric, historically employed for bed upholstery and curtains, and usually white, though sometimes a pattern is printed on it in colors."

One I particularly liked was "ridicule" which turns out to be a variation on the spelling of "reticule." This was a small drawstring purse that women carried in the 18th century when dresses no longer had pockets and that eventually evolved into a fashion accessory.

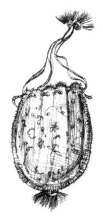

Other items sent me to Webster's Unabridged and the Oxford English Dictionary. "Marseilles" is a thick cotton fabric; "black florence," a fancy lace; "lutestring," a glossy silk material resembling satin; "cassimere," a soft, twilled woolen fabric now called cashmere; "cassinette," a thin cloth with a cotton warp and a weft of wool. "Toilinet" is a fine cloth with silk warp and woolen weft, and "swansdown" is a soft, thick fabric of wool with a little silk or cotton; both were used to make fancy waistcoats. In weaving, weft refers to thread which is drawn through at right angles to the lengthwise warp thread. "Bombazett," or "bombazine," is a twilled dress material of worsted, often used for mourning clothes.

"Bounce" is a liqueur made by infusing brandy with cherries and sugar. "Copperas" is a mineral of ferrous sulfate used at that time to make ink and dye wool. Interesting that whiskey sold by the gallon or by the barrel. (I was unable to identify "levinthine," "pinknot sleeves" and "arronita.")

Based on the goods offered by just one business, it appears that our early stores were well stocked for their day and age. Nothing like Walmart or Lowe's today, of course, but hey, this was more than two hundred years ago.

Sources
The Advertiser, November 19, 1814; *Kentucky Advertiser*, November 9, 1816; Clark County Deed Book, 9:96, 118, 254, 405, 10:67, 77, 342.

28
Betty Ratliff Smith
A Master Storyteller

March 17, 2017

In some ways, a community can be defined by the stories it tells about itself. Knowledge about our past often resides in the memories of our older citizens. A few that come immediately to mind here locally are Frank Vermillion, Jerry Cecil, Vic Bloomfield, Joan Mayer, Bob Tabor, the late John Venable, the indomitable Mike Rowady, and the one to whom this article is dedicated: Betty Ratliff Smith. While no one could be more pleased than I about the recent resurgence of the *Winchester Sun*, I do still miss reading Betty's column in the evening paper.

Betty was born in nearby Millersburg, and her family soon after moved to Winchester. Her father, Bruce Ratliff, ran Ratliff Furniture Company with his two brothers, Francis and Burbridge. Her academic career began at the old Hickman Street School and culminated with a degree from Kentucky Wesleyan College in 1952. She went to work for the *Sun* in 1957.

By the time she retired after 32 plus years of service, Betty had performed about every job at the paper. She began as society editor, covered city and county governments, the police and fire departments, was the newsroom receptionist and archivist, and even served a stint as sports editor. I remember her best for her column, Betty's Babblins, where she covered a wide range of topics based on her memories of Winchester, old and new. She recounted funny incidents about herself, her family and fellow townspeople. Her early columns were published in book form in 1994 (available at Clark County Public Library). Sadly, her most recent columns have not yet been compiled.

It was once said of Betty that she knows almost everything that happens in Clark County as soon as it happens—and sometimes before.

If you know Betty, you know she enjoys people and loves her community. She has received many honors, including

Winchester-Clark County Citizen of the Year in 2004 and a Commendation from the Kentucky Senate upon her retirement in 2008. I have never seen Betty that she wasn't smiling, and that includes photographs from childhood on. She is not only a talented writer, but also a gifted storyteller. Even if you had read her account of the Patio tornado or the rooster on the Kerr Building, you would still enjoy hearing her talk about those events.

I thought it fitting to reproduce a few snippets from Betty's articles that I have saved in my files. From "Test your memory of Winchester" (August 6, 2007):

"Can you remember diagonal parking in the middle of Broadway?

"A hatchery near the site of the present Maple Street and another, Anderson's on North Highland Street?

"Browning's Processing Plant where Beverly White Towers and Ecton Station of the Winchester Fire Department now stand?

"Flynn's, Dailey's and Quisenberry's as popular high school hangouts?

"Blue Ribbon Days when children marched down Main Street near the end of the school year?

"Reynolds Village on the west campus of today's College Park, then homes for veterans returning from World War II and their families while attending Kentucky Wesleyan College?"

From "Changes come, but memories remain" (August 13, 2007):

"The North Main Street Dairy Queen stands where Hollar's Grocery once stood. I remember during World War II my mother would order groceries, and when we got them home, once in a while a can of Dole pineapple was in the box. That was hard to come by, but the Hollar family—Cora, Mary and Bill—knew our family loved pineapple (I'm sure other families got a can, too), so when the store got pineapple, we got pineapple."

From "Downtown no stranger to forces of change" (October 3, 2003):

"St. Agatha Academy, now a modern educational facility, was once a two-story residence that at one time had been a private home. I attended St. Agatha in the seventh grade and recall going outside from the room that housed seventh-eighth graders to a kitchen at the rear of the structure. I am certain that we had other food for lunch, but the lumpy mashed potatoes stand out in my mind!"

From "Names and places of the past" (January 22, 2007):

"A question came up the other day about early Winchester and I turned to my hidden treasure. That's what I call the city directory of 1911-12-13, because it contains lots of information that is not readily available today.

"On the inside cover of the hardback book was a picture of the Citizens National Bank located at the corner of Main and Court streets and home today of Subway. But I have a question. In the photograph there are steps leading up to the entrance. So where did they go, and how did today's building get even with the street?

"Winchester's post office was located at 4 S. Main St. The Brown-Proctoria Pharmacy offered pure drugs, Huyler's candies and the coldest soda water. The Baldwin Brothers, located under the Sign of the Big Watch, were jewelers and opticians and J. A. Hughes was proprietor of Broadway Livery, Food and Sale Stables. Kerr & Bean were undertakers and embalmers and offered ambulance service. Sam Jett was proprietor of the Winchester Poultry Farm specializing in S. C. Leghorns. Many of the names mentioned are familiar names today, some totally unknown, but for lovers of history of our hometown, this makes good reading."

So do all of Betty's old columns. And I think it especially fitting to recognize her contributions during Women's History Month. If you see Betty before I do, tell her I still miss her.

29
John Robert Shaw, Well-Digger

March 31, 2017

I like to read and am especially fond of writers who make me laugh. Among my favorites are P. G. Wodehouse, David Sedaris, Gerald Durrell (brother of more famous Lawrence) and Bill Bryson. Bryson's *Walk in the Woods* led me to a whole series of his autobiographical comedies. He introduced the misfit Katz, with whom he hiked the Appalachian Trail, in the uproariously funny *Thunderbolt Kid*.

One of the most hilarious reads I have discovered of late was written at a surprisingly early date. *A Narrative of the Life & Travels of John Robert Shaw, the Well-Digger* was published by John Bradford, editor of the *Kentucky Gazette*, in 1807. Born in England, Shaw joined the British army and came to America in 1778. He described his plights with the military from Rhode Island to South Carolina. He stayed on after the war, trying desperately to assimilate in the fledgling nation. Our preeminent historian, Dr. Thomas D. Clark, praised the book. He wrote, "The peripatetic Yorkshireman found his way to Lexington, where fortune, but not fame, avoided him. Shaw was a man who found solace in a bottle. Well digger, turnpike worker, dam builder, and faithless husband, he lived out his turbulent life in and near Lexington."

The best way to get acquainted with Shaw is to sample his remarkably accessible prose. In one episode after the war, he went on a drinking spree with a friend in Philadelphia. At the "Sign of the Three Jolly Irishmen," they started off with a gallon of wine and a quart of whiskey, "in the punishment of which we were joined by half a dozen fine girls with a piper and fiddler." The group broke up late that night "pretty well done over." He continued, "Being determined to enjoy the pleasures of the night as well as the day, I proceeded with my doxy to her lodgings" and "was invited upstairs into a room, with a good bed and otherwise fully equipped for entering on the wars of Venus."

There he would learn that his lassie was a trickster.

"But alas! how disappointed were my hopes; for when ready to jump into the arms of my fair one, I unfortunately, at her request, stopped to put the candle out, when lo! the floor sunk, and in a few seconds I found myself safely landed in a back street, with no other covering to guard me against the inclemency of a cold winter night, than my shirt."

The Wonderful recovery of JOHN R. SHAW

A drawing from Shaw's Narrative

Each chapter begins with an outline of its contents: "Chapter 9. The author proceeds to Frankfort—experiences a variety of vicissitudes and works at different places until he arrives at Lexington; at which place and its vicinity he meets with a number of adventures, particularly that of seeing a vision, and likewise the anxiety of mind which he laboured under from an excess of spirituous liquors and the result thereof—swindled by Prothroe—was blown up—loses the use of one eye—proves the infallibility of bletonism [water divining or dowsing]—blown up a second time—gets married—has a son—a daughter—another son, etc."

The deplorable situation of JOHN R. SHAW, late Well-Digger of Lexington, surrounded by his Friends and distressed Family—23d August, 1806.

A drawing from Shaw's Narrative

In his adopted professions of quarrying and well digging, Shaw used quantities of black powder to "blow rock" and succeeded in blowing himself up multiple times. In 1806, the *Gazette* published his obituary:

"John R. Shaw, of Lexington, killed Saturday, August 17, 1806, by a blast being used in a well for Lewis Sanders, near Lexington"

To paraphrase Mark Twain, reports of Shaw's demise were greatly exaggerated. However, he came very close. This was the fourth time he had blown himself up and his injuries were described by his attending physician, Dr. James Fishback, in a letter to the *Gazette*. Shaw suffered a fractured skull, a broken eye socket, broken shin bone, left arm broken with the loss of two fingers, right arm broken in two places, as well as "considerable injury of the hand, the skin upon the breast, and stomach was very much bruised and cut, from which I inferred he was leaning nearly over the blast. The surface of his remaining eye ball was considerably bruised and torn by a number of small pieces of stone, in addition to the above, his face was enormously swelled and covered with blood, gunpowder and dirt, so that it was utterly impossible to recognize the lineaments of John Robert Shaw." In spite of his dire injuries, Dr. Fishback noted that "ultimately the wounds healed in the most friendly manner."

Shaw's story does have a Clark County connection. In the course of his travels he did a job for Hubbard Taylor at Spring Hill on present-day Colby Road.

"I then proceeded on to Mr. Hubbard Taylor's, living in Clarke county, for whom I dug a well and for which he honourably paid me. I then went on to Strode's station, where I spent all my money."

At Strode Station, he met up with several old acquaintances. They purchased "goods in Cock and Lytle's store to the amount of eighteen pounds." This is the first report I have seen of this store, presumably located at Strode Station, which was then a small community west of Winchester.

Afterwards, Shaw "jogged on with them to Clark court house, and there commenced a roaring frolic, with a set of as jovial fellows as ever sat over a half pint of whiskey, amongst whom was a jolly Irishman, who cut as many didos as I could."

At the conclusion of their frolic, "I exchanged all my goods for whiskey; then turned to jobbing about the town, and shewing Mr. [John] Baker, the proprietor of the land, a number of places where water may be found. He kept me there a considerable time, endeavouring all in his power to acquire of me some knowledge of bletonism, after which he sent me off without either fee or reward."

In concluding his book, Shaw recounted the price he had paid for acquiring some material success. "In consequence of accumulating property [in Lexington] I have been equally if not more disabled in battleing with the rocks than the gallant [Lord]

Nelson has been in battleing against the enemies of his country,[*] as I have lost no less than one eye, four fingers, one thumb and seven toes."

At the end of the book, Shaw listed the names of subscribers who purchased a copy of his Narrative. There were twenty-seven from Clark County; Hubbard Taylor was among them.

Shaw continued digging wells and advertised regularly in the *Kentucky Gazette*. The latter were described by a biographer as done "in the shape of the most execrable poetry, 'written by himself.'" Sadly, it was the *Gazette* that announced his end.

"John R. Shaw, well-digger and stone quarrier, of Lexington, died Monday evening, September 6, 1813, when blown up in a well he was digging for Robert Wilson. He was the author of the biography bearing his name."

Sources

Thomas D. Clark, *Bluegrass Cavalcade* (Lexington, KY, 1956), p. 82; *Kentucky Gazette*, July 25, 1806, September 7, 1813; William H. Perrin, editor, *History of Fayette County, Kentucky* (Chicago, IL, 1882), p. 404.

---

[*] Lord Horatio Nelson was wounded several times in combat, losing most of one arm in the unsuccessful attempt to conquer Santa Cruz de Tenerife and the sight in one eye in Corsica. He was shot and killed during his final victory at the Battle of Trafalgar in 1805.

30
Charles Mitchell
The Coca-Cola Man

April 14, 2017

In the early 20th century two of Kentucky's best-known beverage bottlers called Winchester home. Both were in the soft drink business. There can't be many people living here who have not heard of G. L. Wainscott, inventor and producer of Ale-8-One (locally known simply as Ale-8). The company is still in business and now has a national presence. Wainscott, widely known in his day, founded the Kentucky State Bottlers Association. I suspect fewer of us will recognize Charles Mitchell, who was once acknowledged to be at the "head of Coca-Cola business in Kentucky."

Charles Mitchell (1868-1927) came to Winchester from Carlisle with his parents, William and Achsah Mitchell. William began here selling shoes and "gents furnishings" at 9 South Main Street, and Achsah (axe-suh') kept house upstairs. Her name has a biblical origin; Achsah was the daughter of Caleb, prince of the tribe of Judah. At the time of his death in 1908, William, then retired, lived in the house he purchased at the northwest corner of Maple and College Streets.

Charles sold shoes in his father's store for a time, then in 1904 incorporated the Coca Cola Bottling Works of Lexington "to install and operate a bottling plant for the purpose of bottling Coca Cola and other carbonated waters." The plant was located on West Water Street in Lexington. He later added bottling plants in Danville and Somerset.

The 1920 census lists Charles, single, living with his widowed mother at the house on Maple Street. Three years later he married Myrtle Mae Critchfield of Princeton, Indiana; he was 55, she was 38. They had two children who died in infancy. The couple moved to Lexington, where they purchased a fine home at 449 West Second Street. In 1927 Mitchell built a new bottling plant at 451 West Short Street outfitted with the latest equipment and accompanied by a modern fleet of delivery trucks. The plant was located a few doors west of St. Paul's Catholic Church.

Mitchell's bottling plant at 451 W. Short St.
(Lafayette Studios, Lexington, KY)

Mitchell and Wainscott had business connections. They operated in the same central Kentucky counties, socialized at bottlers association meetings and, in due course, had a squabble over their empty bottles. The latter may have been what led to a famous lawsuit: Coca-Cola Company sued Carlisle Bottling Works (a Wainscott subsidiary) for trademark infringement. The formal complaint began when Mitchell company drivers asked local grocers in Carlisle for a Coke and were sold Wainscott's Roxa Kola. That brought in the big guns from Atlanta. Coca-Cola had sued dozens of times when bottlers tried to use similar names for their soft drinks—and Coca-Cola always won. In June 1927, U.S. Circuit Court denied Coca-Cola's request for a preliminary injunction.

Bullies with lots of money have been suing little people for centuries, and sometimes the underdog wins. After Mitchell died, the suit continued through district court, court of appeals and the U.S. Supreme Court. Coca-Cola lost at each stage, their first defeat.

In December 1927 Mitchell, who suffered from asthma, contracted pneumonia and quickly succumbed at his home in Lexington. His wife had him buried in Winchester Cemetery where his parents were interred. There are eight handsome ledger markers[*] in the family plot, and the Mitchell obelisk appears to be the tallest in the cemetery. All the obituaries referred to Mitchell's "great wealth" or "considerable fortune." His estate was valued at more than $500,000.

Mitchell obelisk in Winchester Cemetery

---

[*] A ledger marker is a thick slab of stone covering the entire grave, as shown in the photo.

Myrtle Mitchell took over as president and general manager of her husband's bottling works. She seems to have had a natural talent for business, as the company continued to flourish under her leadership. She was deeply involved in civic affairs and local charities. After her death in 1964, her estate built the Mitchell Fine Arts Center at Transylvania University.

Mitchell's bottling company passed through a succession of owners until it was acquired by Warren B. Terry in the 1960s. He moved the bottling plant to Leestown Road. In the 1990s, the operations were acquired by the Coca-Cola Company.

Sources

Joshua 15:16; Judges 1:12; William M. Ambrose, *Soda Pop: The Soft Drink Industry in Lexington, Fayette County, Kentucky* (Lexington, KY, 2007); Winchester City Directories, 1892 and 1980, Clark County Public Library; *Lexington Leader*, May 3, 1904, December 16, 1927; *Lexington Herald*, December 17, 1927; *Winchester Sun*, December 16, 1927; *Coca-Cola Co. v. Carlisle Bottling Works*, https://casetext.com/case/.

31
Remembering Leeds Theatre

April 28, 2017

Leeds Center for the Arts held its grand reopening on Saturday night, April 15, and a grand evening it was. A full house was on hand to hear cellist Ben Sollee, who thrilled the audience with a two-hour concert. The weekend began Friday morning with a yoga class at the theatre. Erin Smith led a class of more than 50 participants, who filled the stage and spilled out into the aisles, while Sollee accompanied the class with his heavenly cello. He took part is several other events at the theatre before the concert.

Not taking anything away from Ben Sollee, the real star that weekend was the theatre itself. Simply put, the place is a knockout. I wish I could adequately describe all the work done on the building. Every surface, inside and out, seemed fresh and new in the near-century old movie house. Tracey Miller, her group of volunteers and the Winchester Council for the Arts deserve a huge thank you for this gift to the community.

The story of Leeds Theatre began with its predecessor, the Liberty Theatre on North Main Street. At 7:00 p.m. on May 8, 1925, a fire started in the projection booth at the Liberty during a screening of the silent film "Proud Flesh." According to an article in the *Winchester Sun*, the operator, Albert Conn, was rewinding a reel when the celluloid somehow caught fire. He was briefly trapped by the flames and had to fight his way out with a fire extinguisher. The fire department arrived on the scene and put the blaze out in short order. The projection machines were destroyed along with 18 of the 20 films on hand.

Theatre manager, Morris B. Levy, stated in an interview that the fire was a rare occurrence that "would never happen in the new theatre being erected across the street, as the very latest of fire-proof apparatus was being installed in the steel-concrete booth." He added that future shows would be cancelled and "the new picture theatre would be rushed to completion."

The newly remodeled Leeds Center for the Arts

A *Sun* headline on Tuesday, May 12, read "Liberty To Be Opened Tonight." The new theatre was "informally thrown open to the public" due to the fire that closed the old theatre. Seats from the old theatre were temporarily installed. Winchester Amusement Company took out a large ad to announce the showing of Paramount Picture's "The Crowded Hour" starring Bebe Daniels at "7 O'Clock Sharp."

The theatre began daily performances from 2 to 5:30 p.m. and 7 to 10:30 p.m. Admission was 25 cents for adults, 10 cents for children and there was a "balcony for colored patrons." For the next two months, the movie house would be referred to as

"Winchester's New Theatre Beautiful."

The company announced a naming contest for the new theatre. They asked for an original and distinctive name of one word not exceeding ten letters. Judges were Mayor G. E. Tomlinson, C. B. George (of the St. George Hotel) and M. T. McEldowney. First prize was $25; second and third prizes were free passes for six and three months, respectively.

Leeds opening night ad for "The Little French Girl"

The grand opening on July 8 featured the 1925 hit film "The Little French Girl" and was preceded by several pages of advertisements in the *Sun*. "Better, grander and more palatial than ever before seen in Winchester [and] which will operate on a scale seen only in cities of much larger population." After entering the theatre by "the beautiful French doors," patrons would enter "a most spacious lobby, the walls of which are made in marble." In the foyer, "to the left and right are mirrors surrounded by handsome mahogany woodwork, while underfoot one treads upon noiseless tile floorings and overhead the soft subdued lights attract the attention, and immediately the noise of the city street is forgotten." Advancing further into "the playhouse, earthly cares are entirely forgotten and one is enveloped in the midst of the best in amusement and entertainment that can be offered."

The manager, Morris B. Levy, had directed operations at the old Liberty Theatre for more than three years, and J. A. Conn Jr. reprised his role as projection engineer. The company furnished the theatre with the latest equipment: "Powers G-B Improved models of motion picture machines, a Brenkert Spot-Light Machine, and a two-arc 75-ampere General Electric Generator to produce direct current for the machines." The screen made by Minusca eliminated the glare that was common in other theatres.

The president of Winchester Amusement Company was S. D. Lee, said to be "a leader in business and social circles" and a "typical Southern gentleman." Slaughter B. Sparks,[*] the secretary-treasurer, brought years of theatre experience and had been superintendent of the Phoenix Amusement Company of Lexington.

The name chosen, Leeds Theatre, was a play on the president's name. I have not yet identified the contest winner.

Thanks to the Winchester Council for the Arts, this magnificent restored facility is truly "Winchester's New Theatre Beautiful."

Sources

Winchester Sun, May 9, 12 and 16, June 27, July 6, 8 and 10, 1925, June 29 1929; *Winchester Democrat*, June 28, 1929.

---

[*] Slaughter Sparks began his career as an usher in Lexington theatres and later became manager of the Strand Theatre. Gregory A. Waller, *Main Street Amusements* (Washington, D.C., 1995), p. 116

32
Early Movie Theatres in Winchester

May 12, 2017

Silent Film Era

The silent film era in Winchester began in 1907 and ended with the first "talkie," which made its appearance at the Leeds in 1929. Anyone who happens to watch one of these old films today can be forgiven for wondering what all the excitement was about. These early movies had no spoken dialog, relying instead on the actors' gestures and mime with occasional title cards to convey plot and key dialog. Today these films seem primitive and barely watchable, but this is more due to their poor state of preservation.

Silent films were usually accompanied by a piano and sometimes a small orchestra. The music was improvised and keyed to the action shown on the screen. The first silent film theatres were called "nickelodeons." These were small affairs established in existing storefronts by addition of a projector, screen and chairs. The name came from the nickel admission charge.

I recently had a pleasant visit with Vic and Mary Bloomfield discussing early Winchester theatres. They both assured me that those old silent movies had made a bigger impression on them than television did when it came along. They attributed this partly to the fact that the sources of amusement were so sparse in those days.

Vic's father and uncle, Clarence and Arthur Bloomfield, were both involved in Winchester's emerging movie business. So it was natural that Vic became a huge fan. He recalled going to the theatre every time the program changed. In his youth, the films played Sunday-Monday, Tuesday-Wednesday, Thursday-Friday, with westerns and serials on Saturday. He even managed to set up his own small theatre in his parents' basement, where he had friends over to watch films he ordered by mail.

Clarence Bloomfield once prepared a list of the Winchester theatres he could recall, giving their names and locations. Vic was kind enough to share the list with me, and it was most helpful in writing this article.

Lexington ushered in the silent film era at the Woodland Park auditorium, which commenced in June 1906. According to *Main Street Amusements*, a history of Lexington's early theatres, Nicholasville, Paris and Versailles followed in July 1907 "and four months later in Winchester."

Court View Theatre

The author was incorrect regarding Winchester. On February 7, 1907, the *Sun-Sentinel* reported, "The Electric Theatre opened in the Court View Hotel last night. The show consists of moving pictures and illustrated songs." The latter involved a vocalist and pianist performing while a film projected images on the screen; these were used as a means of marketing sheet music. Regular ads began appearing for Court View Theatre: "Open every night from 6 to 10 o'clock; we give a clean, moral up-to-date show; come one, come all; admission 5 cents; Cox & Patterson [of Cincinnati], managers."

Clarence Bloomfield's list referred to this as the "Band Theatre," a name not found in newspaper ads but may have been a local nickname. The Court View Hotel was destroyed in a spectacular fire in January 1909. Opened thirty years earlier as the Central Hotel, it had been considered one of the finest in the area. The city purchased the property to build City Hall.

Bijou Theatre

According to Clarence Bloomfield's list, Winchester's first theatre was the Bijou on East Broadway. It was located in the turn-of-the-century building with the three projecting bay windows that now houses Bill's Place. The theatre is difficult to document, as they apparently did not advertise in the newspaper. We find it shown on a 1907 Sanborn Fire Insurance map, where the right half of that building is designated "Moving Pictures." The only other information comes from an article in the *Winchester News*, February 1, 1909: "Moving Picture Sale. The chairs, piano machine and other fixtures of the old moving picture theatre on East Broadway were sold at auction Monday morning to satisfy a debt. A large crowd attended." David Matlack purchased 100 chairs and the "picture machine."

Winchester Theatre at the Opera House

Opera House fare at the Winchester Theatre mainly consisted of fine plays, musical performances, distinguished lecturers and vaudeville acts. However, in August 1907 they began showing silent films. Moving pictures played at 2:30 every afternoon and 7:30 in the evening. The films, usually advertised as "3000 feet of moving pictures," were not movies as we know them with actors and plot. For example, they might show film footage shot from a moving train or at a scenic location like Niagara Falls or some exotic foreign location. Admission was five cent.

After several years, Opera House moving picture ads ceased. Then in July 1912, an industry magazine—*Motion Picture World (MPW)*—reported that "Sil Dinelli of Winchester, Ky. has opened a theatre in that town, utilizing the opera house. A Powers machine is in use, and the new house has received liberal patronage." The Winchester Theatre showed feature films until about 1917, when advertising for motion pictures ceased and may have ended with the death of Sylvester Dinelli in April of that year.

Winchester Auditorium

Winchester Auditorium began the early 20th century as a roller skating rink on Main Street, where the parking lot now stands adjacent to the Brown-Proctor. The Auditorium held indoor baseball and basketball games, as well as broomball—hockey on roller skates—that was hugely popular at the time.

In 1909 the newspaper reported on plans to open a movie theatre at the Auditorium. "The rink will be partitioned off in two sections. The front of the rink will be used for a soft drink emporium, and the rear end will be used for a moving picture theatre."

The grand opening of the Winchester Auditorium summer garden and motion picture theatre was held on April 3.

Films were shown every afternoon from 3 to 5:30 p.m. and evenings from 7:30 to 10 p.m., except Sundays. Admission was 5 cents, except on Saturday nights when 3000 feet of film was shown and admission was increased to 10 cents.

D. B. Scobee managed the theatre; Fred Dakin sang and played piano; Arthur Bloomfield and Sol Ratliff were proprietors. The theatre closed in summer and reopened in the fall.

Winchester Auditorium's "moving picture" ad (*Winchester News*, 1910)

In 1910 the Auditorium advertised itself as "the only continuous show house in the City." That year the theatre began showing feature films produced by movie studios. The first named film advertised in Winchester was "Go West, Young Woman, Go West," a western comedy featuring Tom Mix, which played at the Auditorium on November 29. This was followed by a string of films from the Biograph Company in New York City, including several by the famed silent film director, D. W. Griffith (a Kentucky native). Biograph was the first film studio dedicated solely to making movies. These early feature films only ran 15 or 20 minutes and are called "shorts" today.

By 1912 movie ads ended and the Auditorium returned to a full time skating rink. Their demise may have been hastened by the rise of local competition.

33
Early Movie Theatres in Winchester, Part 2

May 20, 2017

Lyric Theatre

The Lyric was the next to open in Winchester. Henry H. Phillips and Woodson Moss leased a room on the first floor of the Fraternity Building on Court Street where they showed their first film on December 6, 1911.

The Lyric announced their schedule of first run films for January and February 1912: "Maud Miller," "Auld Lang Syne," "Durbar," "Vanity Fair," "The Three Musketeers," and "Cinderella." They claimed that "the patrons of the Lyric are being shown the very best that is on the market. The management is booking all the best pictures just as fast as they are issued."

The Lyric may have been the first theatre to use a lighted marquee. As reported in *MPW*, "The Lyric Theater has added a hundred 100-candle power lights to the illumination in front of the theater on Court Street. The string extends from the theater to the next corner, and converts the thoroughfare into a 'white way.'"

In mid-year the theatre moved to a new location. "H. H. Phillips and Woodson Moss, owners of the Lyric Theater in Winchester, Ky. have leased property in the downtown district of that city from the Lexington Lodge of Elks for a period of five years and will remodel the present building to constitute one of the handsomest moving picture theaters in Central Kentucky. The auditorium of the new Phillips & Moss Theater will be 116 by 28 feet in dimension. Work of equipping the establishment for business is to be begun at once and rushed to completion (*MPW*)."

The new theatre on South Main Street, seating 500 persons, opened in July 1912. Clarence Bloomfield's list gave the location as the "Finance Office." In the 1960s through the '80s there were several finance companies on South Main:

Kentucky Finance, Winchester Building Savings & Loan and Winchester Federal Savings and Loan. The only building that fits the theatre dimensions (28 x 116) is Winchester Federal at 57 South Main (became Winchester Federal Bank in 1987).

The Lyric would last until 1914. The theatre was losing money, and the owners decided to sell out to their competitors at the Pastime and Colonial.

Pastime Theatre

The next entry in Winchester's motion picture scene was the Pastime Theatre. *MPW* reported on the planning phase in late 1911. "Arthur Bloomfield, of Winchester, Ky. is preparing to invest about $7,000 in an up-to-date picture theater, having leased a suitable building for his enterprise. Plans for the new house are now being prepared, and it will be erected as soon as possible." Bloomfield leased the building at 24 North Main Street from Mrs. C. R. West.

"The Pastime Theater, the new picture theater at Winchester opened Thursday, April 4, 1912. It has a seating capacity of 333 persons and is well lighted and ventilated. An orchestra of five pieces provides music for the pictures. Arthur N. and Clarence Bloomfield are the managers. A ten-cent admission is charged (*MPW*)."

In 1913, the Pastime became the first Winchester theatre to present color films. The new technology was referred to as "Kinemacolor," the first successful process for making movies in color.

In 1915 Vic Bloomfield took a seventeen-year lease on the building and announced plans to enlarge the theatre. In May *MPW* reported, "The Pastime theater has opened its house after the building was overhauled and thoroughly remodeled. The building, as now arranged, is one of the most complete moving picture and vaudeville houses in the eastern part of the state. The auditorium has been extended back twenty-five feet and a stage has been erected with dressing rooms beneath. A small balcony with a seating capacity of twenty-five has been constructed at the front of the house. The theater now has a seating capacity of 450 in all. A gold fibre screen and new chandeliers have been installed. Another motion picture machine has been purchased, as the operator was handicapped with only one machine. Mary Pickford, in the Paramount production of 'Such a Little Queen' was shown as the opening subject."

In early 1918, the theatre was disrupted by a fire in the basement engine room. The gasoline engine and dynamo the theatre used to generate electric power were damaged. The audience exited the darkened theatre without injuries.

Aftermath of the Pastime Theatre Tragedy
Photo by Hunt Owen in the *Winchester Sun*. Owen was entering the theatre when the roof collapsed.

Disaster struck on Saturday evening, March 9, when a wall collapsed killing eleven instantly and injuring scores, many of them children. Two days before the adjoining hardware store had been gutted by fire leaving a tall masonry wall unsupported. High winds on Saturday night caused the wall to fall on the theatre. A standing room only crowd was on hand to watch "The Quiet Man," a western starring William S. Hart. As usual, children packed the rows nearest the screen. The front ten rows of the theatre were in a one-story section of the building. The collapsing wall came through the roof dropping tons of bricks and debris on the audience. It is recorded as one of the worst tragedies in Winchester's history.

34
Early Movie Theatres in Winchester, Part 3

May 26, 2017

Lincoln Theatre

The third theatre launched in 1912 was at 51 North Maple Street, adjacent to Central Bank where Tax Matters has a business today. *MPW* reported that "plans for the erection of a theater for colored people exclusively have been completed in Winchester, Ky. The new structure will go up on Maple Street. Experienced theater men are backing the proposition and work will begin at once." The venture was led by "Senator" R. F. Bell, owner of the Gem, one of Lexington's early African-American theatres.

Its March inauguration was reported in *MPW*: "The Lincoln Theater has opened. The house is built on modern lines, electric lights and other essentials being in evidence. Early business indicates that the venture will be a success." In May, W. W. Banks wrote in the *Sun's* Colored Column that "the Lincoln Theatre is said to have record-breaking crowds under its new management."

In 1913, the Winchester Commercial Club inspected the theatre, found it well-conducted and gave its endorsement. The Lincoln was still a going concern in 1914. It closed before 1926, but the exact date is uncertain.

Colonial Theatre

The Colonial became the fourth new theatre in Winchester in a little over a year. They held their grand opening on January 3, 1913, with D. W. Griffith's "In the Watches of the Night." According to a review in *MPW*, "The Colonial Theater, recently opened by Sphar Swift, has met so far with distinct success, and its seating capacity of 280 has been kept filled pretty regularly. An orchestra imported from Cincinnati, Ohio, has proved an attractive feature. Steve McKenna, an expert electrician, formerly of Lexington, Ky., is the operator, and Miss Mary Hackett is cashier. Mr. Swift is himself managing the theater."

Colonial Theatre at the corner of Washington and Main
(Bluegrass Heritage Museum)

The theatre was located on the first floor of the Colonial Building at the corner of Main and Washington. The name "Colonial" may still be seen in the floor tile near the entrance.

The Colonial was eventually acquired by Winchester Amusement Company (owners of the Liberty and Leeds theatres). In the 1920s the Colonial played matinees and the Liberty nights. The Colonial and Leeds were the only early theatres to survive into the talking film era.

In later years the Colonial opened irregularly. Vic Bloomfield recalled that when Leeds ran hit movies to sold out crowds, the overflow would sometimes be accommodated at the Colonial. When the first reel ended at the Leeds, it was run across the street and cued up to play at the Colonial.

The Colonial, which closed and reopened under a succession of owners, finally closed for good in the late 1940s.

Queen Theatre

The Queen Theatre opened on the night of January 25, 1915. The crowd was so large some had to be turned away. The theatre was located in the Fraternity Building, previously occupied by the Lyric. The manager, Chris Sideris, offered a $5 prize for the best name, which was submitted by Mrs. E. E. Quisenberry.

MPW described the elegant interior: "The 'Queen' looks inside like a Pullman car [lined] with panels, on each of which is a hand-painted picture of some noted place in the world. On each side of the mirror screen stands a life-size statue. The front is Gothic. The lobby is arched with plate glass mirrors. Statues on pedestals stand at every convenient place in it." By mid-year the theatre had closed and Sideris declared bankruptcy.

Cozy Theatre

In September 1916 a new concern opened a theatre in the space vacated by the Queen. The Cozy Theatre was organized by some of the city's leading businessmen, including M. D. Royse, D. S. Haggard, C. H. Bowen, Matt Bean, J. F. Winn, Dr. W. A. Bush, J. E. Grubbs, A. G. Locknane and J. N. Renaker. F. A. Ogden was the manager. Sadly, the Cozy did not last much longer than its predecessor.

Family Theatre

In mid-1917 Arthur Bloomfield and Fonda Minor leased the space vacated by the Cozy and opened the Family Theatre. By March 1918 the Family was a thing of the past, and the space was converted back to a store room.

Liberty Theatre

September 1918 saw yet another new movie house open its doors, the Liberty Theatre on North Main Street. This venture of the Winchester Amusement Company had a successful run until 1925, when the company replaced it with the luxurious new Leeds Theatre. The Liberty closed due to a fire in the projection booth on May 8 that rendered the theatre inoperable. The only documented clue we have to its location is "across the street from the Leeds."

Talking Picture Era
Leeds Theatre

Winchester Amusement Company built Leeds Theatre on the lot at 35-37 North Main Street. Due to the fire that closed the Liberty, Leeds was pressed into service before construction was completed. Leeds began showing films on May 12, 1925, and held a grand opening on July 8. (More information about Leeds Theatre may be found in my *Sun* column of April 28.)

The Leeds is considered by far the finest in the city's long theatre history. It was the Leeds that introduced "talkies" to Winchester in 1929. The first talking picture shown here was "Syncopation," a musical featuring Fred Waring and the Pennsylvanians. It opened on Monday, July 1, with a newly installed Western Electric sound system called "Vitaphone." The sound was recorded on a 16-inch phonograph record. Due to severe synchronization problems, the sound-on-disk system was soon replaced by sound-on-film technology.

Vic Bloomfield, an early fan of the Leeds, recalled their early "cooling system." He said that 100-pound blocks of ice were loaded into cutouts at the front of the stage. Fans under the ice blew cool air out over the audience.

By the 1960s Michael Chakeres had acquired the Leeds, Town Hall and Skyview Drive In. He closed the Leeds on July 14, 1986. That summer the Winchester Council for the Arts began their "Save the Theatre" campaign. The council's original board—Helen Becker, Barbara Falmien, Molly and Craig Stotts, Mary Davis, Janie Johnson, Fara Lowry, Mary Buckner, Ralph

Tyree, Charles Witt, Vanessa Oaks and Vic Bloomfield—managed to save the city's premier movie house. The present board and volunteers under Tracey Miller finally succeeded in restoring the theatre to mint condition. The "new" Leeds held its grand reopening on April 15, 2017.

Ad for "Syncopation," Winchester's first talkie (*Winchester Sun*, 1929)

Clark Theatre

George Myers and Harry Schwatrz's Clark Theatre opened with much fanfare on November 14, 1940. The 40 by 125 foot building could seat 500. "Kentucky's newest and most modern theatre" claimed perfect viewing from all seats, high fidelity sound ("a thrill for your ears"), brilliant projection on a silver screen, sound-absorbing acoustical walls, and many other features "that will surprise and delight you." Weekday matinees cost 10 cents, nights 16 cents; Sunday and Monday nights were

22 cents.

The Clark apparently closed after two years, when advertising ceased. The building is gone. It was located on West Broadway, where the present parking lot stands between Wall Alley and the Kerr Building.

Town Hall

The last of Winchester's early theatres was the Town Hall at 22 North Main Street, next door to the building that housed the Pastime Theatre. Opened in 1941, Town Hall never achieved the popularity of the Leeds.

Town Hall, 1948, white building at right center of the picture
(James Mann)

By 1967 the theatre only opened on Friday, Saturday and Sunday. On April 29 that year, Town Hall advertised its last shows, double feature horror movies "Destination Inner Space" and "Frozen Alive."

Sources
Clarence Bloomfield's list of theatres is referred to as "Bloomfield list," *Motion Picture World* magazine is cited as *MPW* (available online at *http://mediahistoryproject.org/earlycinema/index.html*), and Sanborn Fire

Insurance maps as Sanborn maps. Winchester newspapers from 1906 through 1944 were scanned for movie theatre ads; only select dates are cited below. **Introduction**: Gregory A. Waller, *Main Street Amusements* (Washington, D.C. 1995). **Court View**: *Winchester Sun-Sentinel*, February 7, 1907; 1907 Sanborn map; *Winchester News*, January 7, 8, 11 and 28, 1909. **Bijou**: Bloomfield list; 1907 Sanborn map; *Winchester News*, February 1, 1909; Bloomfield list. **Opera House**: *Winchester Sun-Sentinel*, August 1, 1907; *Winchester News*, January 15, 1909; *MPW* (1912) 13:162, (1917) 32:1165. **Auditorium**: *Winchester News*, February 24, March 4, April 1 and 3, 1909, November 3 and 29, December 10, 1910. **Lyric**: *Winchester News*, October 21, 1910, January 15, 1012; *MPW* (1911) 10:1000, (1912) 11:220, 226, 12:352, 746, 13:56, 162, (1914) 21:981. **Pastime**: *Winchester News*, February 8 and 16, 1912; 1912 Sanborn map; *MPW* (1911) 10:404, (1912) 11:220, 702, 12:234, 352, (1913) 18:856, (1915) 23:548, 24:250, (1918) 35:559, 1829. **Lincoln**: *Winchester News*, February 16, 1912; *Winchester Sun*, May 25, 1912; 1912 Sanborn map; *MPW* (1912) 11:220, 1186, (1913) 15:480; Caron's City of Winchester Directory (1914). **Colonial**: *Winchester Sun*, December 31, 1912, January 8, 1921; *MPW* (1914) 19:827. **Queen**: *MPW* (1914) 22:1550, (1915) 23:106, 1010, 1291. **Cozy**: *MPW* (1916) 29:2004, (1917) 32:1972. **Family**: *MPW* (1917) 32:1972, (1918) 35:1548. **Liberty**: *Winchester Sun*, September 6, 1918, May 9, 1925, September 6, 1986. **Leeds**: *Winchester Sun*, May 12 and 16, June 27, July 6, 8 and 10, 1925, June 29 1929; *Winchester Democrat*, June 28, 1929. **Clark**: *Winchester Sun*, November 13, 1940. **Town Hall**: First newspaper ads in 1941; *Winchester Sun*, April 29, 1967.

35
Newspaper Bits and Pieces

June 9, 2017

While researching Winchester's early theaters in local newspapers, I came upon numerous unrelated but eye-catching tidbits. It never fails. If you start scanning old papers on microfilm, you may not find what you were searching for, but you will certainly see items that grab your attention and make you stop to read. I hope you will find some of these as interesting as I did.

In 1907 a local jeweler, Bowen & Whitehead, placed an ad in the *Sun-Sentinel* with the heading "Swastika—A Sign of Welfare." Reportedly found "among the relics of all ages," the swastika "has been considered as a talisman, a charm to drive away evil and bring good luck." The word comes from Sanskrit meaning conducive to wellbeing or auspicious. The symbol was indeed used in many Asian, European, African and North American cultures, and took on different meanings at different times and places. It found a popular use in the early 20th century on jewelry, especially rings, pendants and stickpins. According to Bowen & Whitehead, "It is the very latest fad." The swastika quickly went out of fashion after it was adopted as the symbol of the Third Reich in Nazi Germany.

The year 1908 brought a whistle-stop visit to Winchester by presidential candidate, Judge William Howard Taft. His train stopped at Union Station on October 15. I've often heard people talk about President Truman's visit here in 1948, but no one ever mentions Taft. (Of course, almost no one alive here today was born before 1908.) More than 3,000 people turned out to greet Judge Taft. Local Republican dignitaries escorted him from the train to a platform erected for the occasion in front of the depot, where he addressed the crowd. After a brief speech, he left on the campaign trail and was elected to office in November. Weighing in at over 330 pounds, Taft is said to have been our largest president. There is an old wives tale that he started a diet after getting stuck in a White House bathtub—most recently mentioned in the June 5 issue of *Time* magazine. Taft did in fact install a super-sized tub in the master bathroom at the White House. The rumor probably began from there and was gleefully spread by his political opponents.

Judge Taft speaking at Union Station (*Winchester News*)

I was briefly mystified after stumbling on the following headline in the *Sun* from September 2, 1940: "Roosevelt Train Due In City Early Tuesday En Route To Capital." Why had I never heard of this? The paper announced that F.D.R.'s itinerary included a stop at Union Depot. Alas, the 200 people who showed up at the station at 1:55 a.m. did not get to see the president. He was fast asleep during the whole forty-minutes it took to check the train and shunt it from the L&N line to the C&O for the trip back to Washington.

In 1910 John W. Murphy provided the *Winchester News* with reminiscences about his old friend, Joel Tanner Hart. Early in his career Hart built stone chimneys in this area. His last was for a Mr. Horton in Flat Rock, Bourbon County. Hart cut his name on every stone in that chimney. Asked why he did it, Hart replied, "The day would come when they would know [me]." He went to Lexington to work in the shop of Pat Doyle at the corner of Upper and Second Street, where Hart worked, ate and slept. John S. Wilson, a druggist with a shop nearby, recognized his skill and helped Hart launch his career as a sculptor. His genius was recognized after he carved a bust of Chief Justice George Robertson. "It only lacked breath to be Mr. Robertson." His next model was the Honorable John [J.] Crittenden, "which was perfect." He then took a cast of Henry Clay and left for Florence, Italy, where he carved three life-like statues that sold for $10,000 each. Hart spent 21 years working on his masterpiece, "Woman  Triumphant," rendered in Carrara marble. The piece stood under the bell tower of the Fayette County Courthouse and received the admiration of thousands. In 1897 a fire broke out in some waste paper and trash. When the blaze reached the cupola, it burned through the timbers supporting the bell, which fell on the statue crushing it to pieces. (My apologies to Joel T. Hart scholars if some of Mr. Murphy reminiscences prove inaccurate.)

There is a delightful sequence of stories in the 1913 *Sun* about Professor Herman D. Kline, "Psychic Medium and Clairvoyant." He installed a chair at 101 Highland Street and gave personal readings for as little as 50 cents. He inserted daily ads in the paper claiming that "a true clairvoyant is born not made" then offered "an honest proposition": He guaranteed there would be no charge "if I fail to tell your name" and anything "you wish to know concerning business changes, love, marriage, divorce and [whether] your sweetheart is true or false." The subjects upon which he promised "infallible advice" went on for two more paragraphs. He announced his hours were 10 a.m. to 8 p.m. seven days a week. Less than a week later the newspaper reported, "Whereabouts Of Clairvoyant Are Now A Mystery." It seems he left an empty suitcase and some dirty clothes in his room at John A. Bishop's boarding house on Maple Street and absconded. The paper said that "he made many friends by his genial manner and honest appearance. He saw 75 to 100 people at his headquarters the night before he left town." There was suspicion that many left money or valuables with him, and at least one person filed a formal complaint. The police speculated that he had taken the night train to Cincinnati. Three days later a report came from Mt. Sterling that a flim-flam man had victimized many people there a few weeks before. That self-styled clairvoyant had made the same claims under the name "Professor Harry A. Swell" and had "departed by the light of the moon."

A 1925 article in the *Sun* described the unveiling of Chief Justice James Simpson's portrait at the state capitol in Frankfort. Judge J. M. Benton of Clark County delivered the portrait on behalf of the family and gave a brief biographical sketch at the event. Simpson was born in Ireland in 1796, came to Winchester with his parents as a young man, was admitted to the bar in 1817 and rose "immediately to a front place in his profession." He represented Clark County twice in the legislature and was appointed to the Kentucky Court of Appeals. After the office became elective, he won a seat in 1851 and served as Chief Justice. The Court of Appeals was then the highest court in

Kentucky. Opposed to "electioneering," he was defeated for the seat in 1860. Judge Simpson died in 1876 and is buried in Winchester Cemetery. His portrait no longer hangs in the capitol and could not be located by staff at the capitol or the Kentucky Historical Society. A portrait of Judge Simpson—possibly a copy—hangs in the second floor courtroom at the Clark County Courthouse.

Sources

Swastika: *Sun-Sentinel*, February 7, 1907. **Taft**: *Winchester News*, October 15 and 16, 1908. **Roosevelt**: *Winchester Sun*, September 2 and 3, 1940. **Hart**: *Winchester News*, December 19, 1910. Hart's "Woman Triumphant" is from the Wilson Family Photograph Collection, University of Kentucky. **Prof. Kline**: *Winchester Sun*, January 22, 25 and 28, 1913. **Simpson**: *Winchester Sun*, June 16, 1925.

36
The Sad Tales of
Thomas Scott & Mollie Abbott

June 23, 2017

Thomas Scott's handsome monument in Winchester Cemetery bears a lengthy inscription that serves as a thumbnail biography: "Thomas Scott was born in 1763 in the State of Delaware and settled in Winchester in 1795. He was successively a representative in the state legislature, county surveyor, justice of the peace, high sheriff of Clark County. He died 1839."

Thomas Scott's monument in Winchester Cemetery

In April 1796, not long after Scott brought his surveying skills to town, he was appointed a trustee of Winchester. The board of trustees served as the city government until the mayor-council system was adopted in 1882.

In October 1796 Scott performed a survey of the town, which turned up an interesting result. Our familiar history credits John Baker as the "founder" of Winchester for laying out the town lots on his land and for donating land for erection of our public buildings (courthouse, jail, etc.). The trustees divided the town into 96 lots separated by six streets and six alleys. These were drawn up on paper, then the corners of each lot were staked. The first lots were sold at a public auction held in March 1794. The trustees held the sales but the moneys were paid to John Baker as owner of the land.

At some point, it was recognized that all the lots were not within the boundaries of Baker's land. No record exists to tell us how this happened or who first noticed the aberration, but it became crystal clear after Scott performed his town survey in 1796. The result showed that the twelve lots north of Washington Street were on the property of Josiah Hart (father of Joel Tanner Hart) and therefore, when these lots sold, the purchase money had to be paid to Hart.

Scott purchased several town lots for himself. He bought a lot at the southeast corner of Washington and Water (Maple) Street at auction and a lot at the southeast corner of Main and Broadway from William Miller. He bought and sold a number of other town properties over the years. Land sales usually included the wife's name as one of the sellers. None of Scott's deeds indicate he had a wife in Winchester. He may have come to Kentucky as a widower of, perhaps, he never married.

In 1813 Scott was elected to represent Clark County in the Kentucky General Assembly and served one term. He supervised the laying of a brick floor in the courthouse in 1815— it had been a dirt floor until then. After serving for a decade as a county magistrate (1806-1816), Scott accepted the sheriff's job in 1817. He had problems properly fulfilling his duties, which led to his securities being charged for his omissions. The problem, according to Goff Bedford's Clark County history, was that "Scott was drinking heavily and was badly in debt." I have not found the evidence for that yet, but it may be true. He did face a number of lawsuits at this time; the plaintiffs included Dudley Wells, Samuel Patterson, Edward Bullock, Thomas Gardner, Austin Trimble and Alfred Stevens.

Up into the 1820s the county cared for the poor by paying responsible citizens to house, feed and clothe them. When the numbers finally got to be too great, the county appointed Scott and James Lampton to find land on which to erect a poorhouse. In 1829 the county purchased 110 acres on Ironworks Road where 17 people were housed. The land is now known as the "county farm" and is the site of the animal shelter, fairgrounds and county cemetery.

The story takes a turn with Scott's death in 1839. Records indicate that the court paid Dr. John Mills to treat Thomas Scott in his last illness—at the county poorhouse! A local attorney, George Smith, went to the poorhouse to record Scott's will. He left $50 to Mrs. Sarah Jackson "for her attention and care to me during my old age and sickness." The rest of the estate was left to the county court "to be appropriated in the manner they shall think best." The inventory of his estate included a note from William and Wade Hampton for $21.43 and two from Richard Baxter and John Evans for $3.06 and $4.24. No real or personal property was listed.

The county court paid to put up Scott's monument at the cemetery in 1846.

* * *

The case of Mollie Abbott displays a similar turn in fortunes but is more tragic. Mollie was a daughter of Barzilla D. and Evaline (Rankin) Abbott. Abbott was a well-to-do farmer in the eastern end of the county. He had a gristmill and distillery on Lulbegrud Creek, a few miles south of Ironworks Road. After Barzilla died in 1847, Evaline inherited the mansion house, 100 acres of his 330-acre farm and one-third interest in the mill and distillery.

The 1850 census lists Evaline, 42, with a household of four sons—John, 22, William, 19, Daniel, 16, Washington, 14— and two daughters—Nancy, 8, Mary "Mollie," 6. In 1870, Mollie was still single and living with her aged mother. By 1880 Evaline had died and Mollie was living alone.

B. D. Abbott's Mill on Lulbegrud Creek (L&E Railway, c1901)

Tragedy struck in early 1900. Mollie was still living alone in the old family home, when two men tried to rob the place. They fired several shots through a window, presumably hoping to scare Mollie. One of the bullets, however, struck her in the side. Mollie ran from the house to seek help from her brother-in-law, John Swope, who lived on the next farm. She had to wade a creek along the way, and when she arrived water had frozen on her clothes and her whole body was bloody. She never recovered from the wounds. Several men were arrested for the crime, tried and found innocent.

In June of that year the *Winchester Democrat* reported that "Mollie Abbott, an inmate of the poor house, was tried before Judge Evans and a jury Wednesday on a charge of lunacy. She was adjudged a lunatic and was taken to the asylum at Lexington." She died at the asylum several months later. The same paper added a poignant note to the story:

"We have been pained to see recently the name of Miss Mollie Abbott in The Democrat in its several connections. The history of this poor, unfortunate woman reads like a romance with a sad and pathetic ending. Forty years ago she was the beautiful and popular daughter of the wealthy Boswell [Barzilla] Abbott. She dressed in silks and satins and happy was the young lady who was so fortunate as to be her friend and companion. But reverses came, the father died, the fortune left was soon dissipated by bad management and unprincipled parties. The widow and mother, bent with care, sorrow and privations, in a few years followed her husband, and Miss Mollie was left comparatively alone in the world. Poverty, wicked and shameful treatment, poor house, insane asylum, marks the last sad steps of a life once so beautiful, propitious and happy. And thus it is that 'Fortune's furious, fickle wheel' makes rapid and capricious revolutions."

Mollie's older brother William had earlier come to the same unfortunate end, as reported in the *Democrat* in 1887: "William Abbott, who lived in the Eastern part of this county and who was sent to the Lunatic Asylum at Lexington last Thursday, died there the next day of brain disease, aged 57 years. His remains were brought home and buried at Log Lick. He was a member of Capt. George M. Jackson's Company, 4th Kentucky Federal Infantry."

Sources
Scott: Winchester Trustees Minute Book, 1794-1806, pp. 13, 17, 32; Clark County Deed Book 8:37, 43:357; Richard H. Collins, *History of Kentucky, Vol. II* (Covington, KY, 1874), p. 774; Clark County Order Book 5:420, 11:425; A. Goff Bedford, *The Proud Land, A History of Clark County, Kentucky* (Mt. Sterling, KY, 1983), pp. 400, 403-404, 465, 525; Thomas Scott's estate settlement in loose papers in the Courthouse attic; Will Book 9:341, 602; **Abbott**: Clark County Order Book 12:23-24, 14:125; *Winchester Democrat*, November 30, 1887, March 2, June 8 and 12, 1900; *Winchester Sun*, October 30, 1913; L&E Railway, *Natural Bridge in the Kentucky Mountains* (Louisville, KY, c1901), p. 8.

37
Early
African-American Churches

July 7, 2017

I have collected information on black churches in Clark County with the thought of preparing brief sketches of those established in the 19th century. With two exceptions, all of our known African-American congregations began after the Civil War. However, it was not until after emancipation that they were able to form churches. The favored denominations were Methodist and Baptist. According to Dr. Thomas D. Clark's *Clark County, Kentucky: A History*, "Documentary evidence describing the number and location of the colored Baptist congregations is skimpy." And the same is true for Methodist congregations.

Establishment dates given in this article are taken from deeds of trustees purchasing property on which to build a church.[*] While this may not be precisely accurate, other data are simply not available. Other documentation comes from county records and a few published church histories. The list of churches is fairly impressive, and it's possible I may have missed a few.

Allen Chapel CME

The first black church established was a Methodist congregation that later became Allen Chapel CME. Their history states that "a number of years before the Emancipation, the black people of this locality were permitted to worship in the basement of the First Methodist Church." Then, in February 1866, Joshua Neale and his wife sold a lot at the corner of Broadway and Highland Street to John Allen, James Winn and John Massie, trustees for the church. In 1870 the congregation joined the newly formed Colored Methodist Episcopal (CME)

---

[*] An exception was made for Providence Missionary Baptist Church (see below).

denomination. They built a frame church and parsonage; the former was replaced with a brick edifice in 1898 that still stands.

Allen Chapel CME today

The church had a long history but membership declined in recent years. The congregation is no longer active, and their building has been purchased by First Baptist Church.

First Baptist Church

First Baptist Church was established in 1867. According to a church history prepared by Rev. Alvin W. Farris, the congregation first met in the home of Henry and Dullie Ecton. Members were drawn from Old Friendship Baptist and other churches around the county. In August 1867 John and Anne Madigan sold a lot on North Highland Street to Madison Gentry, John Woodford and Lewis Hood, trustees for the Missionary Baptist Church. Rev. Farris stated that the congregation rented a building on South Church Street (Church Alley) until members could erect a 30 by 36 foot structure on their lot.

A brick church was built in 1893, and it was replaced in 1930 by the present brick structure on Highland Street. The sanctuary has now been completely updated and beautiful stained-glass windows installed. Their expanded campus now includes a Family Life Center/gymnasium. The Harris Hoops Summer Basketball League was inaugurated there in June. The congregation is ably led today by their community-minded pastor, Rev. Marvin King.

Providence Missionary Baptist Church

The first black congregation that has come to light began as members of Providence Baptist Church on Lower Howard's Creek. This church, which came to Clark County in 1784, accepted its first black member in 1786. Church minutes indicate that, beginning in September 1849, "the coloured brethren" were permitted to hold irregular meetings on their own. Then, in October 1854, the church agreed to allow regular Sunday meetings with the condition that "some two or more of the white brethren be present at each meeting." The black congregation continued to meet in this manner until after the Civil War. Finally, on July 4, 1868, nineteen "Coloured Brethren & Sisters of this Church" were granted letters of dismission, presumably in order to form their own separate body.

White Providence members erected a new meeting house in 1870 on the road to Boonesborough, and in 1872 they sold their old church to "Thompson Ragland, Robert Bush, John Covington, Silas Gentry and Lewis Woodford, trustees of the Colored Baptist Church." All except Covington had previously been members of Providence.

Although the deed was made in 1872, the evidence above suggests an establishment date of July 1868. This congregation, today known as Providence Missionary Baptist Church, has been meeting continuously ever since. Their place of worship, long known as the Old Stone Church, is now the oldest operating church in Kentucky.

The nearly illegible gravestone of Louis Woodford at the Old Stone Church. Woodford, one of the first trustees of Providence Missionary Baptist Church, was a Civil War veteran, having fought in the 109th U.S. Colored Infantry. (Photo by Wallace B. Guerrant Jr.)

Dry Fork Colored Methodist Church

In November 1869, Dry Fork Colored Methodist Church purchased a lot from Pleasant Conkwright and wife Annie. Trustees Andrew Rucker, Peter Buckner and Click Vivion paid $50 for two acres of land on the Dry Fork of Upper Howard's Creek. This would have been in the Ruckerville area. Their pastor in 1870 was Reuben Taylor. No other information found.

Clark Chapel AME

The third Methodist congregation, Clark Chapel AME, is now known as Clark United Methodist Church. Its original members came from Allen Chapel CME. They withdrew from that congregation when it departed from the much older African Methodist Episcopal (AME) conference. They purchased a lot at the corner of Church Alley and Broadway known as "the Old William Factory." The sale was made in January 1870 to trustees Reuben Ragland, Shelton Jones and William Irvin. An 1872 deed indicates the congregation first met in the old factory:

"The brick house that was formerly used as a carding Factory but is now owned by the African Methodist Church and used as a Meeting House...."

They sold this building to Ernest Jordan in 1926 and moved to a new church at the corner of Broadway and Burns

Avenue.

Clark United Methodist is an inclusive, neighborhood-focused church currently pastored by Chrysanthia Carr-Seals. Their original building on East Broadway has been purchased by Pillar of the Community and is currently being restored by Mt. Folly Enterprises.

The old AME Church today

Thanks to Lyndon Comstock, who prepared voluminous, detailed information on the African-American members of Providence Baptist Church and whose book will soon be forthcoming.

This article corrects some incorrect information about the formation of Allen Chapel CME and Clark Chapel AME that appeared in the Winchester Sun February 10, 2016 and in Where In The World II, pages 198-201.

Sources

Allen Chapel: Church history in the Centennial Edition of the *Winchester Sun*, September 9, 1978; Clark County Deed Book 42:216. **First Baptist**: Church history in *Winchester Sun* Centennial Edition; Clark County Deed Book 43:27. **Providence Missionary Baptist**: Clark County Deed Book 45:9; Providence Church Minute Books 1, 2 and 3. **Dry Fork Colored Methodist**: Clark County Deed Book 43:541; *C. H. Phillips, History of the Colored Methodist Episcopal Church in America* (Jackson, TN, 1925), p. 46. **Clark Chapel**: Church history in *Winchester Sun* Centennial Edition; Clark County Deed Book 44:158, 45:67, 104:230.

38
Early
African-American Churches
Part 2

July 21, 2017

This is the continuation of an article that appeared in the Winchester Sun on Friday, July 7.

Pine Grove Baptist Church

In April 1872, James S. Lane sold one acre on Holder's Road to James Baker, Charles Fishback, John Green and Civil War veteran, Jack Rones, "trustees of the Colored Baptist Church of Pine Grove." The land was on what is now Venable Road, a half mile from Old Pine Grove. The church building is long gone, but the foundation stones, spanning about 30 feet by 30 feet, are still in place. Hillcrest Cemetery is located on the adjacent site. The successor congregation, Gentile Pine Grove Baptist Church, now simply Gentile Baptist Church, moved to Winchester, where it stands at the corner of Elm and Fifth Street.

Broadway Christian Church

In March 1876, W. N. West sold a lot fronting on the south side of Broadway to the "Colored Christian Church of Winchester" represented by trustees John Judy, Granville Woodward and Alfred Frazier. The frame church that burned here in about 1896 was replaced by a larger frame building. In 1957 the latter building was torn down and the present brick church erected on the site. Broadway Christian Church is still an active congregation led by their charismatic pastor, Rev. Raymond H. Smith Jr.

Pleasant Hill Baptist Church

In March 1881, Lewis McVane, Nelson Seals and Dudley Irvine, "committee men for the Pleasant Hill Baptist Church," purchased a small lot on Jouett Creek from Lydia Aldrich. The church stands on the south side of Athens-Boonesboro Road, where the road crosses the creek. An early colored school also stood on the site. The church and grounds are still well maintained, and a small cemetery has been fenced off to protect the gravestones.

Pleasant Hill Baptist Church

Murray's Chapel ME

In August 1881, Jeremiah McKinney sold an acre of land to trustees Newton Murray, Joseph Murray and James Johnson, for "a place of Divine worship for the use of the Ministry and Membership of the Methodist Episcopal Church in the United States of America." Four years later, Joseph Murray sold the trustees of "M. E. Church of Howard's Lower Creek" a small parcel of land "on which to build a church edifice." The deed description places the lot in a bottom on the north side of the creek, less than a half mile downstream from the Old Stone Church. Murray's deed states that the church was to be known as "Boone's Chapel." In 1892 when they sold off part of their lot the church was referred to as "Murray's Chapel." No other information found.

Corinth CME Church

In November 1883, George and Phillis Gaitskill sold an acre of land to William Wilson, Manson Vivion and Harry Haggard, who were trustees of the "Colored M. E. Church of Corinth." A black congregation met here for more than a century, but Corinth CME Church is no longer in use. The handsome frame building, located on L & E Junction Road, is listed on the

National Register of Historic Places. The church has begun to fall into disrepair.

Corinth CME Church
(National Register of Historic Places)

Colored Baptist Church at Becknerville

In October 1888, D. P. and Charlotte Scott sold a lot to Clark Tibbs, Jackson M. Taylor, Lee Mason and Perry Richardson, who were "trustees of a Colored Baptist Church being organized in Clark County." These men represented "the Colored Baptist Church at Becknerville." A 1926 map of the county shows the "Colored Church & School" on the west side of Waterworks Road at Becknerville. Now known as Houston Baptist Church, with Rev. Timothy F. Lynem pastor of the congregation.

Houston Baptist Church at Becknerville

Stoner Creek CME Church

In November 1889, Wayne Morton, Thomas Miller and Sanford Miller, trustees for the "Colored Methodist Episcopal Church in America," paid $20 for one quarter acre of land "on the waters of Stoner Creek." The premises were to be used "as a place of divine worship" and "for public school purposes." Two years later a deed of correction was signed stating that the original purchaser "of the lot on which a church is now being built" was actually the Colored School District #7. Church trustees and school trustees agreed to joint ownership of the lot and building that would be used by both parties, and further agreed to share expenses equally. Deed records indicate that the church and school were located on Goose Creek Road, a dirt lane at that time. When Sanford Miller's estate was divided among his heirs in 1896, the accompanying map shows the church lot on the left side of Goose Creek Road, about 100 yards south from where the road crosses Goose Creek. The school was not mentioned. No other information found regarding the church.

Broadway Baptist Church

According to their written history, Broadway Baptist Church was formed by 60 former members of First Baptist Church on Highland. Their charter was granted in December 1889. Rev. R. T. Huffman served as the first pastor. In April 1890, Isaac Skinner sold a lot in Winchester to Edward Turner, Charles Dedman and Beverly Jackson, "as Trustees for the Broadway Baptist Church." The church paid $300 of the $1,350 purchase price, giving notes for the remainder. A black architect from Nashville drew up plans, and the cornerstone of the new church was laid in 1890. The handsome brick building with its tall steeple was erected on the north side of Broadway near Maple Street.

Construction costs put the congregation further in debt. The church was almost lost to indebtedness on several occasions but somehow managed to survive. Deed records indicate that in 1904, the congregation paid George Nelson $1,335 in cash to regain the title to their church. At that time, trustees were Orrin W. Bates, Sid Boone, Charles Wills, Silas Coach and Charles

Dedman. The last of a series of mortgages was paid off in 1923.

The church was led for 38 years (1955-1993) by Rev. Henry E. Baker Sr. Reverend Baker was a tireless worker for the black community of Winchester. He played a prominent roll dealing with integration of local government and schools. Baker was the first African-American elected to public office in Clark County, serving as a city commissioner and vice mayor from 1980 to 1984. A month before his death in 2014, the new Henry E. Baker Intermediate School was named in his honor.

Broadway Baptist Church

Much more work needs to be done to document these historic churches. My apologies for any errors that may be found in this work. I would appreciate receiving corrections or additions (henoch1945@gmail.com).

Many thanks to Jerry Cecil for help with this article.

Sources
Pine Grove Baptist: Clark County Deed Book 44:493. **Broadway Christian**: Clark County Deed Book 48:102, 52:499. **Pleasant Hill Baptist**: Clark County Deed Book 48:549. **Murray's Chapel ME**: Clark County Deed Book 49:61, 51:449, 61:94. **Corinth CME**: Clark County Deed Book

50:303. **Becknerville Baptist**: 54:492. **Stoner Creek CME**: Clark County Deed Book 56:541, 57:377; Clark County Division of Lands Book 1:187. **Broadway Baptist**: Church history, *Winchester Sun* Centennial Edition, September 9, 1978; Clark County Deed Book 56:559, 72:630; Betty Ratliff Smith, *Winchester Sun*, September 9, 1989.

39
Old Stone House with Portholes

August 4, 2017

In the late 1920s a pair of Clark County historians, Lucien Beckner and S. J. Conkwright, became interested in the location of McGee's Station, one of the earliest settlements north of Kentucky River. Conkwright later wrote, "[We] knew that the location of the Station was somewhere near Hayden Corner, so on making inquiry of some of the old citizens of that neighborhood [we] learned that there was an Old Stone House with port holes in its walls, about one mile south of Hayden Corner." Hayden Corner, at the intersection of Waterworks Road and Combs Ferry Road, was named for Samuel Hayden, an early landowner there.

Old Stone House with Portholes

Beckner and Conkwright eventually concluded that the station stood at the headwaters of Jouett Creek on David McGee's 400-acre settlement. The site is on the farm of

Harkness and Cathy Edwards on Jones Nursery Road. The old stone house with portholes still stands on the east side of Combs Ferry Road on the farm of Eck Rose. The house has an interesting and confusing history, clouded in controversy.

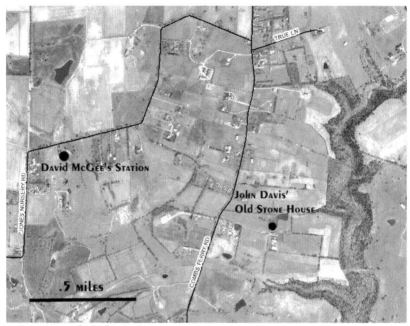

**Location of McGee's Station and the old stone house with portholes.
The serpentine shape at the right side of the map is West Fork.**

David McGee with some men from his neighborhood headed west in 1775 in search of new lands. McGee stated in a deposition, "[This] deponent and other adventurers set out from Virginia for Kentucky with an intention to explore the country and acquire land. That as soon as they reached the place of their destination they began to make small improvements and claimed the adjoining land by occupancy, expecting that they would be confirmed to them by the State, as soon as a land office would open for the country."

In 1779 McGee appeared before the Virginia Land Commission at Boonesborough to present his claim for a 400-acre settlement where he had erected his fort. He also presented to the commission the claim of Bryan McDonald, his Botetourt County neighbor, for a 400-acre settlement on the West Fork of

Lower Howard's Creek. Both had raised corn and built a cabin on their respective tracts in 1776. When surveyed, McDonald's 400 acres lay on both sides of West Fork. A 1792 court decision reveals that McDonald and McGee had made an agreement that McDonald's claim would not cross West Fork.

The court decision came too late for John Frame, who settled on McDonald's claim on the west side of West Fork. John Davis acquired 103 acres of this tract in 1795 and built the stone house with portholes soon after. The original house, approximately 18 feet by 27 feet, was two stories plus a basement. The first floor was divided into two rooms with a chimney at each end. The house has had numerous additions and alterations over the years. At this time, only one of the portholes is visible from the outside—in the east

(Photo by Clare Sipple)

basement wall. The opening is about 3 inches wide on the outside and about 18 inches wide on the inside. Such an opening would give a defender inside a good range of view and field of fire but would provide a very small target for someone outside.

It is uncertain whether Davis built the house himself or hired a mason. The dry-laid, undressed stone gives the construction a rough appearance, quite unlike the fine workmanship of stone houses that would appear on Lower Howard's Creek a few years later. The roof has kept the house in remarkably good condition considering that it has been vacant and otherwise open to the elements for decades.

Davis apparently left the house, and presumably the

county, after being informed that McGee held a superior claim to the land. Davis and his wife Ann were members of Providence Baptist Church. They obtained letters of dismission from the church in 1797, and his name disappeared from the county tax roll. McGee gained full possession of the house and land a few years later. Davis was never paid for the house he erected that stands to this day.

Sources
Morgan v. Robinson, Fayette County Complete Record Book A:64; "Certificate Book of the Virginia Land Commission, 1779-1780," *Register of the Kentucky Historical Society* (1923) 21:68; copy of McDonald's settlement survey, Kentucky Land Office online, http://apps.sos.ky.gov/land/ nonmilitary/patentseries/vaandokpatents/; *Dryden v. McGee*, James Hughes, *Report of the Causes Determined by Late Supreme Court for the District of Kentucky* (Lexington, KY, 1803), p. 71; *Morgan v. McGee*, Clark County Complete Record Book, 1818-19, pp. 24-65; Clark County Deed Book 1:458; George F. Doyle, *First Record Book of Providence Church* (Winchester, KY, 1924), pp. 15, 28.

40
Boone Family in Clark County

August 18, 2017

It's hard for me to believe I have lived in Clark County almost eighteen years now—and still feel like a newcomer. I grew up in Mt. Sterling, where my love of history dates from a visit by our Cub Scout den to the site of Morgan's Station, a pioneer fort on the eastern edge of the county. We were told Indians had burned the station and taken a large group of captives. Morgan's Station was said to have been "the last Indian raid in Kentucky." There were Indians in Montgomery County? Wow! That made quite an impression on this ten-year old. My passion for history grew from there. My special interest is the pioneer era or settlement period in Kentucky.

Montgomery County got split off from Clark in 1796, so study of the early times there meant going into the records of Clark, and also Fayette from which Clark was formed in 1792. One doesn't have to go very far back in the records before one runs into the Boone family. This brief article can only begin to lay out a history of all the Boones who lived here over the last 200 plus years.

As it turns out, the most famous Boone left his footprints all over Clark County—from Lulbegrud Creek in the east (named by Daniel Boone in 1770) to Boone Creek in the west (named for Daniel Boone before 1779). Kentucky's earliest pioneers were allowed to claim 400 acres for their settlement and an adjoining 1,000 acres called a preemption. Daniel Boone selected a site on George's Creek, a branch of Stoner, for his Kentucky settlement.

After having his 1,400 acres surveyed, Boone decided not to live there and sold the land to William Scholl. William's sons—Joseph, Peter and Abraham—erected a small fortress there called Scholl's Station. The station, located near present-day Schollsville, provided for protection of the neighborhood in the event of an Indian raid.

Map of Daniel Boone's 400-acre settlement and 1,000-acre preemption near Schollsville.

    Boone's daughter Levina married Joseph Scholl. She lived and died in the Schollsville neighborhood. According to the Clark County Chronicles, written in the 1920s, Levina and her sister Rebecca Boone Goe are buried in the Scholl Graveyard near there. This family cemetery has been lost for many years.

    Daniel's brother, Samuel Boone, left children with Clark County connections. In the summer of 1786, several of his offspring joined Providence Baptist Church on Lower Howard's Creek—sons Squire and Samuel Jr., daughters Mary who married Leonard K. Bradley and Elizabeth who married William White, and son-in-law Roger Jones who married daughter Rebecca. There is not a shred of evidence to support the notion that Daniel Boone attended church there. Scholarly studies of the church have been prepared by Baptist historians and Clark

County historians with no mention of his name, not even so much as an "it has been said...." Furthermore, Boone is known to have shunned organized religion all his life, going back to the time of his father's ill treatment by the Quakers in Pennsylvania.

Samuel Boone Jr. (1758-1843) left a rich history in the county. He was a Revolutionary War veteran and received a pension for his service while residing here. When he was 78 years old, Samuel wed Susan House. She married with the consent of her father, so Susan must have been under age 21. Samuel's will left all his estate to Susan, then she died only four years after Samuel. Her will left everything to her House nieces and nephews, indicating that she and Samuel had no surviving children.

Samuel Jr.'s brother Thomas was killed and brother Squire was badly wounded at the battle of Blue Licks in 1782. Squire became a licensed Baptist minister in 1790 and pastored Boggs Fork Church in Fayette County. Squire's son Thomas "Tommy" Boone was a well-known Baptist preacher in Clark County for many years. He was ordained in 1815 and pastored Log Lick, Dry Fork (on Upper Howard's Creek), New Providence (near Kiddville) and Lulbegrud churches. In 1832 Providence Church on Lower Howard's Creek received permission from New Providence for Reverend Boone to serve them with one-fourth of his time, presumably one Sunday a month.

Thomas Boone married Sallie Muir and they raised twelve children. Their son Ira became a Baptist preacher, and daughter Polly married a Baptist preacher, James Edmonson. Sallie was interviewed by Rev. John Shane and made some amusing comments about Eli Cleveland, yet another pioneer Baptist preacher, for whom Cleveland Road takes its name: "Was shot at several times. Shot once in his bed. Had a good many adventures."

Rev. Tommy and Sallie are buried in the Lulbegrud Churchyard in Montgomery County. Their son George kept Boone Tavern in Winchester (southeast corner of Main and Broadway) during the Civil War. George had twin sons who chose to fight on opposite sides in the war, epitomizing the maxim "brother against brother." Tommy and Sally left numerous descendants who will be the subject of a future article.

Grave of Rev. Thomas Boone in Lulbegrud Church Graveyard
(Courtesy of Sue Rife)

Daniel's brother Edward "Ned" Boone was killed by Indians in 1780 while the pair were out on a hunting trip. Ned married Martha Bryan, a sister of Daniel's wife Rebecca. After Ned's death, Martha left Boone's Station (near Athens) and purchased 100 acres of land on Boone Creek in Clark County. Martha died in 1793, leaving a will that named six children. Four later left Kentucky, while daughter Mary and son George remained in Clark County. Mary married Peter Scholl, who was in the battle of Blue Licks and was a brother of Joseph, mentioned above. The couple lived on the Daniel Boone tract—the 1,400-

acre settlement and preemption—surrounding Schollsville and raised fourteen children there.

Ned and Martha's son George lived on Boone Creek in Clark on land he purchased from Eli Cleveland. George married twice—Patty Hazelrigg in 1793 and Hester Lock in 1801. They had a number of children but all eventually left the county, many following George and Hester to Daviess County.

It was surprising to find an unrelated Boone in the same area. George G. Boone also lived on Boone Creek. He was raised in King George County, Virginia, a son of William Boone and Keziah Green. George married Mary Plunkett in Clark in 1835; they are listed in Clark in the 1850 census. Coincidentally, he was also a Baptist minister and served for three years as pastor of Providence Church on Lower Howard's Creek, 1828-1830. He later moved to Fayette where he was pastor of Boone Creek Baptist Church.

To do a thorough job of describing the Boone families of Clark County would require a book—and would be one I'd like to work on if I ever get the time.

Sources

Harry G. Enoch, *Deposition Book*, pp. 109-113; *Certificate Book*, p. 82; John Hedge interview, Draper MSS 11CC 20; James M. Stevenson interview, Draper MSS 11CC 51; Nancy O'Malley, "Stockading Up," Archaeology Report 127, April 30, 1987; (George F. Doyle, *First Record Book of Providence Church* (Winchester, KY, 1924), pp. 4, 138, 143, 161, 158-159; George F. Doyle, *Marriage Bonds of Clark County*; Clark County Will Book 1:7, 10:279, 11:222; S. J. Conkwright, *History of the Churches of the Boone Creek Association*, p. 72; J. H. Spencer, *History of Kentucky Baptists*, Vol. 1, pp. 261-262, 280, 479, Vol. 2, pp. 350-351, 373; Clark County Deed Book 12:6, 13:131, 15:26, 17:223, 244, 26:93; Clark County Chronicles, *Winchester Sun*, June 21 and July 5, 1923; Hazel A. Spraker, *The Boone Family* (Rutland, VT, 1922); Samuel Boone's Revolutionary War pension papers, S. 1168, SC; Harry G. Enoch, *Pioneer Voices* (Winchester, KY, 2012), p. 98.

41
Keeping Up with the Joneses

Joan Pursley Mayer, who grew up in Clark County, has penned a memoir entitled "Of Family and Place." Her book of memories, written for her children and grandchildren, relates many adventures of her parents, Fauntleroy and Charlotte (Bowman) Pursley, in the Iroquois Hunt Club. The book is a most enjoyable read. Joan also provides a history of the hunt country as well as the whole area of southwest Clark County. Part of that history journeys back in time to tell the stories of her ancestors who settled there. This article focuses on one of those lines, a branch of the Jones family that arrived in this county just after 1800.

While researching her family history, Joan was aided by a classic work of genealogy: *Captain Roger Jones of London and Virginia*, written by Judge Lewis H. Jones of Clark County in 1891. His tome provides the record of seven generations of her Jones family in America. Joan's narrative adds five more generations of her family, making a remarkable twelve generations in all. I will note each in turn, but the main focus will be the Joneses who settled in Clark County.

The progenitor of this family was Roger Jones (1625-1701), an immigrant of Welsh descent who came to America with his wife, Dorothy Walker, before 1680.

Their son Col. Thomas Jones (d. 1757) married a widow, Elizabeth Pratt, who was the daughter of Dr. William and Elizabeth (Catesby) Cocke of Williamsburg, Virginia.

Following the Welsh tradition, their eldest son bore the name Thomas ap Thomas Jones (1726-1785), meaning "Thomas son of Thomas." He married Sally Skelton, a daughter of James and Mary Bathurst (Meriwether) Skelton.

The eldest son of Thomas and Sally, Maj. Thomas ap Thomas Jones (1755-1800), earned his rank in the Revolutionary War. He inherited the family seat, Bathurst, in Essex County, Virginia. Thomas married Frances Carter, a granddaughter of

Robert "King" Carter, who was reputed to have once been the richest man in Virginia.

Thomas ap Thomas Jones (1784-1843), who represents the fifth generation, married Elizabeth Fauntleroy, a daughter of Griffin and Margaret (Murdock) Fauntleroy of Richmond County, Virginia. Thomas sold the family seat, Bathurst, and moved to Kentucky in the latter part of 1810. He purchased and farmed several large tracts of land between Lower Howard's Creek and present-day Jones Nursery Road, all north of Athens-Boonesboro Road. Thomas established a family reputation for integrity, intelligence and generosity. His wife, Elizabeth, outlived him by 22 years. They are buried in a small graveyard west of Combs Ferry Road.

Roger Jones home, Sunnyside (Photo from Lewis H. Jones book)

Thomas and Elizabeth had nine children. The eldest, Frances, died of consumption in 1833. Son Joseph Lewellin died in infancy. Daughter Sally, who married Armistead Blackwell, died in 1854 leaving four small children. Son Thomas ap Thomas Jr. moved to Missouri, where he served as a Confederate soldier. Son Cad Jones, a bachelor and attorney, served five years as clerk of the county court and died in 1862. Daughter Ann Eliza married Samuel T. Martin, a son of the famed Clark County doctor, Samuel D. Martin, and they moved to Saline

County, Missouri. Son Joseph acquired Caveland, home of Gen. Richard Hickman built in 1797, and was a successful farmer; his sons operated the Jones Brothers Warehouse in Winchester in the late 1800s. Son Roger Jones established the stock farm, Sunnyside, and his fine Greek-Revival home still stands on Combs Ferry Road. Joan's ancestor was son Fauntleroy Jones.

Nursery Place at the corner of Jones Nursery Road and Athens-Boonesboro Road. The old gentleman seated in front of the house is Fauntleroy Jones. (Photo from Lewis H. Jones book)

Fauntleroy Jones (1816-1897) married his neighbor, Martha Jane Browning, a daughter of James and Jane (Morrow) Browning. Fauntleroy was one of the most enterprising citizens of his era. His business life began with failure as he acquired the ill-fated ropewalk and bagging factory in Winchester that had been the downfall of David Dodge and, in turn, cost Fauntleroy a considerable fortune. His obituary in the *Winchester Democrat* describes how he managed to recover from that reversal:

"He obtained permission from his mother to plant the beginning of a nursery on an extreme corner of her farm. He built a shop close to his little cabin home. He employed a man to work in it and from him he learned the trade of a wheelwright. He worked by day in his nursery and at night by lamp light or candle light at his trade, making large spinning wheels on which servants used to spin yarn, and smaller wheels for spinning flax. He made chairs also which then brought higher prices than similar articles now bring, also the tall old fashioned bedsteads, which he turned on a turning lathe at which he became very expert."

Fauntleroy eventually became a learned horticulturist and the most noted nurseryman in Kentucky. It was said that most of the old orchards in Clark and neighboring counties were supplied from Jones' Nursery. Fauntleroy also had a blacksmith shop with five employees, where he manufactured wagons and sleighs. He was postmaster of the Jones Nursery Post Office from 1850 to 1859.

When the Civil War broke out, Fauntleroy was a Union man. But their harsh treatment of Kentuckians during the conflict caused him to sympathize with the Southern cause, which resulted in his arrest and imprisonment for a time in Lexington.

In 1885 Fauntleroy deeded most of his 220-acre farm to his five surviving children, reserving Nursery Place for himself and Martha Jane.

Their son Francis "Frank" served in the Confederate army under John Hunt Morgan; after the war he graduated from the University of Louisville medical school and became a practicing physician in the Becknerville area. Son Lewis, who wrote the Jones history, studied law at Transylvania University and became a judge before giving up the profession to become a Christian Scientist practitioner and educator in Louisville. Daughter Alice married Lewis Woodford, the only son of S. A. B. Woodford, and they lived at the Woodford homeplace, Possum Trot, on Combs Ferry Road (now the Venable home); he is buried there and Alice is buried in Winchester Cemetery. Daughter Elizabeth Jane married Reuben Moore and they resided in Lexington.

Reuben's brother John Moore married Fauntleroy's daughter, Mary (1845-1916). John had served in the Civil War with Mary's brother Frank. John and Mary were Joan's great-grandparents. They set up housekeeping at Nursery Place, and their daughter Mattie (1869-1927) was born there. Mattie married John G. Pursley; their son William Fauntleroy Pursley (1903-1991) was Joan's father.

Joan is the tenth generation in this Jones line. She has two sons, John and Mark, and three grandsons. Joan lives at

Nursery Place.

Sources
Lewis H. Jones, *Captain Roger Jones of London and Virginia* (Albany, NY, 1891); Joan P. Mayer, *Of Family and Place, A Memoir* (n.p., 2016); *Winchester Democrat*, November 23, 1897; U.S. Manufacturers Census, Clark County, 1860, 1870; Robert M. Rennick, *Kentucky's Bluegrass; A Survey of the Post Offices* (Lake Grove, OR, 1993), p. 79; Clark County Deed Book 30:515, 581, 34:324, 52:26, 161, 168, 169, 171; Clark County Will Book 10:220, Red 1:198, 159, Red 2:227.

42
57 Years of Bullocks in the Clerk's Office

September 16, 2017

The Shimfessel family enjoyed a long run—45 years—in the Clark County clerk's office. After several terms as county magistrate, Beckner Shimfessel served as clerk for 16 years. He was followed by his daughter, Anita Jones, who served for 29 years, until her retirement in 2014. Their tenure was exceeded only by the Bullock family who held the office for 57 years.

David Bullock was selected by the court as Clark's first clerk in 1793. Following his resignation in 1814, he was succeeded by his son, James P. Bullock who held the office until 1845. Finally, James was succeeded by his son, James W. Bullock, who served until 1850.

The county clerk has many duties today, some of them dating back to the beginning. The main task has always been to maintain the county's record of deeds, mortgages, marriages and estate settlements. Many of today's records are kept on computer and before that they are typed. But when the office was created, each record had to be written out by hand. The clerk typically employed a stable of "office boys" to do the writing. Yes, they were boys. Micah Taul went to work for Bullock in 1798. Having just turned 13, he also lived with Bullock. "I had a neat hand for a little boy," he later wrote. In his memoirs, Taul paints a vivid picture of our first clerk and is quoted extensively below. It is rare to find such a detailed personal description in the 18th century. It would be difficult to find one in Clark County to exceed Taul's portrait of Bullock.

At that time (1798), Bullock kept the office at his house on Grassy Lick Road (now North Main Street), one mile from Winchester. That was not as unusual as it sounds. We know Fayette's first clerk, Levi Todd, kept the office in a cabin behind his home, "Ellerslie," on Richmond Road. The office burned in 1803 destroying most of the county's records.

Taul begins, "I found Captain B. a plain, sensible well educated & very stern old Virginia Gentleman. He had been a Captain in the Revolutionary War & was a first rate clerk—wrote with more rapidity than any person I ever saw." Taul ventures a guess that Bullock "must have been very poor" when he was appointed, because "they lived poor during my residence with them," then follows with a lengthy description.

"Captain B. was at the time I went to write in his office about 50 years of age inclining to corpulency. Was certainly one of the best & altogether Laziest men I ever saw. He was an inveterate smoker & had a great repugnance to locomotion. He went to the town of Winchester every Saturday, and except that, he scarcely ever went off the place. He was no farmer and did not keep an Overseer. Raised but little stock, perhaps pork enough to supply the family." On his second day at work, Taul was put to work recording deeds, and thereafter "he [Bullock] hardly ever had occasion to come into the office."

He certainly came from notable stock. According to Taul, Bullock was "connected by blood & marriage with several distinguished families in Virginia & Kentucky, particularly the Clarkes, Hendersons & Lewises."

Bullock was married to Susannah Moore—Taul says they were cousins. "I never saw a man & wife so well matched, so perfectly congenial in their dispositions. She too was a great smoker, and they spent the principal part of their time in smoking & conversation. They were perfectly contented & happy. Lived in an indifferent cabin in a plain, simple manner. Their diet was of the most common kind, meat, corn bread & milk being almost the only articles. Tea & coffee were unknown."

The couple raised two sons and five daughters. "They did not educate their children—I never could account for it, particularly as he was himself a well educated man. He was a first rate Greek & Latin scholar. The consequence was, when his children grew up, they labored under great disadvantages. His stingyness might have been the cause of his not educating his children, for he was the stingyest man I ever knew—and yet wife, daughters & all were perfectly cheerful & happy—and so was I." Taul added that "Captain Bullock sent his children to the dancing school, almost the only school he ever sent them to."

Taul remembered his first visit to court day in Winchester. "There was an immense crowd of people at an indifferent Tavern...kept by an old Dutch woman." This was Ann Sphar—tavern keeper and wife of Theodorus—who left him and took up with William Smith in Winchester. Goff Bedford claimed she ran a bawdy house, which may be true. Taul says when the passed the tavern, "so uproarious were the people that Captain B., altho a very moral man, had to stop & go in and, of course, the boys followed. The young Gentlemen of the bar I distinctly remember were there, as happy and as jovial a set of fellows as I ever saw. Many of the most respectful married men of the County were present & that house continued to be the center of attraction during the sitting of the Court."

Taul continues but we must move on. Bullock gave up the office in 1814 and died the following year. His son James P. Bullock took over for a long run. He had served during the War of 1812 in Capt. Joseph Clark's ill-fated company that was slaughtered at "Col. William Dudley's defeat" during the siege of Fort Meigs (Ohio). James was badly wounded, taken prisoner and later paroled. He was allowed a pension on his disability. He married Mildred Didlake and they raised a large family. James resigned his office in 1845 and, soon after, followed several of his children to Sumner County, Tennessee, where he died in 1848. Clark County Public Library has one of his law books on display—William Littell's *Statute Law of Kentucky*, published in 1809.

When James left office, his son James Werter Bullock took over and held the position for five years, rounding out the family's service at 57 years.

Sources

Micah Taul, "Memoirs of Micah Taul," *Register of the Kentucky Historical Society* (1929) 27:343-380; *Kentucky Gazette*, February 1, 1803; James Patterson Bullock's War of 1812 pension file, www.fold3.com. The Bullocks service in the clerk's office was determined by searching the county's deed books.

43
Memoirs of Micah Taul

September 29, 2017

The description of David Bullock, first clerk of the Clark County Court, in my last column was provided by Micah Taul. This remarkable gentleman began writing his 163-page memoir at the age of 63. A digital copy of his handwritten document is available from the Kentucky Historical Society. A transcription was published in their journal, the *Register*, in 1929.

Micah Taul
(Young, *Battle of the Thames*)

Micah Taul led an eventful life. He was born in Maryland in 1785 and came to Kentucky with his parents. His father, Arthur Thomas Taul, settled on his 950-acre land grant located on the dividing ridge between Stoner and Hinkston creeks, near the Clark-Montgomery border. He went to work as one of David Bullock's "office boys" in the Clark County clerk's office at the age of 13. He himself would be appointed the first clerk of newly formed Wayne County in 1801—two months shy of his sixteenth birthday.

Taul raised a company during the War of 1812 and soon after was promoted to colonel in command of the 7th Regiment of Kentucky Volunteers. After the war, he was elected to the U.S. Congress and served one term before eventually moving to Winchester, Tennessee, to practice law. By an odd coincidence, this was where John Holder's and Richard Callaway's children had settled and with whom Taul was acquainted. Taul later moved to Alabama and died there shortly after completing his memoirs.

The recollections from his youth throw light on the early times of Clark County. One of the boys he worked with in Bullock's office was named John Mitchell. He described Mitchell as "a very unpromising looking young fellow, probably 16 or 17 years of age, exceedingly awkward, uncouth in his appearance & wretchedly dressed. And yet this 'ogre' was a natural son of Gen. Daniel Morgan of Revolutionary Memory."

"His father sent for him & had him taken to Virginia where he put him to school, intending as I understood to adopt him as one of his children. But before his death his legitimate children contrived to prejudice him against him & he died without making any provision for him.

"Upon Mitchell's return to Virginia, his name was changed to Willoughby Morgan. He by some means obtained a liberal education & afterwards read law in the office of a distinguished lawyer of Winchester [VA] & in a short time gave promise of future eminence."

Willoughby would distinguish himself in the War of 1812. Taul met him again in 1820 at St. Louis. "He was beyond all question one of the noblest looking men I ever saw. His height 6 feet 2 or 3 inches with a perfect symmetry of form & with a many commanding face, and all in all a most elegant & accomplished Gentleman."

I considered it quite a surprise that a son of Gen. Daniel Morgan worked in the Clark County clerk's office.

Taul went on to describe what court day in Winchester were like in his youth. "The taverns were full of people from early in the day until the next morning. The people would quarrel and fight, as it seems to me now, just for the love of it."

According to Taul, cock fighting "was a common and favorable sport in those days." "On Christmas day 1798, a main event was fought on the Public Square in Winchester for a large wager." One of the parties was from Lexington, the other from "Slate Furnace," near Owingsville. "A Pit was prepared & an Amphitheatre erected around it for Spectators." Nothing else was talked about for days.

Taul described the contest in hilarious detail. "One of the Cocks in quick time cut down his adversary. The proud Victor Cock strutted round & about [then] jumped upon his prostrate foe & crowed. The dying Fowl, cut down in the prime of life, felt that his last end was near, but to be trampled upon & crowed over by his ungenerous foe was too much for the brave Cock, even in the last agonies of death. He summoned up all his expiring energies, threw his foe off his body and run one of his Gaffs entirely through his [opponent's] head which produced instantaneous death." The victor "did not survive long enough to receive the congratulations of his friends on his unexpected victory."

Taul reported other things people did for fun back then. "Horse racing was an almost every day business. The people indulged in almost all sorts of amusements: playing cards, fives or ball, throwing long bullets & even pulling an old Gander's head off, was no uncommon sport. Shooting, running foot races, wrestling, hopping, &c. was practiced at all public gatherings. A fist fight followed as a matter of course." Several of these are unknown today. Fives was a game resembling handball. Throwing long bullets was a game to see who could throw a heavy stone or metal ball (the bullet) a certain distance, say a mile, in the fewest throws. The game was usually played in public roads and was eventually outlawed everywhere.

Taul gave personal descriptions of the illustrious members of the Clark County bar in 1798. They included Gen. Levi Todd, James Brown, Henry Clay, George M. Bibb, and Jesse Bledsoe. "General Todd was an old man, was called the father of the bar, tho' I don't expect he was much of a Lawyer.

A man of high character & universally esteemed. His brother, Col. John Todd, was killed at the battle of the Blue Licks. Mr. Brown was a gentleman of high literary & legal attainments. Was a man of towering & majestic person, very proud, austere & haughty. Was afterwards Senator to Congress & Minister to France. Mr. Clay, Mr. Bibb & Mr. Bledsoe were all three great favorites with the people & considered very promising. Mr. Clay, however, took the lead & kept it. Young as I then was, I paid particular attention to the speeches made at that Court & I determined then to be a Lawyer. Mr. Clay's success & career are well known. Mr. Bibb also became highly distinguished as a Lawyer & has twice been on the bench of the Supreme Court of Kentucky, Senator in Congress & Secretary of the Treasury of the U.S. Mr. Bledsoe was a man of the first order of talents, a classical scholar, a man of exquisite wit, a poet & Orator. He soon acquired great eminence at the bar & was considered one of the best advocates in the State. He was afterwards in the Senate of the U.S. and a judge on the Circuit Court bench in Kentucky. He married [Sally,] the eldest daughter of the late Col. Nathaniel Gist of Clarke County. She was at the time one of the 'belles' of Kentucky. His besetting sin was 'intemperance' that impaired his usefulness."

Taul came back to Clark County for a time (1817-1825). He was a delegate to the Kentucky convention that nominated Henry Clay for president in 1824. The election was thrown into the House of Representatives when no candidate received a majority of electoral votes. This was the election when Clay was accused of making a "corrupt bargain" by supporting John Quincy Adams in return for being appointed Secretary of State.

In a show of support, Clark County citizens called on Taul to invite Clay "to partake in a dinner at Col. [Hubbard] Taylor's, five miles from Winchester on the Lexington road. Mr. Clay attended and...delivered a very handsome and eloquent speech. The Dinner was one of the very best I ever sat down to. The day was spent in the utmost gaiety and hilarity. Conversation, eating, drinking, dancing etc. etc." This places Henry Clay at Spring Hill, Taylor's home which still stands today on Colby Road.

Sources

Micah Taul, "Memoirs of Micah Taul," *Register of the Kentucky Historical Society* (1929) 27:354-359, 625-627; Bennett H. Young, *Battle of the Thames* (Louisville, KY, 1903); U.S. Congressional Biographies, http://bioguide.congress.gov/scripts/biodisplay.pl?index=T000054.

44
Rock Fences of Clark County

October 13, 2017

The rock fences of Clark County are one of the most iconic symbols of our heritage, and one of the most-noted landscape features observed by visitors. It is surprising then that many of us who see these fences every day have no idea why they are here, when they were built or by whom. Some, but not all, of these mysteries are cleared up in a book—*Rock Fences of the Bluegrass*—written by Carolyn Murray-Wooley and Karl Raitz. Most of what follows is from their research.

For starters, we are blessed with plentiful sources of limestone, the preferred building stone in our region. This rock has been quarried here from pioneer times to the present. Nowadays rock quarries are huge open pit operations or underground mines. Neither of these was used in early times. The first quarries took rock out of small hillside ledges and stone-bottomed creek beds. In addition to these two sources, rock fences also were constructed using field stone, the rocks picked up when clearing fields for plowing.

Three different types of fence construction are recognized: plantation, turnpike and edge-laid.

Plantation fences were used to mark boundary lines and to enclose stock pens, pastures, gardens, house yards and graveyards. The earliest date from the late 1700s. The construction method is interesting, if not a little surprising. They are actually double walls, usually built by two workers, one on each side. The fence begins with foundation stones, followed by horizontal courses of stone laid so as to overlap the joints, much like brick is laid. The walls are battered, or tapered, meaning they are wider at the bottom than at the top. The spaces between the two walls are filled with small stones. The most important structural components are so-called "tie rocks," which are laid perpendicular to the face of the wall and serve to tie the two walls together (*refer to the drawing*). The top courses of stone are covered with large horizontally-laid cap rocks, which in turn are topped with a row of vertical rocks, called coping stones. A typical rock fence might be 5 feet tall, 3 feet wide at the bottom and 2 feet wide at the top.

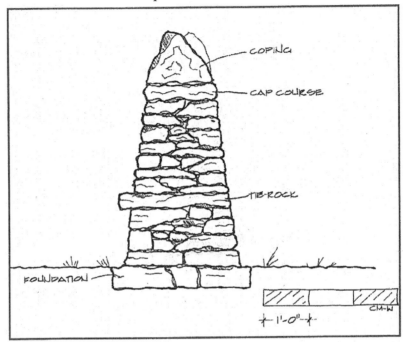

COPING

CAP COURSE

TIE-ROCK

FOUNDATION

1'-0"

CM-W

**Cross-section of a plantation fence
(Dry Stone Conservancy)**

Perhaps the most characteristic feature of these walls is that they were dry laid, meaning no mortar was used in their construction. Intuitively, you might think the mortar would add stability to the wall. But the wall's strength comes from the friction of stone touching stone, the weight of the stones and gravity. The open spaces in dry-laid fences allow water to enter and drain away, whereas mortar can trap water inside. Trapped water undergoing freeze-thaw cycles will eventually destroy the integrity of the fence.

This type of fence came into general use after the Kentucky General Assembly passed a law in 1798 to prevent stock from damaging a landowner's crops or property. The act stipulated that property owners could sue if they had erected a suitable barrier to keep out stock. They defined a suitable barrier as "any grounds being enclosed with a strong and sound fence five feet high and so close that the beasts breaking into the same could not creep through." This gave rise to a local description of fences being "horse high, hog tight and bull strong."

The second type of rock fence common here are turnpike fences. These were the fences built lining turnpikes, the toll roads built by private companies beginning in about the 1830s and lasting through the end of the century. The turnpike companies hired hundreds of stonemasons—often referred to as "turnpikers" in census schedules—to build stone fences, retaining walls and bridges. Landowners then began filling in with their own fences, so that in many places stone fences lined both sides of the turnpike. Clark County still has a few places where they may be observed—Athens-Boonesboro Road and Old Boonesboro Road come immediately to mind. It is along our roadways that tourists first become acquainted with our rock fences.

Turnpike fences on Old Boonesboro Road
(University of Louisville Archives)

Construction of these fences was very similar to plantation fences. Turnpike fences were narrower, less tapered, and the space between the two walls was filled with rubble or gravel. The latter practice greatly reduced the cost of stone as well as the cost of labor.

The third type—edge-laid fences—came into wide use in the mid-1800s in hilly regions. They began with a stone pier to anchor the fence, then stones were laid on edge leaning against each other. The stones lean toward the downhill side allowing gravity to strengthen the wall. Field stone is used rather than quarried stone, so these fences are not only cheaper to build but also very simple to construct. This writer recently built a 25-foot long edge-laid fence in a matter of a few hours, and by far the greatest part of that time was spent hauling rock. (By contrast, several years ago I took a rock fence workshop at the Bluegrass Heritage Museum. My partner and I spent two full days to complete a 4-foot section of a plantation-style fence.)

There are many examples of early quarries in Clark County. Several are located in the Lower Howard's Creek Nature and Heritage Preserve, both the creek bed and hillside ledge variety. Two well-known stonemasons resided there— Richmond Arnold and Robert Martin.

It is generally agreed now that the first builders of rock fences in the Bluegrass were Scotch-Irish immigrants. They brought the craft here from their homeland in Northern Ireland. Slaves would have performed much of the manual labor involved in construction and eventually learned the art. In the 1850 census, the first to list occupations and country of birth, stonemasons were most often Irish. Later censuses show that free blacks came to dominate the profession.

The hardest question to answer is when our rock fences were built. Most were constructed in 1800s, perhaps peaking around mid-century. But except in the rarest cases where family papers or deeds mention them, it is almost impossible to say when any particular fence was built.

Our county is fortunate to have so many attractive fences remaining, but it is sad to see them accumulating more damage each year from careless drivers. More distressing are the fences that disappear when property owners dismantle them or allow trees to destroy them. On an encouraging note, however, many conscientious landowners have removed covering vegetation, repaired collapsed sections and in some cases rebuilt substantial lengths of their rock fences. We are also fortunate to have an experienced stonemason, Stuart Joynt, in our community.

Over the next few weeks, as you drive around the county observing the fall colors, keep an eye out for our rock fences— and enjoy.

Sources

Carolyn Murray-Wooley and Karl Raitz, *Rock Fences of the Bluegrass* (Lexington, KY, 2014).

45
William Beckner
The "Horace Mann of Kentucky"

October 27, 2017

William Morgan Beckner (1841-1910) earned a glowing obituary in the newspaper he founded. "He advocated for better schools, better roads, better streets, turnpikes and railroads, and public improvements of all kinds. He was not afraid of increased taxation if the community secured corresponding benefits. He was largely responsible for the removal of Kentucky Wesleyan College to this city. Much of the most progressive school legislation of the State was due to his influence. He was also a great advocate of increased rights and privileges of women."

Beckner followed his beliefs with action. "Judge Beckner was by nature a leader of men. What he believed was right he advocated with all his might whether or not it was popular at the time." This was especially true regarding the issue of public education. Here Beckner left his most enduring mark, and the principles he fought for are still relevant in Kentucky today.

You may recall Kentucky's education crisis that resulted in a 1985 lawsuit, *Council for Better Education et al. v. Martha Layne Collins, Governor, et al.* Former governor, Bert Combs, and his legal team argued that the poorer counties of Kentucky could not provide an adequate education for their children due to an insufficient local tax base compared to wealthier counties. Statements such as "48 percent in this county can't even read" were undisputed by the defense. Judge Ray Corns heard the case and his opinion declared Kentucky's entire system of school finance unconstitutional.

The General Assembly immediately appealed to the Kentucky Supreme Court. That court's final opinion issued in 1989 found "the system of common school education in Kentucky to be unconstitutional." The state's widely publicized Education Reform Act of 1990 (known as KERA) was the result of the court's sweeping mandate.

So what does the Kentucky constitution say about education? Section 183 requires that "The General Assembly shall, by appropriate legislation, provide for an efficient system of common schools throughout the State." Both courts cited this clause as the basis for throwing out the existing education framework. And this clause was the work of William M. Beckner, Clark County's representative to the Constitutional Convention of 1890.

William M. Beckner
(in *Lawyers and Lawmakers of Kentucky*, 1897)

Beckner was born in Moorefield, Nicholas County, and attended neighborhood schools, the Richeson and Rand Academy in Maysville, and Centre College. Leaving college after five months due to lack of funds, he taught school while reading law in Maysville. Beckner settled in Winchester in 1865, where he began his law practice, and was soon elected Police Judge. He also served as principal of Winchester public schools and was founder and editor of the *Clark County Democrat*. In 1866 he was County Attorney, four years later County Judge, in 1880 State Prison Commissioner, and in 1882 State Railroad Commissioner. In 1893 he served in the General Assembly and a year later was elected to fill a vacancy in the U.S. House of Representatives occasioned by the death of Marcus C. Lisle.

Beckner's passionate belief in the value of education led to his effort to reform the state's system of common schools. Kentucky, like most of the rural South, had a deplorable record of educating its citizens. Our first state law dealing with common schools was not passed until 1838—and compliance was voluntary. Slight progress was made in the 1840s and 50s with enactment of a small state school tax. The Civil War disrupted progress, as did hostility to local taxation, political infighting, racial tensions and citizen apathy.

In the 1870s Beckner began advocating for better education in his newspaper columns and eventually was able to secure passage in the legislature of a graded public school system in Winchester. Following this, he began speaking out around the Commonwealth on the need for more state funding of schools. Condemning the level of illiteracy, he argued that "the free school has been the foundation of New England's power and greatness." He urged citizens to raise local taxes and to provide adequate education for black children—at that time the state had grossly unequal school systems for white and black children.

One of his speeches, entitled "A Problem To Be Solved," was reprinted in newspapers across the state in 1882. He organized a state Education Convention in Frankfort in April 1883 and the Inter-State Educational Convention in Louisville that September. These efforts resulted in Kentucky's Common School Act of 1884 that created a "uniform system of schools." but did nothing to address their inadequate funding. In 1889 he was invited to speak at a symposium in New York City on the question, "Shall the Negro Be Educated or Suppressed?" There Beckner expressed "a Christian hope that prejudices of the past would die, racial antagonism cease, and equal rights before the law endure for all races of men."

Elected to represent Clark County at the 1890 Constitutional Convention, Beckner was easily the most widely recognized advocate of public education. He worked tirelessly during the 226-day convention to advance his ideas in the Committee on Education. When the convention took up debate on the committee's report, Beckner asked if he might "say a word or two." He then launched into a two-hour oration that touted education's "power to break down class barriers, prevent crime and poverty, enrich democracy, and improve the general economic condition of the state." The convention ultimately voted to approve his committee's six sections on education. For his efforts he was recognized by the other delegates as the leader of the "friends of education" and dubbed "the Horace Mann of Kentucky."

Beckner had no way of foretelling that 100 years later, his Section 183 would be the justification to remake Kentucky's education system.

Sources

James C. Carper, "William Morgan Beckner: The Horace Mann of Kentucky," *Register of the Kentucky Historical Society* (1998) 96:29-60; H. Levin, editor, *Lawyers and Lawmakers of Kentucky* (Chicago, IL, 1897), pp. 657-661; *Winchester Democrat*, March 18, 1910; Biographical Directory of the U.S. Congress, http://bioguide.congress.gov.

46
The Myth Regarding
Mark Twain's Mother

November 10, 2017

The famous author, Samuel L. Clemens, was the son of John M. Clemens and Jane Lampton. Jane was well-known in Columbia, Kentucky, where she grew up. There are many reports by locals of her charm and beauty. "She was a belle in the society in which she moved, admired and loved most by those who knew her best." Another stated, "She was the prettiest girl ever reared in Columbia, with the exception of my wife." Her girlhood home there is commemorated by a Kentucky historical highway marker.

Jane Lampton Clemens, c1870
(Steamboat Times, unknown photographer)

Thus, it was a surprise to find the claim that Jane Lampton was born in Winchester. Since that claim appeared in print, it was probably inevitable that the same is still being repeated today, especially on the Internet. For example, the most widely used cemetery documentation website, findagrave.com, which records more than 165 million graves, lists Jane Lampton Clemens' birthplace as Winchester [*corrected since this article was published*]. I am unaware of where this originated, but A. C. Quisenberry made the claim in a 1922 article published in the *Register of the Kentucky Historical Society.*

"James Lampton was the father of Jane Lampton, who married John Marshall Clemens, of Lexington, Ky., and became the mother of Samuel Langhorne Clemens, who won a worldwide and lasting fame under the pen name of 'Mark Twain.' Jane Lampton was born in Winchester in a brick house on the corner of Main and Hickman streets (then called 'Highland' street). This house is still standing, and used to be known as 'the Trowbridge place.'"

The paragraph contains several inaccuracies but most directly to the case at hand: James Lampton was not the father of Jane; that was James' brother, Benjamin, who is confirmed as Jane's father by the Lampton family bible.

Quisenberry may have drawn from an earlier source called "local tradition." The following is taken from a letter Lucien Beckner wrote to Kathryn Owen, "At the northwest corner of Hickman and Main Streets, where now stands a filling station, was an old brick mansion in which *tradition states* that Mark Twain's mother was born."

Since no birth record has been found for Jane, we look to other authorities for information. Jane Lampton's biographer, Rachel Varble, states that Jane was born in Adair County, Kentucky. The "Mark Twain Project," a group operating out of the University of California at Berkeley, has gathered "more than four decades' worth of archival research" on Mark Twain, and they also place Jane's birth in Adair County. Similar conclusions may be found in *The Encyclopedia of Mark Twain*, the Mark Twain Boyhood Home & Museum and the work of Adair County historian, Judge H. C. Baker.

All these separate works appear to draw on compelling circumstantial evidence to "prove" that Jane Lampton was born in Adair County. Her father, Benjamin Lampton, married Margaret "Peggy" Casey, a daughter of Col. William Casey, the noted pioneer settler of Adair County. Casey County, adjoining

Adair, was named in honor of Colonel Casey. Peggy Casey was living in Adair County with her parents when Benjamin first met her. There would have been no reason for the couple to go to Winchester either to get married or to reside. And, indeed, there is no marriage for them recorded in Clark County, nor does Benjamin appear on the tax rolls there.[*]

All nonsense aside, the Lampton family had a long and honorable history in Clark County. The progenitor was an immigrant, William Lampton (1734-1790) who married Martha Patsy "Patty" Schooler in Page County, Virginia. Together they raised eight sons and three daughters. Four of the sons appear as residents on early Clark County tax lists—John, William Jr., Wharton and Joshua. Two of the daughters are found in early county marriage records—Nancy and Sally. William Sr.'s widow gave consent for her daughter Nancy's marriage in 1796, so Patty must have come to Clark County after her husband died.

James Lampton (1787-1862), who is also recorded in the family bible, is the best known of the Clark County family. He married Susan Ryon, a daughter of John B. Ryon, and she is named ("Susan Lampton") in her father's will.

James had a topsy-turvy career in Winchester. He purchased land on Fourmile Creek and several lots in town, including one at the northwest corner of Main and Hickman, where the "local tradition" arose. He served briefly as a deputy sheriff to Thomas Scott and kept a tavern in Winchester at various locations in the late 1810s and early 1820s. Records show that he borrowed heavily from banks and individuals and repeatedly had to mortgage his personal property and real estate to satisfy creditors. One of the mortgages lists his "tavern house & other buildings thereunto attached, a distillery with two Stills and other articles to carry on the distilling, and one horse mill with one pair of Stones and all other articles necessary to keep the mill in opperation, the Stables and all other out houses attached." James eventually moved onto his Fourmile land and lived in a house that still stands today on the west side of Muddy

---

[*] Records exist showing that Benjamin visited his brothers in Winchester after Jane was born, but no evidence has been found that he resided there earlier.

Creek Road, about 4 miles southeast of Winchester. James later moved to Greenup County where he died in 1862.

James Lampton House on Muddy Creek Road

James' son, William Henry Lampton, in later life lived in the Captain John Tramel House on West Hickman Street, now gone. Beckner's letter to Miss Owen, cited above, recalled his memories of the family. He wrote that William, "who was Mark Twain's first cousin, was almost as full of fun as Twain himself. He kept the crowd laughing where ever he stopped to talk. I talked to Mark Twain about him and Twain seemed to know about his remarkable sense of humor. He would walk across the street and talk to Miss Nannie Hickman, a lively old maid of eighty, who lived in the old Hickman house. We could always tell when Mr. Will was around by the shrieks of laughter from Miss Nannie."

William's son, William James Lampton, was a New York newspaperman and noted humorist. He was famous for his "Yawps," droll poems that were popular around the turn of the century. He is buried in Winchester Cemetery. His gravestone is marked "Plain Poet of the People."

One final tidbit regarding Samuel L. Clemens' middle name. Mark Twain's sister Permelia quoted her mother saying,

"My son Sam was named Samuel Lampton Clemens after my uncle in Kentucky, one of the best men I ever knew." His later adoption of "Langhorne" is unexplained.

Thanks to Ernestine Bennett and others at the Adair County Public Library for their assistance with this article.

Sources

H. C. Baker, "Sketches of Adair County," *Adair County News*, February 27, 1918; www.findagrave.com; A. C. Quisenberry, "Clark County, Kentucky, in the Census of 1810," *Register of the Kentucky Historical Society* (1922) 20:69; Lucien Beckner letter to Kathryn Owen, December 5, 1961, at the Bluegrass Heritage Museum; Clark County Chronicles, *Winchester Sun*, July 12, 1923; "Lampton Bible," Julia S. Ardery, *Kentucky Records, Vol. 1* (Lexington, KY, 1926), p. 151-152; William M. Clemens, "Genesis of Mark Twain," *Genealogy Magazine* (1922) 10:92-101; Rachel M. Varble, *Jane Clemens : the Story of Mark Twain's Mother* (Garden City, NY, 1964); Mark Twain Project, www.marktwainproject.org/; J. R. LeMaster and James D. Wilson, *Encyclopedia of Mark Twain* (New York, NY, 1993), p. 152; Mark Twain Boyhood Home & Museum, www.marktwainmuseum.org/; Clark County tax lists, 1794-1810; Clark County Will Book 5:197; George F. Doyle, *Marriage Bonds of Clark County, Kentucky* (Winchester, KY, 1933); Clark County Deed Book 10:432, 11:175, 14:157, 159, 15:336, 470, 472, 22:151, 165, 23:338; Kathryn Owen, *Old Homes and Landmarks of Clark County, Kentucky* (Winchester, KY, 1967), p. 39; W. J. Lampton letter to James Lampton, September 18, 1914, at the Bluegrass Heritage Museum; William J. Lampton, *Yawps and Other Things* (Philadelphia, PA, 1900).

47
Clark County's
Confederate Soldiers

November 24, 2017

The Local History Room at Clark County Public Library contains "many a quaint and curious volume of forgotten lore." One of the more curious is a volume entitled, "The Confederate States of America Roll of Honor." It consists of 212 pages of Application Blanks filled out in pen or pencil and bound in alphabetical order. There are listings for 144 Confederate veterans. The first entry gives an example of the type of information provided for each:

> Name—Richard Add
> Company—A
> Regiment—11th Kentucky Cavalry
> Command—J. H. Morgan
> Enlisted—September 10, 1862
> Age—18
> Died—In Service
> [Information] Entered by—E. G. Baxter
> Date—February 9, 1906

Ellis G. Baxter filled out forms for a number of soldiers who served in the 11th Kentucky Cavalry. The few Applications with dates are all from 1906, apparently the year this project unfolded. Many of the Applications have a handwritten narrative attached, such as the following for Ellis Baxter:

"I inlisted the 15 of June 1862, before I was 13 [on] the 10 of September 1862, in the 2 Kentucky Cavelry, Morgans old ridgement. I was transferd to the 11 Kentucky, same brigade, the first of October 1862. Was mayed 2 leutenant of Company A of that ridgment in July 1863. I was parled [paroled] at appomattix, when Lee surrenderd, to go home and stay til duley exchanged. I have never bin exchanged and I stil have my parale."

Baxter's Application states he was twice wounded,

captured during Morgan's Indiana-Ohio Raid in 1863, and imprisoned in the Ohio Penitentiary at Columbus. Ellis Baxter died in Winchester in 1909, when his delivery wagon was struck by an L&N passenger train on Maple Street.

While reviewing each of the 144 Applications, I tallied the following statistics:

130 of the men served under Gen. John Hunt Morgan, 6 in the Orphan Brigade, and 3 in Gen. Humphrey Marshall's brigade.

The most frequently mentioned regiment was the 11th Kentucky Cavalry, which drew many Clark County men.

48 enlisted when they were teenagers, under the age of 20.

A total of 87 were captured during the war, most during Morgan's ill-fated Indiana-Ohio Raid.

37 died in service, a few in battle but most while imprisoned.

The narratives that go with some of the Applications provide personal descriptions of the veterans' wartime experiences. Such accounts for soldiers, North or South, are quite rare for Clark County. Some are brief.

"Joe Hampton was the first Confederate soldier buried in the county." E. G. Baxter, who filled out the Application, added that Hampton was killed in a skirmish at Red River on October 22, 1862. According to official records, Hampton enlisted at Richmond, Kentucky, on September 10, 1862, was wounded on November 17 and died on November 30. Hampton is buried in Winchester Cemetery, but his gravestone has not been found.

John S. Gamboe, "He was the son of William Gamboe. Was born July the 6th, 1842. In 1863 he was drowned while out swimming with several soldiers in a pond near Monticello, Kentucky. He was buried nearby in Mr. Williams' garden."

Many soldiers described their capture and imprisonment. Few were more descriptive than Lt. William Berry Ford of Roy Cluke's Regiment.

"He was captured at Bluffington Island, Ohio, with Morgan's command then taken to Cincinnati and confined for a few days in a station house in that city. From Cincinnati he was taken to Camp Chase near Columbus. Being an officer, he was sent to Johnson's Island in Lake Erie. From there he was taken to Alleghany City, Pennsylvania, where he was confined in the penitentiary at that place. From here he was taken to Fort Delaware, Pennsylvania, and thence to Fort Lookout, Maryland, and then to Morris Island near Charleston, South Carolina. From here he was transferred to Fort Pulaski near Savannah, Georgia. Here he suffered from want of food, and he was very glad when the order came for removal to Fort Delaware. Here he remained until after Lee's surrender when he came back to his old Kentucky home in Clark County."

Francis Jones in uniform
(*Captain Roger Jones of London & Virginia*, **1891**)

Francis Jones enlisted at 17, served in Cluke's regiment, was captured and imprisoned at Camp Douglas in Illinois. "After the war he studied medicine and in 1872 graduated an MD with honorable mention at the University of Louisville. He located in Clark County near Winchester and continued the practice of his profession with increasing and gratifying success. He died July 28, 1898."

John D. Duvall was taken prisoner at the same place and sent to Camp Chase, Ohio. "Was taken sick and the vigilance of the guards being somewhat relaxed, he made his escape through the wall, but was so weak he got but a short distance. And old gentleman & his wife saw his distress, took him in, secreted him, wrote to his father of his condition saying if he was sent back to camp he would die. He was paroled & returned home."

Officers of Morgan's Command in Western Penitentiary, Pennsylvania, Captured in the Indiana-Ohio Raid
(*From the left*) Capt. William E. Curry, Lt. Andrew J. Church, Lt. Leeland Hathaway, Lt. Henry D. Brown, and Lt. William Hays.
(University of Kentucky Special Collections)

Obediah Tracy, one of the oldest soldiers in the 11th Kentucky Cavalry, enlisted at the age of 65. He was captured during Morgan's raid in 1863 and died in prison at Camp Douglas the following year. "He was a brave old soldier. A parole was offered him on account of his feeble health, which he refused."

Orlando Hensley participated in the battle of ironclad vessels in Hampton Roads, Virginia, in 1862. "I Desire to say that Pollards Description of the Battle of the *Virginia*, also called the *Merrimac*, against the men of war ships the *Congress*, *Cumberland* & *Monitor* and other war vessels and gun boats, that

I witness the Battle, being at Sewells point. Battery Company F of the 41st regiment, the same regiment that I belong to, Served the hot shot gun that set the *Congress* afire and Burned her up."

George Crutchfield described his experiences serving in the Orphan Brigade. "Lived in Clark County but enlisted in Shelby County under Capt. James Johnson, and was with his company when it was reorganized at Bowling Green under Ben Hardin Helm. Surrendered at Fort Donaldson but escaped. At Laverne next and then at Shiloh. Heard [Albert Sidney] Johnston's famous command to his men, 'Cavalry, water your horses in the Tennessee river tonight. Infantry, sleep on its banks.' Was at the battles of Richmond and Perryville and for 45 days in the saddle, fighting every day. In Tennessee next and at the 3 days battles of Murfreeborough. Next in Georgia & around old Lookout [Mountain]. Was captured on Peachtree Creek & carried to Nashville, Louisville, Camp Chase & last to Fort Delaware."

Will Emerson, who also served under Morgan, gave his account of the Battle of Winchester. This occurred in 1862 when he, Stephen Sharp and four other soldiers "captured" Winchester and sent a Federal company scurrying out of town. They had claimed to be the advance guard of John Hunt Morgan's army, who was headed for the town. After the war, Emerson earned a medical degree and lived in Pinchem, Clark County.

The little volume contains many more personal accounts, some quite lengthy, but space permits only a sampling here.

Sources
Winchester Democrat, August 13, 1909; *Report of the Adjutant General of the State of Kentucky. Confederate Kentucky Volunteers, War 1861-65* (Frankfort, KY, 1915), pp. 76-77; Edward A. Pollard, *The Lost Cause; A New Southern History of the War of the Confederates....* (New York, NY, 1866); for the full story of the Battle of Winchester, see Harry G. Enoch, *Where In The World II* (Winchester, KY, 2017), p. 214.

48
House at the Corner
of Hickman and Main

December 8, 2017

Several weeks ago in a column about the Lampton family, I stated that James Lampton owned a house that once stood on the northwest corner of Main and Hickman Streets. After the article appeared, Bobbi Newell sent me a photograph showing the actual house. Having this fascinating old picture in hand made me wonder who erected the building and when, and who the subsequent owners were?

Robert Griffing may have built the brick house on the corner of Main and Hickman, 1813-1818. The frame house attached is referred to in deeds as the "old Fitch place." The photograph is part of a larger panoramic view of the Methodist Church, circa 1920s. (Courtesy of Bobbi Newell)

Much of Winchester's early development took place on an extension of Main Street referred to as "the southern vicinity of the town," which at that time meant south of Ogden Court. Speculators purchased parcels of land and sold them off in pieces. The buyers in turn further subdivided the land before reselling and so on.

Thruston M. Taylor acquired the one-acre tract enclosed by present-day Main and Hickman Streets, Wall Alley and Ogden Court. Thruston was married to Mary Clark, a daughter of Robert Clark Jr. (brother of Governor James Clark).

In 1812 Taylor sold Jesse W. Garner one-half an acre off the south end of his tract. That same year, Garner divided his tract and sold William Vaughn a one-eighth-acre lot that fronted 26 feet on Main and ran back along Hickman (not then opened) 210 feet to the alley. A few years later Jesse Garner moved to Howard County, Missouri. William Vaughn became a noted frontier Baptist minister. He was still preaching when he died in Bloomfield, Kentucky, at age 92.

Rev. William Vaughn (Smith, *History of Kentucky*)

Vaughn split his narrow lot, selling the east end to Robert Griffing and the west end to Thomas and James Palmer. Coincidentally, Reverend Vaughn solemnized the marriage of Robert Griffing and Apphia Gray. Griffing was a saddler and Master Mason in the Winchester Lodge.

Up to this point, deeds refer to Garner's and Vaughn's land as "lots" with no houses. The lot Griffing purchased in 1813 for $140 fronted 26 feet on Main and 110 feet on Hickman (still not opened). When he sold the lot to Dr. John Mills in 1818 for $2,000, the conveyance included a house. Thus, we infer that Griffing built the house shown in the photograph sometime between 1813 and 1818. Thereafter, the house would change hands numerous times.

Doctor Mills sold the house almost immediately (1818) to Willis R. Smith for $2,500. Smith was a veteran of the War of 1812 and Winchester merchant. He moved to Bourbon County and sold the property to Henry Kohlhass (1826). In 1838 Kohlhass sold the house to Valentine Lingenfelter, a tanner, and his wife Mary "for one dollar and love and affection for daughter Mary, wife of Valentine." The deed states Valentine and Mary were then living in the house.

The couple sold the house to Henry Grant (1842) for $1,000. Grant turned around and sold to the Presbyterian Church (1845) for $700. At that time, Rev. William Matthews was living in the house, which became the church parsonage.

In 1871 church trustees sold the house to Jonathan Trowbridge for $3,000. When Trowbridge died in 1890, he was remembered as a highly esteemed merchant and "one of the oldest and best known citizens of this city." His will conveyed "to my nieces, Sarah and Belle Nelson who live with me, the house and lot of ground where I live on the corner of Main and Hickman Streets." Belle, unmarried, lived with her parents in Illinois. She died of "la grippe" in 1899. In 1900, Samuel N. Ballard and wife, "formerly Sarah Nelson," sold the house to Sarah H. Scobee.

Sarah, the widow of Robert Scobee, was living at Sewell Shop when she died in 1901 at the age of 82. Her obituary stated that "she fell and broke a thigh bone, and owing to her extreme age, the accident proved fatal.... She bought a residence in this city and had made arrangements to come here to live." Sarah's will left the house in Winchester to her step-children, who sold it to Mrs. Allie H. T. Vaught "for a valuable consideration."

Allie Hubbard Taylor Vaught
(Courtesy of Bobbi Newell)

Alice "Allie" Hubbard Taylor Vaught was the wife of Dr. John C. Vaught and a daughter of Hubbard B. Taylor. They lived half a block north in the "Coulter House," which I wrote about on June 3, 2016. In 1930, Harvey Lisle, master commissioner, sold Vaught's property on the corner—80 feet on Main and 100 feet on Hickman—at auction to the Texas Company for $13,000. Presumably, the houses shown in the photograph were razed soon after. A Texaco station—South Main Auto, operated by Robert Smith and Yantis B. Conkwright ("Bob and Conkey")— stood on the site for many years.

In 1977, Texaco Inc. sold the property to William E. Bonfield. A year later, Bonfield sold the property—where John and Roy Myers were leasing and operating the service station— to Winchester Bank for $110,000. The site presently serves as a parking lot for Community Trust Bank; however, the corner where the houses stood is now a shady little park with several benches.

* * *

Alert readers will have noticed the chain of title for the house that stood at the corner of Main and Hickman never mentions James Lampton. In a previous article I examined the myth that Jane Lampton, mother of Mark Twain, was born in Winchester. A. C. Quisenberry had claimed Jane was the daughter of James Lampton and that she was born "in a brick house on the corner of Main and Hickman streets...known as the old Trowbridge place." We now know that James was not the father of Jane Lampton (it was Benjamin), and we must doubt whether James ever lived at the corner of Main and Hickman. When Jane was born in 1803, the house had not been built and would not be for at least a decade. If James Lampton ever resided in the house or kept a tavern there, he certainly did not own it.

James Lampton at one time owned the west end of William Vaughn's lot. Lampton acquired the tract bordering 26 feet on Wall Alley and 100 feet on Hickman. James sold the tract to his brother Joshua in 1818. The property was described in the deed as having a brick house formerly owned by James and a brick livery stable built by Joshua. Perhaps this was the source of the confusion.

Sources

Clark County Deed Book 8:307, 9:235, 237, 10:359, 14:160, 15:44, 46, 22:258, 20:81, 22:258, 29:30, 30:350, 32:31, 44:365, 67:621, 69:447, 108:223, 232:555, 239:99; Clark County Will Book (Red) 2:100; **Garner**: Walter Williams, *History of Northwest Missouri, Vol. 2* (Chicago, IL, 1915), pp.910-911; **Smith**: *Memorial and Biographical History, Dallas County, Texas* (Chicago, IL, 1892), pp. 907-909; **Vaughn**: William Cathcart, editor, *Baptist Encyclopedia* (Philadelphia, PA, 1881), pp. 1191-1192; **Griffing**: *Winchester Advertiser*, November 12, 1814; **Trowbridge**: *Winchester Democrat*, February 26, March 26, 1890; **Nelson**: *Winchester Democrat*, February 17, 1899; **Scobee**: *Winchester Democrat*, May 25 and June 4, 1901; and various Winchester directories.

49
V. W. Bush Warehouse

December 22, 2017

This is the first installment in a series of articles on the V. W. Bush Warehouse. This 2-story brick structure stands at the intersection of Main Street and Depot Street in Winchester. Better known locally as the "Sphar Building," it has always been referred to in county deed books as the V. W. Bush Warehouse. This landmark building—the city's first railway warehouse—is Clark County's most recent addition to the National Register for Historic Places (March 2017).

Introduction

Valentine White Bush erected his warehouse in 1880 adjacent to the tracks of the Elizabethtown, Lexington & Big Sandy Railroad, the rail line that launched a building boom in Winchester. The structure stands about 300 feet from the site of the depot shared by the EL&BS and Kentucky Central Railroads. The warehouse was designed to store hemp, wheat and other grains for local sale and shipment by rail and to provide a market for the county's agricultural products.

V. W. Bush
(Handbook of Clark County and the City of Winchester, 1889)

The 27,000 square foot building has two stories and a full basement.

The original building had wooden platforms on the south (Depot Street) and west (Main Street) sides. At some point, the platforms were replaced with concrete sidewalks, now mostly absent. A defunct set of scales adjoins a remnant of sidewalk on the south side.

The original structure was modified by two additions.

The present trapezoidal-shaped building has a rear or east addition constructed sometime between 1880 and 1886 and a north addition built between 1912 and 1926.

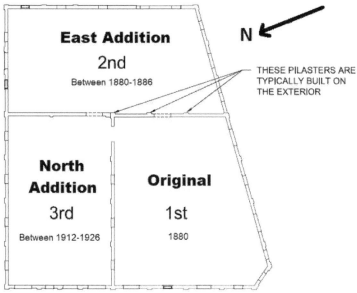

The warehouse was built in phases, as shown in the above diagram.

Exterior masonry walls are three bricks thick with a laid stone foundation and a flat wood roof. Interior framing is heavy timber post and beam. The diagonal entrance on the southwest corner facing Main Street leads into a small office area. A sign over the entrance reads, "Sphar & Co. Puritan Field Seeds." Except for the office and two adjoining rooms, the building has an open floor plan. One freight elevator remains of the three that were present in 1926. A front stairwell provides access to the second floor, a rear stairwell goes to the basement.

Four grain silos were installed at the rear of the building by Sphar & Co. sometime in the 1930s or 40s. These structures were added during the heyday of the bluegrass seed industry and could hold raw or cleaned seed. The silos allowed the warehouse to handle bulk quantities of grass seed without having to receive and ship it in bags. Highly sophisticated grain-cleaning equipment was mounted inside the building, much of it still in place.

Many of the window openings still have their iron-clad wooden shutters, which probably helped reduce the risk of fire. The building has a number of decorative architectural elements on the exterior. These include brick pilasters, arched doorways, and a brick parapet surrounding the roof. The parapet has a dentillated cornice and a recessed rectangular brick feature in each bay. The brickwork features a modified Flemish bond pattern.

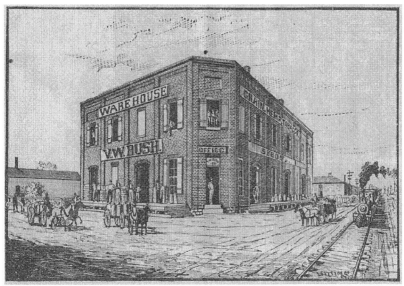

V. W. Bush Warehouse as pictured in the *Handbook of Clark County and the City of Winchester*, 1889.

In its first 125 years, the building housed a variety of commercial concerns, mostly focused on the seed industry: V. W. Bush, Goff & Bush, Sphar & Co. and Sphar Feed & Seed. After Sphar Feed & Seed Company closed in 2005, the warehouse stood empty. Unused portions of the building had been deteriorating for many years due to lack of maintenance, and the warehouse was in danger of being razed due to code violations.

The warehouse is now poised to return to service. Recognizing the historic value of the building and its importance in revitalizing the North Winchester area, the City of Winchester and Clark County Fiscal Court stepped forward to rescue this landmark. The City acquired title to the property in April 2016. Funding—nearly $2,000,000—has been secured for rehabilitation. GRW, the architect and engineering firm for the project, has completed construction drawings, specifications and cost estimates. Bid documents are currently under review by state agencies in Frankfort. Construction should begin in the spring of 2018 and, optimistically, could be completed by the end of the year. Plans call for rehabilitating the warehouse and repurposing it to serve as Winchester's welcome center and professional office space for local agencies including Tourism, Industrial Development Authority, Chamber of Commerce, and Main Street Winchester. This historic icon (1880-2016) is on its way to serving the community through the 21st century.

50
V. W. Bush Warehouse II

December 30, 2017
This is the second installment in a series of articles on the history of the V. W. Bush Warehouse, better known locally as the "Sphar Building."

Farm Markets in Clark County Before 1880

Clark County settlement began in 1779 with establishment of two pioneer stations, John Strode's and David McGee's. The county, created in 1792 from parts of Fayette and Bourbon, had an agricultural economy for its first two centuries. Finding markets for surplus agricultural products had always been a challenge for the county's farmers. Winchester had a market house (1794-1856) that provided limited opportunities for selling produce to town residents. Local merchants accepted certain farm products, notably tobacco, in exchange for goods. However, nineteenth-century roads were too poor and unreliable to move products to more distant markets.

The major transportation route for the county's farm produce was the Kentucky River. Beginning in 1789, flatboats began making annual springtime runs down the Kentucky, Ohio and Mississippi Rivers to reach markets in New Orleans. From there, goods could be loaded onto seagoing vessels and shipped to the east coast and Europe. Boatyards and warehouses were established along the Kentucky River to facilitate this vital commerce. Riverside warehouses, established by the state for the inspection of flour, tobacco, hemp and cured meats, served as storage facilities for these products until they could be loaded onto boats for the run to New Orleans on the spring tides. Interestingly, the first warehouse in Clark County was established by William Bush, the great-uncle of V. W. Bush, in 1792.

According to Dr. Thomas D. Clark, the Kentucky River was a lifeline for Clark County farmers until the Civil War, when southern shipment of Kentucky goods was curtailed. The year

1860 marked the high point for Kentucky's and Clark County's agricultural output. That year "Kentucky ranked fifth among the states in the value of its livestock and general farm products. Never again was Kentucky to attain such a high rating in the area of agricultural statistics." For example, Kentucky ranked first in wheat production in 1840 and had fallen to 8th by 1870; Kentucky ranked first in corn production in 1850 and had fallen to 6th by 1870.

Kentucky still ranked first in hemp but production fell off dramatically—from 39,409 tons in 1860 to 7,777 tons in 1870—due to loss of the cotton bagging market. Most of the cotton bales produced in the South had been wrapped in hemp bagging and tied with hemp twine.

Breaking hemp, circa 1900 (Clark County Public Library)

What little hemp production was left in the U.S. was centered in Kentucky. In 1879, the whole country harvested only 5,025 tons of hemp, of which 4,583 tons came from Kentucky. After that, loss of the binder twine market resulted in a further shrinking of hemp production. Wheat continued to be an important commodity in Clark County during this era, but it would also undergo steep decline, making way for locally produced bluegrass seed to rise in its place. "Throughout the history of Clark County there have been changing patterns of crops produced.... By the mid-nineteenth century many Clark

County farmers, especially those once devoted to livestock production, turned to the culture of non-row grasses and clovers." The most important of these for the future would be Kentucky bluegrass.

The Rise of Warehousing in Winchester

Thomas Clark observed, "The inception of the railway era wrought deep and fundamental changes in the transporting and marketing of farm products." Clark County's first railroad was the Elizabethtown, Lexington & Big Sandy, completed from Lexington through Winchester to Mt. Sterling in 1873. The line was later extended to Catlettsburg (1881), connecting there to the Chesapeake & Ohio Railroad, which allowed shipments through to the eastern seaboard. The EL&BS eventually became part of the C&O system. Winchester continued to add rail lines in the 1880s: Kentucky Central in 1883, Lexington & Eastern in 1889-1890. The last to be constructed was the L&N Railroad's line from Winchester to Irvine-Ravenna in 1914.

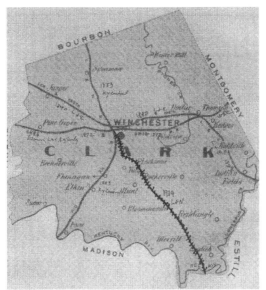

**1889 Clark County map showing seven railroad
lines leaving Winchester.**

Warehouses played an essential role in this rail-driven transformation of the town. Prior to the arrival of the railroad and construction of warehouses, a farmer selling his produce in

Winchester had to find numerous customers to purchase his harvest in small lots. Products like tobacco, hemp, wheat and other grains presented special problems. To market these crops, the farmer usually needed a middle man, and this role was filled by the warehouse operator. A proprietor purchased the farmer's product, processed it—wheat and bluegrass seed were cleaned, hemp was hackled—then stored it, and finally shipped it out by rail. For convenience, the first warehouses were located in North Winchester near the rail lines. Later warehouses were constructed along specially built spur lines.

With the entry of warehouses into the commercial arena, sales of agricultural products accelerated in two ways. Farmers could sell their entire harvest, in bulk quantities, to a single purchaser, the warehouse operator. And the warehouse operator then used the railroad to sell those products in distant markets. Hemp was shipped to factories producing binder twine, wheat went roller mills for production of flour. V. W. Bush was the first to venture into the warehousing business in Winchester. His experiment proved so profitable he enlarged his building twice. And his success motivated others to construct additional warehouses in the area.

When markets for Kentucky wheat and hemp slumped in the late 19th century, the Bush Warehouse supported an emergent business: seed production. Starting in about 1900, bluegrass seed production in Kentucky, and Clark County in particular, experienced astounding growth. During this period, the Bush Warehouse expanded from wholesale into retail sales. Local farmers not only sold their seed at the warehouse but also began purchasing products as well, such as fertilizer at first, and then field and garden seeds.

51
V. W. Bush Warehouse III

January 5, 2018

This is the third installment in a series of articles on the history of the V. W. Bush Warehouse, known locally as the "Sphar Building."

V. W. Bush Leads the Way

V. W. Bush (1831-1899) had the foresight and good luck to build his warehouse beside the railroad, ushering in a new era in Winchester—integration of the agriculture and transportation industries. The warehouse was erected initially to store his purchases of hemp, wheat, and other grains. It had the capacity to store 80,000 bushels.

According to the *Clark County Democrat*, Bush commenced the building in August 1880: "Mr. V. W. Bush has made arrangements with the town authorities by which Main Street just beyond the railroad will be still further widened twenty feet. Mr. Bush is going to build an elegant and commodious commission house adjoining the railroad on the north, and work will begin in a few days."

A week later, Bush placed the following notice in the paper: "Wheat Wanted! 50,000 Bushels for which I will pay the highest market price. Call and see me before selling."

This was followed by another ad in November: "V. W. Bush, dealer in Hemp, Tobacco, Grain, and County Produce generally. Warehouse on Main Street, at railroad crossing, convenient to depot." The latter ad ran unchanged the rest of the year and into the next.

The mention of tobacco raises an issue resolved by another newspaper notice that year: "V. W. Bush will at once engage in the tobacco trade when his splendid new warehouse is completed and our farmers will find a profitable market for their crops of the weed at home."

Based on local tradition, Bush's hemp and grain warehouse was the first one ever built in Winchester, and I was hopeful of finding proof. The best sources to track new building construction are newspapers and Sanborn Fire Insurance Maps.

V. W. BUSH,

Ware-House Cor. Main Street, near R. R. Depot, Dealer in

Grain, Hemp, Tobacco, Wool, Corn,

WHEAT AND SEED.

Also, All Kinds of FARMING IMPLE-
MENTS and FARM WAGONS,
BUGGIES, BAROUCHES.

AGENT FOR THE

WALTER A. WOOD SELF-BINDING HARVESTERS,

WINCHESTER, KY.

Ad for V. W. Bush's warehouse, 1880

In order to determine if there were other warehouses in Winchester in 1880, all issues of the *Clark County Democrat* for that year were reviewed. No other warehouse besides Bush's was mentioned. Warehouse operators regularly advertised the products they wished to purchase. No ads appeared that year for the purchase of hemp, grain or tobacco except the ones placed by Bush.

There was a notice that S. P. Kerr had purchased 5,000 bushels of wheat. Kerr was the owner-operator of the Eclipse Mills and, later, the Winchester Roller Mills that produced "White Pearl" and other brands of flour. This sizeable quantity of wheat had to be stored, but his building was simply a "storage warehouse" and had a limited function. Bush's Warehouse purchased goods, stored, processed and then shipped these goods by rail to distant manufacturers. The term "railway warehouse" was coined to describe the latter concern.

The second line of evidence that Bush was the first comes from Sanborn Fire Insurance Maps that show all the significant commercial buildings in the city. The first Sanborn maps for Winchester were made in 1886. Examination of the maps revealed only two railway warehouses: the "V. W. Bush Grain

Warehouse" and the "Jones Brothers Grain Warehouse." Both were brick buildings located on North Main Street adjacent to the railroad. The substantial warehouse of the Jones Brothers— Thomas B. and Henry M.—was constructed sometime after August 1884, when they purchased their building lot from V. W. Bush. Their warehouse was across Main Street from Bush's.

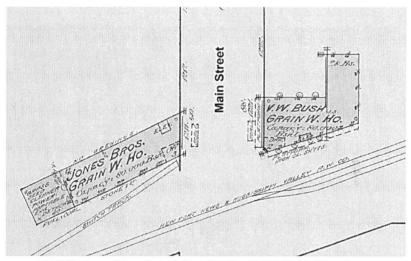

**1886 Sanborn Map detail showing the V. W. Bush Warehouse
and Jones Brothers Warehouse**

Thus, available evidence appears to verify that V. W. Bush had the city's first railway warehouse. It seems appropriate to recognize him as the pioneer of the warehousing industry in Winchester. By 1890 he also had constructed a tobacco warehouse on Winn Avenue adjacent to the railroad.

The Jones Brothers Warehouse burned in a spectacular fire on March 11, 1887. "About 6:30 o'clock Friday morning those of our citizens who were astir were startled by the loud clang of the fire bell and the unearthly screeching of the locomotives at the depot. The location of the fire was indicated by the dense volumes of smoke which were issuing from the large grain and commission warehouse of Jones Brothers on North Main street. This was a large, four-story brick building and was filled from roof to basement with hemp, wheat, bluegrass seed and other combustible material." The fire department was hindered from throwing water into the building as all the windows were blocked by bales of hemp and sacks of grass seed. "It was evident the building was doomed, and as the flames reached the stairways and elevator, they leaped from floor to floor, until in a short time the interior of the edifice was in a seething mass of fire. The dense columns of smoke were soon succeeded by tongues of flame which burst from every window, forming a magnificent picture of destruction."

The above newspaper article went on to give the loss of the Jones Brothers at $10,000 then listed the losses of hemp and grass seed suffered by J. W. Prewitt, D. A. Gay, J. Hood Smith, S. P. Kerr and others. From this detail we infer that a "commission warehouse" would store commodities belonging to second parties and then take a commission out of their eventual sale.

The Joneses together with a new partner, David S. Gay, rebuilt their warehouse. The 1889 *Winchester Handbook* gives a description of the first two hemp and grain warehouses:

"Hemp and Wheat Warehouses. Jones & Gay have a very complete warehouse for storage of hemp, wheat and other produce. They have connected with their establishment a hackling house where their hemp is cleaned and prepared for market. They do an immense business.

"V. W. Bush has another large warehouse of the same kind which is now leased to Levi Goff. It has the proportions of a city establishment and is always full."

V. W. Bush's long-time associate in the warehouse business was Levi Goff (1852-1941). Winchester city directories for 1908 and 1928 identify the business concern as "Goff & Bush Warehouse, dealers in seeds, grain and wool" and "Goff & Bush, warehouse," respectively.

By 1895 Winchester's warehousing industry was expanding rapidly. The Sanborn maps show the David S. Gay Warehouse, the V. W. Bush Warehouse and one other "Grass Seed Warehouse," otherwise unidentified, which stood adjacent to the C&O Railroad where the Winchester Cemetery is now located. Five tobacco warehouses were in operation—V. W. Bush, J. W. Glover, J. R. Stroud and R. P. Scobee had two. In 1901 there were five grain warehouses six tobacco warehouses.

David Gay, who bought out the Joneses, was stunningly unlucky, as his warehouses suffered two more disastrous fires. From a newspaper account in June 1903 we learn: "The grain and seed warehouse of D. S. Gay burned today, including the largest stock of bluegrass seed in the world. Loss $100,000." Then in November 1905: "The Bluegrass seed factory and warehouse of David S. Gay was burned together with most of its contents. Besides machinery it contained about $15,000 worth of bluegrass seed." Undaunted, Gay rebuilt his warehouse, an even larger establishment, at the northeast corner of Main Street and Winn Avenue. This pair of brick buildings is shown on the 1907 Sanborn map as the "David S. Gay Hemp, Grain & Field Seed Warehouse."

52
V. W. Bush Warehouse IV

January 13, 2018

This is the fourth and last installment in a series of articles on the history of the V. W. Bush Warehouse, better known locally as the "Sphar Building."

Bluegrass Seed Era in Clark County

Several lines of evidence show the growing importance of grass seed production in Clark County in the late 19th century. Jacob I. C. Naff of Winchester received two U.S. patents related to grass seed implements—one in 1884 for "an improved grass seed harvester" that was pulled by mules, and one in 1885 for an adjustable comb that could be used to harvest seed from "different kinds of grasses—such as bluegrass, timothy, orchard, &c."

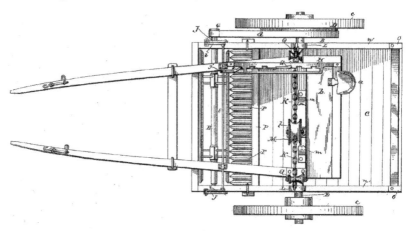

Naff's Grass Seed Harvester, U.S. Patent No. 304,228

Naff's patents were followed by several from the McCormick brothers. Harry T. and William H. McCormick were awarded a patent in 1903 for "an improved grass seed stripper," and Samuel E. McCormick was issued a patent in 1913 for "a bluegrass seed stripper." The brothers manufactured and repaired strippers at their shop on Lexington Road. The business was described in an article in the *Winchester Sun* (1922):

"On or near the site of Strode's Station is now located McCormick's machine shop in which for the past several years has been manufactured a successful make of a machine-operated bluegrass seed stripper. It is the invention of the three McCormick brothers of Clark County, each being a natural mechanic as well as inventors. The machine, a four-wheeled vehicle, is horse drawn, with driver and attendant, is driven across or around the fields, the revolving long-toothed steel combs strip the seed from the grass stems; the seeds being placed in bags by a mechanical conveyor. The grass is left standing, only the seeds are taken."

McCormick Bluegrass seed stripper in the field.
(Clark County Public Library)

Agricultural statistics indicate that substantial production of specialty grass seeds in the U.S. began around the turn of the century. Due to its ease of culture and nutrient value, farmers across the country began planting bluegrass to pasture livestock, and the demand for Kentucky bluegrass seed took off. Total grass seed production in Kentucky in 1870 was 35,806 bushels, which included timothy, clover, rye and others. By 1900, the state was producing an estimated 500,000 bushels of bluegrass seed alone. Production would peak in 1912 at 1,500,000 bushels. Clark County was at the center of this industry.

Kentucky led the nation in bluegrass seed production, which provided an important boost to Clark County's agricultural economy during the first half of the 20th century. The railway warehouses played a significant role in the industry by providing a ready marketplace for seed. They also made seed more marketable by processing and cleaning the raw product supplied by growers. (Bluegrass seed cleaning equipment is still in place in the Bush Warehouse.)

It was the seed industry that helped the Bush Warehouse adapt and survive as a viable commercial establishment while other warehouses went out of business and disappeared. As a result, the Bush Warehouse today is the only building associated with Winchester's early rail history still standing.

Sphar & Co. at the Bush Warehouse, 1948
(Sphar family photograph, Bluegrass Heritage Museum)

Bluegrass seed statistics at the county level are only available from 1949 through 1964. In 1949 Clark County led the state, with 72 farms growing one-third of the bluegrass seed produced in Kentucky. That portion fell to one-fifth of the total by 1959, when 23 farms in the county were still harvesting seed. Clark County also led the state in 1964, but the data indicate that bluegrass seed production had for all practical purposes come to an end—only five farms were still growing and harvesting seed. By 1969 bluegrass seed production had essentially relocated to the Pacific Northwest and Canada.

Riding the strippers provided summer employment for many high school boys in the 1950s and early 60s, including the author. There are still dozens of these machines rusting away on Clark County farms today.

Business Enterprises at the Bush Warehouse

V. W. Bush's warehouse was originally in the business of buying and selling hemp, wheat and tobacco. After Bush died in 1899, the warehouse became heavily involved in the bluegrass seed business. The proprietor was V. W. Bush's wife Kate. At her death in 1927, she left the warehouse to her son, V. W. Bush Jr., a Winchester attorney. He died in 1963 and willed the warehouse to his daughters, Clara and Wilma.

Neither Kate, nor V. W. Jr., nor his daughters had a major role in warehouse management. That job appears to have been left to Levi Goff for many years. Levi had day-to-day care of the "Goff & Bush" enterprise, which operated until 1936. Various sources list Levi's occupation as grain warehouse employer, warehouse clerk, grain dealer, and seed buyer.

In 1936 a new company stepped in to operate the warehouse. "That July W. R. Sphar and his son W. R. "Bill" Sphar Jr. formed a partnership—Sphar & Co.—to handle "feed, seed, fertilizer, grain and wool" in a rented section of the warehouse. W. R. Sphar Sr., an active farmer, left operation of the company to Bill Sphar and Gus White, who had previously worked for Goff & Bush. Sphar & Co. retailed feed, fertilizer and Puritan Field Seed to area farmers. The company soon took over the entire warehouse and enlarged their wholesale business in bluegrass seed.

In 1939 the Sphars formed a new partnership—Sphar & Gay Seed Company—which greatly expanded their bluegrass seed operation. The partners, W. R. Sphar Sr., Bill Sphar, H. W. Sphar and J. D. Gay Jr., operated warehouses and processing facilities near the C&O Railroad at Pine Grove in Clark County. Articles of agreement stated their main business was "cleaning, processing, preparing for market, handling, storing, buying, selling, shipping and delivering blue grass seed."

Sphar & Gay Seed Co. Building at Pine Grove, 1945
(Sphar family photograph, Bluegrass Heritage Museum)

Following the decline of bluegrass seed production in Kentucky, the Sphar and Gay partnership was dissolved (1972). Sphar & Co. then filed new principals—Bill and Asa Sphar, Asa Reeves, Clark Barnett and Jack Buchanan. The company continued their retail operation at the Bush Warehouse until 1999, when they sold the business to Spencer Pittman and Wayne Wilson. The latter operated a feed store called Sphar Feed & Seed until 2005.

Although it would be re-invented several times, the warehouse survived as a commercial establishment for 125 years. The building's utilitarian design proved adaptable to each new operation it housed. The V. W. Bush Warehouse—the last surviving 19th-century warehouse in the city—is set to be repurposed yet again. Plans call for the building to serve as Winchester's welcome center and to house several local agencies.

Sources

A. J. Pieters and Edgar Brown, *Kentucky Bluegrass Seed: Harvesting, Curing, and Cleaning* (Washington, D.C., 1902), p. 3, 15

Bill Sphar Jr., "History of Sphar Seed," October 31, 1972, copy at the Bluegrass Heritage Museum, Winchester, KY

Clark County Democrat, August 4 and 11, October 13, and November 3, 1880, June 8, 1881, March 16, 1887

Clark County Deed Book 50:6, 7, 51:127, 53:237, 117:437, 281:169, 359:498, 510:881

Clark County Will Book (red) 4:10, 20:367, 694

George A. Rogler, et al., "Production of Grass Seeds," in U.S.D.A., *Seeds: Yearbook of Agriculture, 1961* (Washington, D.C., 1961), p. 170

Harry G. Enoch, *Captain Billy Bush and the Bush Settlement, Clark County, Kentucky, A Family History* (Winchester, KY, 2015)

_____ *History of the Kerr Building and Eclipse Mills, Winchester, Kentucky* (Winchester, KY, 2005)

_____ *Where In The World? Historic Places in Clark County, Kentucky* (Winchester, KY, 2007)

Henry C. Leister, "Kentucky During the War Decades: A Study in Reconstruction," Bachelor of Philosophy thesis, University of Wisconsin, 1912

Herald Democrat (Colorado), June 15, 1903

Interstate Directory Company, *Directory of Winchester and Clark County Gazetteer* (Marion, IN, 1908)

James F. Hopkins, "Hemp Becomes a Minor Crop," in *History of the Hemp Industry in Kentucky* (Lexington, KY, 1951), pp. 203-208

John E. Kleber, editor, Kentucky Encyclopedia (Lexington, KY, 1992)

John Halley's "Journal of Flatboat Trips to New Orleans in 1789 and 1791," photocopy at the University of Kentucky, M. I. King Library, Special Collections, Lexington, KY

Kentucky Bureau of Agriculture, *Twenty-Second Biennial Report of the Bureau of Agriculture, Labor and Statistics of Kentucky for 1916-1917* (Frankfort, KY, 1918), p. 295

Mary Verhoeff, *Kentucky River Navigation* (Louisville, KY, 1917)

Maury Klein, *History of the Louisville & Nashville Railroad* (New York, NY, 1972)

Mt. Sterling Advocate, April 13, 1910

Mullin-Kille Co., *Winchester Kentucky City Directory* (Chillicothe, OH, 1958), p. 43

Pearson & Peters Architects, "Sphar Seed Building Renovation, Preliminary Estimate of Probable Costs," September 19, 2014

Personal communication from Bill Pumphrey, son-in-law of Bill Sphar Jr., September 28, 2016

Richmond Climax, November 22, 1905

Robert M. Polsgrove, editor, *Survey of Historic Sites in Kentucky: Clark County* (Frankfort, KY, 1979)

Sanborn Map Company, Insurance Maps for Winchester, KY, 1886, 1890, 1895, 1901, 1907, 1912, 1926

Southern Bell Telephone and Telephone Company, "Winchester, Kentucky, Telephone Directory, 1928"

State of Kentucky, *Report of the Railroad Commission of Kentucky* (Frankfort, KY, 1881)

Thomas D. Clark, *Clark County, Kentucky, A History* (Winchester, KY, 1996)

U.S. Patent No. 304,228, August 26, 1884; U.S. Patent No. 325,109, August 25, 1885, U.S. Patent No. 727,412, May 5, 1903; U.S. Patent No. 1,063,812, June 3, 1913

U.S. Population Census, Clark County, Kentucky, 1910, 1920, 1930

U.S.D.A. Census of Agriculture, 1880, 1890, 1900 1910, 1950, 1940, 1945, 1964, 1969

_____ *Index to the Yearbooks of the United States Department of Agriculture, 1901-1905* (Washington, D.C., 1908), p. 88

William Littell, *Statute Law of Kentucky, 5 volumes* (Frankfort, KY, 1809-1819)

William M. Ambrose, *Kentucky Union Railway, Lexington & Eastern Railroad, Lexington, Kentucky, 1852-1915* (Lexington, KY, 2007)

William M. Beckner, *Handbook of Clark County and the City of Winchester* (Chicago, IL, 1889), p. 27

Winchester Democrat, January 31, 1899

Winchester Sun, August 6, 1941, October 26, 2005, April 6, 2016, July 1, 2017, and an undated clipping from 1922, Clark County Public Library, Winchester, KY

Winchester Sun Sentinel, November 16, 1905

53
Whiskey Rebellion in Kentucky

February 2, 2018

In 1791, as Virginia's nine westernmost counties were in the process of gaining statehood, tumultuous proceedings in Philadelphia commanded the attention of Kentucky citizens. The federal government, having assumed the Revolutionary War debts of the states, was searching for a way to raise the money. Since the government's only source of revenue at that time was import duties, Treasury Secretary Alexander Hamilton convinced Congress to pass an excise tax on distilled spirits. The internal revenue act passed that March created an immediate furor in the west, where it was often said "every farmer was a distiller."

At that time Kentuckians often converted their excess corn harvests to whiskey, a more portable and salable product. Instead of taxing wealthy eastern merchants and manufacturers, the government targeted the poor western farmers' most marketable commodity. As a further insult, the whiskey tax had to be paid in cash by citizens who were still subsisting in a barter economy.

In southwest Pennsylvania open hostilities broke out with refusal to pay the tax and a fierce reaction against tax collectors that resulted in numerous violent incidents—assaults, tar and featherings, house burnings and more. In 1794 the situation escalated into gun battles with multiple fatalities. President Washington, faced with an armed insurrection, called out the militia to put down the "Whiskey Rebellion." That October an army of 13,000 men, headed by Gen. Daniel Morgan of Revolutionary War fame, approached Pittsburgh, and the uprising was suppressed without a shot being fired.

For a long time, it was thought Kentucky generally, if reluctantly, complied with the internal revenue law. More recent scholarship uncovered federal court records and Treasury Department accounts that show there was a whiskey rebellion in Kentucky too. Kentuckians were already incensed over failure of the federal government to protect them from Indian incursions and to secure open access to the Mississippi River, the lifeline of western commerce. Violent incidents here were isolated—distillers simply refused to pay the tax. The Treasury Department was certainly aware that no revenues were forthcoming from Kentucky, but they were at a loss how to force compliance. Military action was impractical and could have thrown Kentucky into the arms of Spain.

The chief revenue officer for the Kentucky district was Col. Thomas Marshall, father of John Marshall, the first chief justice of the U.S. Supreme Court. Colonel Marshall had difficulty finding men to serve as tax collectors and could not compel state or county courts to bring lawbreakers to trial. In one of the larger producing counties, where one collector had been assaulted and another robbed, Marshall declared, "No person worthy of trust living in Nelson County could be got to accept the job."

The situation had a theoretical solution. This was a federal law, and the highly respected Virginia attorney, Harry Innes, had been appointed judge of the federal court in Kentucky in 1789. In practical terms, however, violators could not be prosecuted until a competent U.S. Attorney was appointed. That commission went first to William Murray, who refused to bring charges against distillers during the 15 months he held the office. It took the Washington administration four years to find his replacement. The illustrious George Nicholas refused the unpopular appointment three times. Other luminaries who did the same included John Breckinridge and James Brown. Even Marshall's son-in-law, William McClung, turned down the job. Finally, in December 1796 William Clarke of Maryland accepted the appointment.

As an outsider Clarke received no cooperation from a determined populace, and he proved to be less skilled than his adversaries, who took advantage of every loophole in the law. Of the 231 cases Clarke presented in federal court, not one distiller paid the full penalties prescribed by law.

Judge Harry Innes (1752-1816)
Painting by Matthew Harris Jouett

Judge Innes was a stickler for procedure and due process in his court. First, a grand jury had to hear the charges. If they returned an indictment, the case had to go before a petit jury which required a unanimous vote to deliver a guilty verdict. Grand juries initially required 24 members and at many court sessions the summoned jurors failed to show up. Innes decreased the number to 16 but still had little success.

Another factor was the complex nature of the law that subjected distillers of different sizes to different rules. All distillers were required to register their stills and keep complete records of production. In Kentucky they did neither.

Hamilton tried modifying the rules to improve compliance. He agreed to allow payment of the tax in whiskey and followed that by agreeing to forgive taxes owed before 1795. Both failed to result in payment. He then offered to pay informers, a tactic that had worked in Maryland. But Kentuckians refused to turn in their neighbors.

Finally, in 1798 Innes decreed that no distillers be called to serve on grand juries, which had an immediate effect. The number of cases before the court increased dramatically. Sadly for Clarke, these were not followed by convictions, as juries refused to return guilty verdicts against distillers whose only crime was not paying what they perceived as an unjust tax. The bumbling prosecutor often sabotaged his own cases by failing to follow proper procedures.

For example, in December 1796 Clarke charged James Smith with obstructing a revenue collector. The case was continued each month until July 1798, when a jury concluded that Clarke had served the process on the wrong James Smith. Clarke then charged one James Smith, merchant, but could never bring him to court.

According to one account, Clarke managed to earn "the contempt of the judge, censure by the Treasury Department, and the embarrassment of his supporters." In 1800, Colonel Marshall arranged for Clarke's "promotion" to territorial judge in Indiana.

His capable replacement as U.S. Attorney, Joseph Hamilton Daveiss, oversaw a radical turnaround. His first case against a distiller resulted in a conviction, the first up until that time. In all, Daveiss brought 315 cases. Few went to juries. Kentucky distillers got the message and paid their fines. Fortunately for those who had not yet been charged, the law was repealed in 1802 during the Jefferson administration.

Clark County distillers got caught up in the whiskey rebellion too. This will be the subject of the next column.

Sources
Mary K. B. Tachau, *Federal Courts in the Early Republic, Kentucky 1789-1816* (Princeton, NJ, 1978); Leland D. Baldwin, *Whiskey Rebels, Story of a Frontier Uprising* (Pittsburgh, PA, 1939); Bettie C. Cook and Michael L. Cook, *Kentucky Federal Court Records, District and 6th Circuit Order Books, 1789-1804* (Evansville, IN, 1993); Harry Innes biography, History of the Federal Judiciary, www.fjc.gov/history/judges/innes-harry.

54
Whiskey Rebellion in Clark County

February 16, 2018

Reaction of Kentuckians to the whiskey tax of 1791 was swift and universal. They refused to pay. Notices were posted regularly in the *Kentucky Gazette*; these were ignored. There were no immediate consequences to distillers for ignoring the law. That began to change five years later when William Clarke accepted appointment as U.S. Attorney for the Kentucky district. Even then it would be two more years before the prosecutor brought charges in federal court against a Clark County distiller.

Owners of Stills take Notice.
THE law directs that stills shall be entered between the last day of May and the first day of July in every year. My office will be opened at my house on South Elkhorn, in Fayette county, where the inhabitants of Fayette, Clarke and Montgomery, may find due attendance.
T. STHRESHLY, C. R.
May 24, 1797.

Collector of Revenue posting in the *Kentucky Gazette*

At the November 1798 term of court, Clarke obtained grand jury indictments (technically called presentments) against Pleasant Hardwick for having three unregistered stills, William Trimble for distilling spirituous liquors without a license, and Ambrose Bush for having three unregistered stills. The following June five more Clark Countians were indicted— Edmund Hockaday, John Galbraith, Levi Stewart, Robert Peoples and Thomas Wills. None would be convicted.

Trimble and Bush would receive especially harsh treatment from the prosecutor. The author of a book on Kentucky's early federal courts, Mary Tachau, stated, "Nothing in the records explains why William Trimble and Ambrose Bush inspired such attention, but the number and variety of charges against them indicated that they were marked men." Both of these Clark County pioneers resided in the Bush Settlement. We will consider their cases separately.

William Trimble

William Trimble married Mary McMillan, a daughter of James and Margaret (White) McMillan of Augusta County, Virginia. The Trimble and McMillan families settled on Lower Howard's Creek in the spring of 1784. The three Trimble sons all became judges. Robert Trimble, regarded as one of the most brilliant who ever served on the bench, was appointed to the U.S. Supreme Court by President John Quincy Adams.

William was accused of multiple offences, civil and criminal, from the information of two revenue collectors, George Mansell and James Morrison. In July 1799, his civil suit was the first one in Kentucky to go to trial under the revenue act. He pleaded that he "doth not owe the debt" and the jury agreed. The outcome surprised no one, as similar cases were pending against five of the jurors, including three from Clark County—Bush, Peoples and Galbraith. As a further insult, the judge ruled that the "defendant to recover his costs from plaintiff."

William Clarke had to endure a lecture from Judge Innes on the proper manner and form to bring charges in his court. Then William Miller, the Commissioner of Revenue who had succeeded Col. Thomas Marshall, strongly criticized Clarke's handling of the case. "The interests of the United States have been committed by this defeat in a way that is mortifying." As further embarrassment, Morrison filed charges against Clarke (later dismissed).

Following his death in 1806, the inventory of Trimble's personal estate included "1 Still" valued at 13 pounds 16 shillings. This suggests he may have continued his distillery operation after the uproar over the whiskey tax died down.

Ambrose Bush

Ambrose Bush was a younger brother of Captain Billy Bush and perhaps the most ardent Baptist of the family. He was a charter member (1769) of the Blue Run Baptist Church in Virginia. When the family sojourned near present-day Abingdon, he joined a new congregation formed there in 1781 and would later be ordained an elder. Ambrose moved to the north side of Kentucky River with the other church members in 1784. He settled on land he purchased from his brother Billy near the old Providence Elementary School.

William Clarke fared no better against Bush than he had against Trimble. Clarke filed five separate charges—one for each of the three unregistered stills, one for not paying the duties, and one for using an unregistered still to produce peach brandy, two barrels of which were seized by George Mansell, Collector of Revenue. The charges were argued on multiple occasions before the court, with several juries empaneled and discharged. The cases dragged on until June 1800, when Ambrose was tried before two separate juries on the same day. After hearing the evidence, both juries found him not guilty. They also ordered that Ambrose recover his costs from Mansell. Clarke's motions for new trials were denied. The record did not reflect whether the government returned the peach brandy.

Ambrose's estate inventory, recorded in 1816, listed his "still, cap, worm and flake stand," so he, like Trimble, may have continued in the whiskey business.[*] In those days there was no proscription against churchmen producing or consuming alcoholic beverages. Indeed, one of the most famous pioneer Baptist ministers, Elijah Craig, was an early maker of bourbon whiskey—his namesake brand is still produced today. Churches did frown on drunkenness, however. Providence Baptist Church, Ambrose's congregation, frequently excluded members for "drinking too much spirituous liquor." In one remarkable instance, the church charged Ambrose's son, Jeremiah, with intoxication five times in the space of five years.

We might add in closing that Kentuckians' aversion to

---

[*] Purchased by James Duncan for $53.

paying whiskey taxes continued unabated for over two centuries. Colorful tales of moonshiners, revenuers and white lightning became part of our folklore. In an ironic twist of fate, moonshine, or unaged distilled spirits, is now a popular beverage produced commercially—and legally—in a variety of flavors. Winchester will have its own when "Wildcat Willy's Distillery" opens on East Broadway later this year.

Sources

Mary K. B. Tachau, *Federal Courts in the Early Republic, Kentucky 1789-1816* (Princeton, NJ, 1978); Bettie C. Cook and Michael L. Cook, *Kentucky Federal Court Records, District and 6th Circuit Order Books, 1789-1804* (Evansville, IN, 1993); Robert Trimble deposition in William McMillan v. James McMillan Jr., Clark County Complete Record Book 1812-1824, p. 490; William Trimble inventory, Clark County Will Book 3:284; "Robert Trimble," Federal Judicial Center, www.fjc.gov/history/judges/trimble-robert; Harry G. Enoch, *Captain Billy Bush and the Bush Settlement* (Winchester, KY, 2015), pp. 250-260; Ambrose Bush inventory, Clark County Will Book 4:114; George F. Doyle, *First Record Book of Providence Church* (Winchester, KY, 1924); Harry G. Enoch, *Rise and Fall of Orson Martin, Blacksmith* (Winchester, KY, 2013), p. 74.

55
History of "Clarke County"

February 2, 2018

On December 6, 1792, the Kentucky General Assembly formed a new county from a portion of Fayette and Bourbon. After defining the boundaries, the establishing act stated that the county was to be "called and known by the name of Clarke." When the appointed county justices met the following March and began keeping official monthly records, they always used the spelling "Clarke County." Today, of course, we are only familiar with the "Clark County" spelling. This raises several questions. How did the original spelling with the "e" come about? When did the "e" get dropped? (While these sound like trivial issues, they are fascinating to me.)

Our county was named in honor of Gen. George Rogers Clark, who is remembered as the heroic young commander who led a small force of frontiersmen through freezing waters in the Illinois country to capture Vincennes from the British in 1779. Clark always wrote his name without the "e."

A number of historians have speculated that a careless clerk may have been responsible for the "erroneous" spelling of Clarke County. That's not quite fair, or accurate, however, because wherever George Roger Clark's name appeared in print it was just as likely to be spelled with the "e" as not. For example, his first land grant in Kentucky, signed by Gov. Patrick Henry, awarded 400 acres to "George R. Clarke." In 1783, the U.S. Congress set aside 150,000 acres in Indiana for "general George Rogers Clarke" and his men. When his name appeared in military records, newspaper accounts, and even history books, the spelling invariably included the "e."

(A similar thing happened with Daniel Boone's name, in reverse. He always wrote it "Boone." Contemporary records and publications dropped the "e." Thus we had "Fort Boonsborough," "Boon Creek," "Boonville," etc. Why did this happen? Who knows.)

What we do know is *when* the spelling change occurred:

Our official county records—deed books, will books, etc.—
dropped the "e" in Clarke County after May 1850. On the 27th
day of that month, the county court accepted the resignation of
their clerk, James W. Bullock, who moved to Sumner County,
Tennessee. That ended a run of Bullocks in the clerk's office of
57 years: David had served from 1793 to 1814, James Patterson
from 1814 to 1845, and James Werter from 1845 until 1850.
During all those Bullock years, under father, son and grandson,
the county clerk made sure the name was recorded as "Clarke
County."

Cad Jones
(from the *Jones Family History*)

On the same day James W. Bullock resigned, the court
appointed Cadwallo Jones to fill the vacancy. From that day
forward, the county name was rendered as "Clark County."
Although Cad Jones served only a brief term, less than four years,
his revision of the spelling would remained unchanged. A Jones

family history states that Cad could not practice his profession "on account of delicate health." He died, unmarried, in 1862.

JONES' NURSERY,

CLARKE COUNTY, KY.

THE proprietor of this establishment respectfully announces that his stock of Fruit and Ornamental Trees, &c., for sale this fall is unusually large, fine and healthy.

The success and satisfaction which have attended the planting of articles obtained here attest the correctness and care with which they are grown, as well as the great attention paid to preserving the roots uninjured in removing them from the earth.

The prevalence of the yellows in the peach, and the apple tree borer, which are unknown here, and the black knots in the plum, seen only by me in trees from Rochester N. York in other sections, which are all causes of great vexation and loss, together with the injurious effects of exposure of the roots out of the ground for weeks, the danger of freezing and other unfavorable influences consequent upon a voyage from the North or East, are considerations, if there were no others, sufficient to induce Kentuckians to give the preference to Kentucky grown trees.

Purchasers may leave their orders with Mr M. B. Morrison, of Lexington, Messrs. Moss & Wheeler, of Winchester and Mr. Henry Jones of Mt. Sterling, or send them through the Post Office direct, and receive their articles in Lexington or Winchester without additional charge for carriage, and obtain catalogues from either of the above gentlemen gratis or by addressing

F. JONES
Jones' Nursery, Clarke Co., Ky.

Jones' Nursery Advertisement
(Lexington Observer & Reporter, 1855)

While the county remained consistent, the spelling of our name elsewhere took some time to come around. For a decade, area newspapers used "Clark County" and "Clarke County" almost interchangeably, until the latter gradually faded away.

The state of Kentucky took even longer to make the change. The journals of the Senate and House of Representatives used the "Clarke County" spelling until 1866.

Sources

William Littell, *Statute Law of Kentucky, Vol. 1* (Frankfort, KY, 1809), p. 630; Thomas D. Clark, *Clark County, Kentucky, A History* (Winchester, KY, 1995), p. xii; Clark County Order Book 12:289; Clark County Will Book 1:98; L. H. Jones, *Captain Roger Jones of London and Kentucky* (Albany, NY, 1891), p. 70; *Lexington Observer & Reporter*, February 18, 1855; Journals of the Kentucky Senate and House of Representatives, Hathi Trust, https://catalog.hathitrust.org/.

56
100th Anniversary of the Pastime Theatre Tragedy

March 9, 2018

One hundred years ago today Winchester experienced what many call the city's worst ever disaster. About 7:45 on Saturday evening, as the first feature was playing at the Pastime Theatre, a four-story brick wall of the adjoining building collapsed and fell on the theatre. The steel roof, rafters and bricks came down on the audience killing eleven and injuring approximately 100 persons.

On Thursday prior to the accident, fire had gutted the J. T. Luman Building next door to the theatre. The building was a total loss, and the entire stock of the French Hardware and Grocery Company was destroyed. In the aftermath of the fire, a high, unsupported wall on the south side of the theatre was left standing. The Pastime was a two-story brick building on the west side of North Main Street. A one-story extension had been added in the rear a year before. The wall fell on this one-story section, the end near the stage, and the roof collapsed under tons of brick.

The theatre was packed with a standing room only crowd. It was thought as many as 600 people were inside for a showing of "The Quiet Man." The *Winchester Sun* reported that "the front rows were occupied by children who, as is their usual custom, occupy the front rows during the comic pictures." The fatalities and most serious injuries occurred in this area. Others were injured as the panic stricken audience rushed for the exits.

The sound of the crash was heard throughout much of the city, and residents soon began arriving on the scene, joining the fire department, police and doctors. Ambulances found it almost impossible to get through the crowds. Rescuers faced a major challenge inside, because the damaged area was covered with so much debris. While rescuers were working inside, police could hardly keep the crowds away from the front of the building, making it difficult to get the victims out. And the police were concerned that the high wall on the street side of the Luman Building might come down with fatal effects.

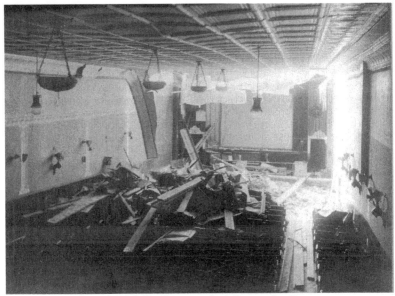

Interior of the theatre after the roof collapse
(Courtesy of Bluegrass Heritage Museum)

The first casualties brought out were carried across the street to the office of Dr. Isaac Browne.   All the injured eventually were taken to the hospital, the deceased to H. H. Hall's on South Main or Kerr & Bean on Court Street. The newspaper gave daily reports on the condition of the victims.

The immediate cause of the accident was a windstorm that, fortunately, kept many people away from the theatre that night. It had been raining and blowing all day. During the afternoon there were reports that the wall of the burned building was swaying in the 60 mph winds. City officials, called in to examine the wall, gave the theatre the okay to open that night.

According to the newspaper account, "All the doctors and nurses of the city were called into service and offered their assistance. The colored physicians of the city were on hand and were assisting...in the efforts to relieve the injured at the hospital and the homes." Nurses arrived from Lexington, Richmond, Mt. Sterling and Paris. The paper gave a list of the dead and their ages:

Abram Feld, 52, proprietor of the Star Store
Houston Noel, 21, son of Ellis Noel
Houston, 12, and George Frisbee, 10, sons of Colonel Frisbee
Coleman Aldridge, 16, son of Bruce Aldridge
J. C. Adams, 18, horseman
Tommy Thomas, 12, son of George Thomas, fruit merchant
Andy Henry, 10, son of Bruce Henry
Russell Smith, 12, son of Sphar Smith
Robert Baber, 33, plumber
Rosie Azar, 16, stepdaughter of James Spears, fruit merchant

The *Sun* article also gave the names of 21 men, women and children who had been seriously injured. It was thought at the time that several of them would not recover.

Funerals for eight of the victims were held on Monday. All local businesses and schools were closed. Another of the casualties, Everett Shindlebower, 33, died at the hospital later that day.

On Wednesday a coroner's inquest was held with Squire Pace presiding. Witnesses testifying included Mayor H. B. Scrivener, Councilman John W. Wheeler, Newt Powell, building contractor, J. W. Crone, architect, and others. Although several persons had warned of the dangers on Saturday, the jury held no one to blame for the accident.

Citizens rallied round the victims' families, and over $4,000 was raised for their relief. The tragedy touched many homes in Winchester. Two of the children, Rosie Azar and Tommy Thomas, were members of the Lebanese community. Long-time Winchester attorney Mike Rowady later recalled that his father had given Tommy the money to attend the movie that night. Mike Butler's stepfather, Elliot Ecton, then aged 10, sustained a serious head injury. Given little hope of recovery, Ecton would go on to serve as Clark County fire chief for 38 years.

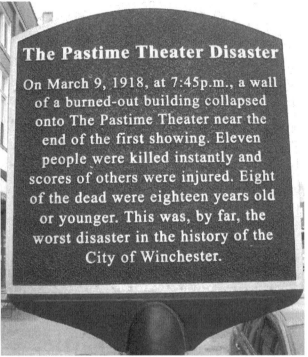

Pastime Theatre Memorial Plaque at 24 N. Main Street
Victims' names appear on the reverse side.

Remembering the tragedy, Butler initiated a fund-raising campaign to install a memorial plaque to the victims. He raised $2,200 for the plaque then had it fabricated and installed. A dedication ceremony was held on April 18, 2013. The plaque stands on the sidewalk in front of 24 North Main Street. Thanks to Mike's efforts, March 9, 1918, is a day that Winchester will never forget.

* * *

Mike Rowady Remembers

Mike Rowady, 99, was born nine months after the Pastime tragedy. This week he recalled many details about the accident that he learned first-hand from the accounts of his family. Mike's cousin, Tommy Thomas, was one of the victims. Mike's father gave Tommy a dime for admission so he could attend that night. "Papa said he always felt badly about that." Tommy's brother, Matry, sat beside him at the theatre. After the roof collapsed, Tommy asked, "Are you hurt?" Matry said, "No. How 'bout you?" and got no answer. Tommy died in the theatre; Matry was taken to the hospital with a broken arm.

Matry had a successful career and was a jack of all trades. In World War II he fought in North Africa and was in the Battle of the Bulge with General Patton. He would graduate from Centre College and had a law practice. Mike called him "a man for all seasons." Sister Helen Thomas was a nationally famous journalist and long-time White House correspondent. Sister Josephine was Miss Michigan and went to become a college professor.

Mike remembered that Elliot Ecton had been in the audience the night the wall fell. He threw himself over Bud Hamilton to protect him and was seriously hurt himself. In the treatment of his injuries doctors put a steel plate in his head.

Mike said that on the afternoon before the disaster, Thomas Dunigan, a blacksmith who had a shop on Maple Street, had seen the high wall of the Luman Building waving in the high winds and called city authorities. They did not knock the wall down as some advised, but simply declared it safe for the theatre to open. Lawsuits against the city were dismissed because local government had sovereign immunity. That law no longer applies in cases of negligence.

Sources
Winchester Sun, March 8, 11-15, 1918, April 16, 2013; *Motion Picture World,* March 30, 1918.

Index

Some women are listed under both their maiden names and married names. In other cases they are listed under one or the other. A few of the names in the Index may refer to different individuals with the same name.

Bloomfield, Arthur 137, 140, 143, 147
Bloomfield, Clarence 137-138, 142-143
Bloomfield, Mary 137
Bloomfield, Vic 121, 137-138, 143, 147-148, 150
Bonfield, William E. 217
Boone, Daniel 9, 32, 47, 88, 94, 177-180, 247
Boone, Edward "Ned" 180-181
Boone, Elizabeth 178
Boone, George 179-180
Boone, George G. 181
Boone, Ira 179
Boone, Lavina 88, 178
Boone, Martha Bryan 181
Boone, Mary "Polly" 179-180
Boone, Mary 178
Boone, Rebecca 178
Boone, Rev. Thomas "Tommy" 179-180
Boone, Sally 180
Boone, Samuel 178
Boone, Samuel Jr. 178-179
Boone, Sid 170
Boone, Squire 178
Boone, Thomas 179
Boone, William 181
Bowen, C. H. 147
Boyle, Terry
Bradley, Leonard K. 178
Bragg, Braxton 73
Brassfield, Wiley 61
Breathitt, Gov. John 38
Breckinridge, John 69, 240
Breckinridge, John C. 102
Breckinridge, Robert 35, 69
Breckinridge, W. C. P. 68
Bridges, James 33-34
Bright, John 76
Bright, Maria 75
Brinegar, Linville 57
Bristoe, James 27
Brooking, Rebecca 75
Brown, Dr. Isaac 252

Brown, Henry D. 212
Brown, James 192-193, 240
Brown, Joe L. 101
Brown, Margaret 79-80
Brown, Samuel 80
Browning, E. G. 56-57
Browning, James 184
Browning, Martha Jane 184
Bruner, John 34, 57, 81
Bryan, Martha 180
Bryan, Rebecca 180
Bryan, William Jennings 66
Bryant, Edwin 55
Bryson, Bill 124
Buchanan, Jack 236
Buchanan, John 93
Buckner, Andrew 79
Buckner, Benjamin H. 72
Buckner, Henry 74
Buckner, Mary 148
Buckner, Peter 165
Buckner, Sophia 79
Bullock, David 187-190, 248
Bullock, Edward 159
Bullock, James P. 187, 189, 248
Bullock, James W. 187, 189, 248
Burch, Ames 81
Burch, Daniel 94
Burch, Eliza 79, 81
Burch, Philip 81
Burch, Samuel 81
Burnau, Eliza 59
Burrus, Sarah Ann 10
Burrus, Thomas 9, 34
Bush, Ambrose 243-245
Bush, Ambrose Jr. 89
Bush, Charles E. 5
Bush, Clara 235
Bush, Dr. W. A. 147
Bush, Frankey 92
Bush, Henry G. 14-15
Bush, James 89, 93
Bush, James S. 5
Bush, Jeremiah 62, 245
Bush, John 34, 93
Bush, Jonathan 5, 85

Made in the USA
Middletown, DE
01 February 2022